Austin Steward

**22 Years a Slave And 40 Years a Freeman**

Austin Steward

**22 Years a Slave And 40 Years a Freeman**

ISBN/EAN: 9783744733076

Printed in Europe, USA, Canada, Australia, Japan

Cover: Foto ©ninafisch / pixelio.de

More available books at **www.hansebooks.com**

# TWENTY-TWO YEARS A SLAVE,

AND

# FORTY YEARS A FREEMAN;

EMBRACING A

CORRESPONDENCE OF SEVERAL YEARS, WHILE
PRESIDENT OF WILBERFORCE COLONY,
LONDON, CANADA WEST,

BY

AUSTIN STEWARD.

THIRD EDITION.

———◆———

ROCHESTER, N. Y.
PUBLISHED BY ALLINGS & CORY, EXCHANGE STREET.
1861.

# FROM GOVERNOR CLARK.

STATE OF NEW YORK,
EXECUTIVE DEPARTMENT,
Albany, May 10, 1856.

MR. A. STEWARD, Canandaigua,

DEAR SIR:—I notice a paragraph in the "Ontario Times" of this date, making the announcement that you are preparing "a sketch of events occurring under your own observation during an eventful life," to be entitled, "Twenty Years a Slave, and Forty Years a Freeman;" and that you design soon to make an effort to obtain subscribers for the book.

Being desirous of rendering you what encouragement I may in the work, you are permitted to place my name on your list of subscribers.

Respectfully Yours,

MYRON H. CLARK.

ROCHESTER, SEPTEMBER, 1856.

Mr. WM. ALLING,

Dear Sir:—The undersigned have heard with pleasure, that you are about issuing a Book made up from incidents in the life of AUSTIN STEWARD. We have been the early acquaintances and associates of Mr. Steward, while a business man in Rochester in an early day, and take pleasure in bearing testimony to his high personal, moral and Christian character. In a world of vicissitude, Mr. Steward has received no ordinary share, and we hope, while his book may do the world good, it may prove a substantial benefit to him in his declining years.

ASHLEY SAMPSON,
THOMAS KEMPSHALL,
FREDERICK STARR,
CHAS. J. HILL,
L. A. WARD,
EDWIN SCRANTOM,
JACOB GOULD.

# RECOMMENDATORY.

Rochester, July 1, 1856.

A. Steward, Esq.,

   Dear Sir:—In reply to your letter upon the propriety of publishing your life, I answer, that there is not only no objection to it, but it will be timely, and is demanded by every consideration of humanity and justice. Every tongue which speaks for Freedom, which has once been held by the awful gag of Slavery, is trumpet-tongued—and he who pleads against this monstrous oppression, if he can say, "here are the scars," can do much.

It is a great pleasure to me to run back to my boyhood, and stop at that spot where I first met you. I recollect the story of your wrongs, and your joy in the supposition that all were now ended in your freedom; of your thirst for knowledge, as you gathered up from the rudimental books—not then very plenty—a few snatches of the elements of the language; of playing the school-master to you, in "setting copies" for your writing-book; of guiding your mind and pen. I remember your commencement in business, and the outrage and indignity offered you in Rochester, by white competitors on no other ground than that of color.* I saw your bitter tears, and recol-

---

* The indignity spoken of was this: Mr. Steward had established a grocery and provision store on Buffalo Street, in a part of Abner Wakelee's building, opposite the Eagle Hotel. He put up his sign, a very plain and proper one, and at night, some competitors, whom he knew, as well as he could know anything which he could not prove, smeared his sign with black paint, utterly destroying it! But the misguided men who stooped to such an act—the victims of sensuality and excess—have years ago ended their journey, and passed to the bar of a higher adjudication.

lect assuring you—what afterwards proved true—that justice would overtake the offenders, and that you would live to see these enemies bite the dust! I remember your unsullied character, and your prosperity, and when your word or endorsement was equal to that of any other citizen. I remember too, when yourself, and others of your kind, sunk all the gatherings of years of toil, in an unsuccessful attempt to establish an asylum for your enslaved and oppressed brethren—and, not to enumerate, which I might do much farther, I remember when your "old master," finding you had been successful, while he himself had lost in the changes on fortune's wheel—came here and set up a claim to yourself and your property—a claim which might have held both, had not a higher power suddenly summoned him to a tribunal, where both master and slave shall one day answer each for himself!

But to the book. Let its plain, unvarnished tale be sent out, and the story of Slavery and its abominations, again be told by one who has felt in his own person its scorpion lash, and the weight of its grinding heel. I think it will do good service, and could not have been sent forth at a more auspicious period. The downfall of the hateful system of Slavery, is certain. Though long delayed, justice is sure to come at length; and he must be a slow thinker and a poor seer, who cannot discern in the elements already at work, the mighty forces which must eventually crush this oppression. I know that you and I have felt discouraged at the long delay, years ago,—when we might have kept up our hopes by the fact that every thing that is slow is *sure*. Your book may be humble and your descriptions tame, yet truth is always mighty; and you may furnish the sword for some modern Sampson, who shall shout over more slain than his ancient prototype. I close with the wish, that much success may attend your labors, in more ways than one, and that your last days may be your best—and am,

Your old Friend,<br>
And obed't serv't,<br>
EDWIN SCRANTOM.

# CONTENTS.

### I.
SLAVE LIFE ON THE PLANTATION, - - - - - - PAGE. 13

### II.
AT THE GREAT HOUSE, - - - - - - - 20

### III.
HORSE-RACING AND ITS CONSEQUENCES, - - - - - 40

### IV.
JOURNEY TO OUR NEW HOME IN NEW YORK, - - - - 52

### V.
INCIDENTS AT SODUS, - - - - - - - - 56

### VI.
REMOVAL FROM SODUS TO BATH, - - - - - - 60

### VII.
DUELING, - - - - - - - - 64

## VIII.

Horse-Racing and General Training, - - - - 69

## IX.

Death-Bed and Bridal Scenes, - - - - - 84

## X.

Hired Out to a New Master, - - - - - - 92

## XI.

Thoughts on Freedom - - - - - - - 106

## XII.

Captain Helm—Divorce—Kidnapping, - - - - 116

## XIII.

Locate in the Village of Rochester, - - - - - 124

## XIV.

Incidents in Rochester and Vicinity, - - - - 138

## XV.

Sad Reverses of Captain Helm, - - - - 145

## XVI.

British Emancipation of Slavery, - - - - - 149

## XVII.

Oration—Termination of Slavery in the British Possessions. 153

## XVIII.

Condition of Free Colored People, - - - - - 164

## XIX.
Persecution of the Colored People, - - - - 173

## XX.
Removal to Canada, - - - - - - - 183

## XXI.
Roughing it in the Wilds of Canada, - - - - 190

## XXII.
Narrow Escape of a Smuggler, - - - - 196

## XXIII.
Narrative of Two Fugitives from Virginia, - - - - 202

## XXIV.
Pleasant Re-Union of Old and Tried Friends, - - - 210

## XXV.
Private Losses and Private Difficulties, - - - - 219

## XXVI.
Incidents and Peculiarities of the Indians, - - - 223

## XXVII.
Our Difficulties with Israel Lewis, - - - - 232

## XXVIII.
Desperation of a Fugitive Slave, - - - - - 245

## XXIX.
A Narrow Escape from my Enemies, - - - - - 253

## XXX.
Death of B. Paul and Return of his Brother, - - 257

## XXXI.
My Family Return to Rochester, - - - - - 268

## XXXII.
The Land Agent and the Squatter, - - - - - 274

## XXXIII.
Character and Death of Israel Lewis, - - - - 282

## XXXIV.
My Return to Rochester, - - - - - - 290

## XXXV.
Bishop Brown—Death of my Daughter, - - - - 299

## XXXVI.
Celebration of the First of August, - - - - 311

## XXXVII.
Conclusion, - - - - - - - - 316

Correspondence, - - - - - - - - 341

# PREFACE.

The author does not think that any apology is necessary for this issue of his Life and History. He believes that American Slavery is now the great question before the American People: that it is not merely a political question, coming up before the country as the grand element in the making of a President, and then to be laid aside for four years; but that its moral bearings are of such a nature that the Patriot, the Philanthropist, and all good men agree that it is an evil of so much magnitude, that longer to permit it, is to wink at *sin*, and to incur the righteous judgments of God. The late outrages and aggressions of the slave power to possess itself of new soil, and extend the influence of the hateful and God-provoking "Institution," is a practical commentary upon its benefits and the moral qualities of those who seek to sustain and extend it. The author is therefore the more willing—nay, anxious, to lay alongside of such arguments the history of his own life and experiences *as a slave*, that those who read may know what are some of the characteristics of that highly favored intitution, which is sought to be preserved and perpetuated. "Facts are stubborn things,"—and this is the reason why all systems, religious, moral, or social, which are founded in injustice, and supported by fraud and robbery, suffer so much by faithful exposition.

The author has endeavored to present a true statement of the practical workings of the system of Slavery, as he has seen and *felt it himself*. He has intended "nothing to extenuate, nor aught set down in malice;" indeed, so far from believing that he has misrepresented Slavery as an institution, he does not feel that he has the power to give anything like a true picture of it in all its deformity and wickedness; especially *that* Slavery which is an institution among an enlightened and Christian people, who profess to believe that all men are born *free* and *equal*, and who have certain inalienable *rights*, among which are *life, liberty*, and the pursuit of happiness.

The author claims that he has endeavored since he had his freedom, as much as in him lay, to benefit his suffering fellows in bondage; and that he has spent most of his free life in efforts to elevate them in manners and morals, though against all the opposing forces of prejudice and pride, which of course, has made much of his labor vain. In his old age he sends out this history—presenting as it were his *own body*, with the marks and scars of the tender mercies of slave drivers upon it, and asking that these may plead in the name of Justice, Humanity, and Mercy, that those who have the power, may have the magnanimity to strike off the chains from the enslaved, and bid him stand up, a Freeman and a Brother!

# CHAPTER I.

SLAVE LIFE ON THE PLANTATION.

I WAS born in Prince William County, Virginia. At seven years of age, I found myself a slave on the plantation of Capt. William Helm. Our family consisted of my father and mother—whose names were Robert and Susan Steward—a sister, Mary, and myself. As was the usual custom, we lived in a small cabin, built of rough boards, with a floor of earth, and small openings in the sides of the cabin were substituted for windows. The chimney was built of sticks and mud; the door, of rough boards; and the whole was put together in the rudest possible manner. As to the furniture of this rude dwelling, it was procured by the slaves themselves, who were occasionally permitted to earn a little money after their day's toil was done. I never knew Capt. H. to furnish his slaves with household utensils of any description.

## WEEKLY ALLOWANCE OF FOOD.

The amount of provision given out on the plantation per week, was invariably one peck of corn or meal for each slave. This allowance was given in meal when it could be obtained; when it could not, they received corn, which they pounded in mortars after they returned from their labor in the field. The slaves on our plantation were provided with very little meat. In addition to the peck of corn or meal, they were allowed a little salt and a few herrings. If they wished for more, they were obliged to earn it by over-work. They were permitted to cultivate small gardens, and were thereby enabled to provide themselves with many trifling conveniences. But these gardens were only allowed to some of the more industrious. Capt. Helm allowed his slaves a small quantity of meat during harvest time, but when the harvest was over they were obliged to fall back on the old allowance.

It was usual for men and women to work side by side on our plantation; and in many kinds of work, the women were compelled to do as much as the men. Capt. H. employed an overseer, whose business it was to look after each slave in the field, and see that he performed his task. The overseer always went around with a whip, about nine feet long, made of the toughest kind of cowhide, the but-end of which was loaded with lead, and was about four or five inches in circumference, running to a point at the opposite or they might from their scanty store bring him such food as they could spare, to keep him from suffering hunger, and offer their sympathy, and then drag their own weary bodies to their place of rest, after their daily task was finished.

Oh, you who have hearts to feel; you who have kind friends around you, in sickness and in sorrow, think of the sufferings of the helpless, destitute, and down-trodden slave. Has sickness laid its withering hand upon you, or disappointment blasted your fairest earthly prospects, still, the outgushings of an affectionate heart are not denied you, and you may look forward with hope to a bright future. Such a hope seldom animates the heart of the poor slave. He toils on, in his unrequited labor, looking only to the grave to find a quiet resting place, where he will be free from the oppressor.

## CHAPTER II.

### AT THE GREAT HOUSE.

WHEN eight years of age, I was taken to the "great house," or the family mansion of my master, to serve as an errand boy, where I had to stand in the presence of my master's family all the day, and a part of the night, ready to do any thing which they commanded me to perform.

My master's family consisted of himself and wife, and seven children. His overseer, whose name was Barsly Taylor, had also a wife and five children. These constituted the white population on the plantation. Capt. Helm was the owner of about one hundred slaves, which made the residents on the plantation number about one hundred and sixteen persons in all. One hundred and seven of them, were required to labor for the benefit of the remaining nine, who possessed that vast domain; and one hundred of the number doomed to unrequited toil, under the lash of a cruel task-master during life, with no hope of release this side of the grave, and as far as the cruel oppressor is concerned, shut out from hope beyond it.

And here let me ask, why is this practice of working slaves half clad, poorly fed, with nothing or nearly so, to stimulate them to exertion, but fear of the lash? Do the best interests of our common country require it? I think not. Did the true interest of Capt. Helm demand it? Whatever may have been his opinion, I cannot think it did. Can it be for the best interest or good of the enslaved? Certainly not; for there is no real inducement for the slaveholder to make beasts of burden of his fellow men, but that which was frankly acknowledged by Gibbs and other pirates: "we have the power,"—the power to rob and murder on the high seas!—which they will undoubtedly continue to hold, until overtaken by justice; which will certainly come some time, just as sure as that a righteous God reigns over the earth or rules in heaven.

Some have attempted to apologize for the enslaving of the Negro, by saying that they are inferior to the Anglo saxon race in every respect. This charge I deny; it is utterly false. Does not the Bible inform us that "God hath created of one blood all the nations of the earth?" And certainly in stature and physical force the colored man is quite equal to his white brother, and in many instances his superior; but were it otherwise, I can not see why the more favored class should enslave the other. True, God has given to the African a darker complexion than to his white brother; still, each have the same desires and aspirations. The food required for the sustenance of one is equally necessary for the other. Naturally or physically, they alike require to be warmed by the cheerful fire, when chilled by our northern winter's breath; and alike they welcome the cool spring and the delightful shade of summer. Hence, I have come to the conclusion that God created all men free and equal, and placed them upon this earth to do good and benefit each other, and that war and slavery should be banished from the face of the earth.

My dear reader will not understand me to say, that all nations are alike intelligent, enterprising and industrious, for we all know that it is far otherwise; but to man, and not to our Creator, should the fault be charged. But, to resume our narrative,

Capt. Helm was not a very hard master; but generally was kind and pleasant. Indulgent when in good humor, but like many of the southerners, terrible when in a passion. He was a great sportsman, and very fond of company. He generally kept one or two race horses, and a pack of hounds for fox-hunting, which at that time, was a very common and fashionable diversion in that section of country. He was not only a sportsman, but a gamester, and was in the habit of playing cards, and sometimes betting very high and losing accordingly.

I well remember an instance of the kind: it was when he played cards with a Mr. W. Graham, who won from him in one sweep, two thousand and seven hundred dollars in all, in the form of a valuable horse, prized at sixteen hundred dollars, another saddle-horse of less value, one slave, and his wife's gold watch. The company decided that all this was fairly won, but Capt. Helm demurred, and refused to give up the property until an application was made to Gen. George Washington, "(the father of his country,") who decided that Capt. Helm had lost the game, and that Mr. Graham had fairly won the property, of which Mr. G. took immediate possession, and conveyed to his own plantation.

Capt. Helm was not a good business man, unless we call horse-racing, fox-hunting, and card-playing, business. His overseer was entrusted with every thing on the plantation, and allowed to manage about as he pleased, while the Captain enjoyed himself in receiving calls from his wealthy neighbors, and in drinking what he called "grog," which was no more nor less than whisky, of which he was extremely fond, notwithstanding his cellar contained the choicest wines and liquors. To show his partiality for his favorite beverage, I will relate an incident which occurred between Capt. Helm and Col. Charles Williamson. The Colonel, believing wine to be a healthier beverage than whisky, accepted a bet made by Capt. Helm, of one thousand dollars, that he would live longer and drink whisky, than the Colonel, who drank wine. Shortly after, Col. Williamson was called home by the British government, and while on his way to England, died, and his body, preserved in a cask of brandy, was taken home. The bet Capt. Helm made considerable effort to get, but was unsuccessful.

Mrs. Helm was a very industrious woman, and generally busy in her household affairs—sewing, knitting, and looking after the servants; but she was a great scold,—continually finding fault with some of the servants, and frequently punishing the young slaves herself, by striking them over the head with a heavy iron key, until the blood ran; or else whipping them with a cowhide, which she always kept by her side when sitting in her room. The older servants she would cause to be punished by having them severely whipped by a man, which she never failed to do for every trifling fault. I have felt the weight of some of her heaviest keys on my own head, and for the slightest offences. No slave could possibly escape being punished—I care not how attentive they might be, nor how industrious—punished they must be, and punished they certainly were. Mrs. Helm appeared to be uneasy unless some of the servants were under the lash. She came into the kitchen one morning and my mother, who was cook, had just put on the dinner. Mrs. Helm took out her white cambric handkerchief, and rubbed it on the inside of the pot, and it crocked it! That was enough to invoke the wrath of my master, who came forth immediately with his horse-whip, with which he whipped my poor mother most unmercifully—far more severely than I ever knew him to whip a horse.

I once had the misfortune to break the lock of master's shot gun, and when it came to his knowledge, he came to me in a towering passion, and charged me with what he considered the *crime* of carelessness. I denied it, and told him I knew nothing about it; but I was so terribly frightened that he saw I was guilty, and told me so, foaming with rage; and then I confessed the truth. But oh, there was no escaping the lash. Its recollection is still bitter, and ever will be. I was commanded to take off my clothes, which I did, and then master put me on the back of another slave, my arms hanging down before him and my hands clasped in his, where he was obliged to hold me with a vise-like grasp. Then master gave me the most severe flogging that I ever received, and I pray God that I may never again experience such torture. And yet Capt. Helm was not the worst of masters.

These cruelties are daily occurrences, and so degrading is the whole practice of Slavery, that it not only crushes and brutalizes the wretched slave, but it hardens the heart, benumbs all the fine feelings of humanity, and deteriorates from the character of the slaveholders themselves, — whether man or woman. Otherwise, how could a gentle, and in other respects, amiable woman, look on such scenes of cruelty, without a shudder of utter abhorrence? But slaveholding ladies, can not only look on quietly, but with approbation; and what is worse, though very common, they can and do use the lash and cowhide themselves, on the backs of their slaves, and that too on those of their own sex! Far rather would I spend my life in a State's' Prison, than be the slave of the best slaveholder on the earth!

When I was not employed as an errand-boy, it was my duty to stand behind my master's chair, which was sometimes the whole day, never being allowed to sit in his presence. Indeed, no slave is ever allowed to sit down in the presence of their master or mistress. If a slave is addressed when sitting, he is required to spring to his feet, and instantly remove his hat, if he has one, and answer in the most humble manner, or lay the foundation for a flogging, which will not be long delayed.

I slept in the same room with my master and mistress. This room was elegantly furnished with damask curtains, mahogany bedstead of the most expensive kind, and every thing else about it was of the most costly kind. And while Mr. and Mrs. Helm reposed on their bed of down, with a cloud of lace floating over them, like some Eastern Prince, with their slaves to fan them while they slept, and to tremble when they awoke, I always slept upon the floor, without a pillow or even a blanket, but, like a dog, lay down anywhere I could find a place.

Slaves are never allowed to leave the plantation to which they belong, without a written pass. Should any one venture to disobey this law, he will most likely be caught by the *patrol* and given thirty-nine lashes. This patrol is always on duty every Sunday, going to each plantation under their supervision, entering every slave cabin, and examining closely the conduct of the slaves; and if they find one slave from another plantation without a pass, he is immediately punished with a severe flogging.

I recollect going one Sunday with my mother, to visit my grand-mother; and while there, two or three of the patrol came and looked into the cabin, and seeing my mother, demanded her pass. She told them that she had one, but had left it in another cabin, from whence she soon brought it, which saved her a whipping but we were terribly frightened.

The reader will obtain a better knowledge of the character of a Virginia patrol, by the relation of an affair, which came off on the neighboring plantation of Col. Alexander, in which some forty of Capt. Helm's slaves were engaged, and which proved rather destructive of human life in the end.

But I must first say that it is not true, that slave owners are respected for kindness to their slaves. The more tyrannical a master is, the more will he be favorably regarded by his neighboring planters; and from the day that he acquires the reputation of a kind and indulgent master, he is looked upon with suspicion, and sometimes hatred, and his slaves are watched more closely than before.

Col. Alexander was a very wealthy planter and owned a great number of slaves, but he was very justly suspected of being a kind, humane, and indulgent master. His slaves were always better fed, better clad, and had greater privileges than any I knew in the Old Dominion; and of course, the patrol had long had an eye on them, anxious to flog some of "those pampered niggers, who were spoiled by the indulgence of a weak, inefficient, but well-meaning owner."

Col. A. gave his slaves the liberty to get up a grand dance. Invitations were sent and accepted, to a large number of slaves on other plantations, and so, for miles around, all or many of the slaves were in high anticipation of joining in the great dance, which was to come off on Easter night. In the mean time, the patrol was closely watching their movements, and evinced rather a joyful expectancy of the many they should find there without a pass, and the flogging they would give them for that, if not guilty of any other offence, and perhaps they might catch some of the Colonel's slaves doing something for which they could be taught "to know their place," by the application of the cowhide.

The slaves on Col. A.'s plantation had to provide and prepare the supper for the expected vast "turn out," which was no light matter; and as slaves like on such occasions to pattern as much as possible after their master's family, the result was, to meet the emergency of the case, they *took*, without saying, "by your leave, Sir," some property belonging to their master, reasoning among themselves, as slaves often do, that it can not be *stealing*, because "it belongs to massa, and so do *we*, and we only use one part of his property to benefit another. Sure, 'tis all massa's." And if they do not get detected in this removal of "massa's property" from one location to another, they think no more of it.

Col. Alexander's slaves were hurrying on with their great preparations for the dance and feast; and as the time drew near, the old and knowing ones might be seen in groups, discussing the matter, with many a wink and nod; but it was in the valleys and by-places where the younger portion were to be found, rather secretly preparing food for the great time coming. This consisted of hogs, sheep, calves; and as to master's *poultry*, that suffered daily. Sometimes it was missed, but the disappearance was always easily accounted for, by informing "massa" that a great number of hawks had been around of late; and their preparation went on, night after night, undetected. They who repaired to a swamp or other by-place to cook by night, carefully destroyed everything likely to detect them, before they returned to their cabins in the morning.

The night for the dance *came* at last, and long before the time, the road leading to Col. Alexander's plantation presented a gay spectacle. The females were seen flocking to the place of resort, with heads adorned with gaudy bandanna turbans and new calico dresses, of the gayest colors,—their whole attire decked over with bits of gauze ribbon and other fantastic finery. The shades of night soon closed over the plantation, and then could be heard the rude music and loud laugh of the unpolished slave. It was about ten o'clock when the *aristocratic slaves* began to assemble, dressed in the cast-off finery of their master and mistress, swelling out and putting on airs in imitation of those they were forced to obey from day to day.

When they were all assembled, the dance commenced; the old fiddler struck up some favorite tune, and over the floor they went; the flying feet of the dancers were heard, pat, pat, over the apartment till the clock warned them it was twelve at midnight, or what some call "low twelve," to distinguish it from twelve o'clock at noon; then the violin ceased its discordant sounds, and the merry dancers paused to take breath.

Supper was then announced, and all began to prepare for the sumptuous feast. It being the pride of slaves to imitate the manners of their master and mistress, especially in the ceremonies of the table, all was conducted with great propriety and good order. The food was well cooked, and in a very plentiful supply. They had also managed in some way, to get a good quantity of excellent wine, which was sipped in the most approved and modern style. Every dusky face was lighted up, and every eye sparkled with joy. However ill fed they might have been, here, for once, there was plenty. Suffering and toil was forgotten, and they all seemed with one accord to give themselves up to the intoxication of pleasurable amusement.

House servants were of course, "the stars" of the party; all eyes were turned to them to see how they conducted, for they, among slaves, are what a military man would call "fugle-men." The field hands, and such of them as have generally been excluded from the dwelling of their owners, look to the house servant as a pattern of politeness and gentility. And indeed, it is often the only method of obtaining any knowledge of the manners of what is called "genteel society;" hence, they are ever regarded as a privileged class; and are sometimes greatly envied, while others are bitterly hated. And too often justly, for many of them are the most despicable tale-bearers and mischief-makers, who will, for the sake of the favor of his master or mistress, frequently betray his fellow-slave, and by tattling, get him severely whipped; and for these acts of perfidy, and sometimes downright falsehood, he is often rewarded by his master, who knows it is for his interest to keep such ones about him; though he is sometimes obliged, in addition to a reward, to send him away, for fear of the vengeance of the betrayed slaves. In the family of his master, the example of bribery and treachery is ever set before him, hence it is, that insurrections and stampedes are so generally detected. Such slaves are always treated with more affability than others, for the slaveholder is well aware that he stands over a volcano, that may at any moment rock his foundation to the center, and with one mighty burst of its long suppressed fire, sweep him and his family to destruction. When he lies down at night, he knows not but that ere another morning shall dawn, he may be left mangled and bleeding, and at the mercy of those maddened slaves whom he has so long ruled with a rod of iron.

But the supper, like other events, came to an end at last. The expensive table service, with other things, which had been secretly brought from the "great house," was hurriedly cleansed by the slaves, and carefully returned. The floor was again cleared, the violin sounded, and soon they were performing another "break down," with all the wild abandon of the African character,—in the very midst of which, the music suddenly ceased, and the old musician assumed a listening attitude. Every foot was motionless; every face terrified, and every ear listening for the cause of the alarm.

Soon the slave who was kept on the "look-out," shouted to the listeners the single word "*patrol!*" and then the tumult that followed that announcement, is beyond the power of language to describe! Many a poor slave who had stolen from his cabin, to join in the dance, now remembered that they had no pass! Many screamed in affright, as if they already felt the lash and heard the crack of the overseer's whip; others clenched their hands, and assumed an attitude of bold defiance, while a savage frown contracted the brow of all. Their unrestrained merriment and delicious fare, seemed to arouse in them the natural feelings of self-defence and defiance of their oppressors. But what could be done? The patrol was nearing the building, when an athletic, powerful slave, who had been but a short time from his "father-

B*

land," whose spirit the cowardly overseer had labored in vain to quell, said in a calm, clear voice, that we had better stand our ground, and advised the females to lose no time in useless wailing, but get their things and repair immediately to a cabin at a short distance, and there remain quiet, without a light, which they did with all possible haste. The men were terrified at this bold act of their leader; and many with dismay at the thought of resistance, began to skulk behind fences and old buildings, when he opened the door and requested every slave to leave who felt unwilling to fight. None were urged to remain, and those who stood by him did so voluntarily.

Their number was now reduced to twenty-five men, but the leader, a gigantic African, with a massive, compact frame, and an arm of great strength, looked competent to put ten common men to flight. He clenched his powerful fist, and declared that he would resist unto death, before he would be arrested by those savage men, even if they promised not to flog him. They closed the door, and agreed not to open it; and then the leader cried, "Extinguish the lights and let them come! we will meet them hand to hand!" Five of the number he stationed near the door, with orders to rush out, if the patrol entered, and seize their horses, cut the bridles, or otherwise unfit them for use. This would prevent them from giving an alarm and getting a reinforcement from surrounding plantations. In silence they awaited the approach of the enemy, and soon the tramping of horses' feet announced their approach, but when within a few yards of the house they halted, and were overheard by one of the skulking slaves, maturing their plans and mode of attack. There was great hesitancy expressed by a part of the company to engage in the affair at all.

"Coming events cast their shadow before."

The majority, however, seemed to think it safe enough, and uttered expressions of triumph that they had got the rascals at last.

"Are you not afraid that they will resist?" said the weaker party.

"Resist?" was the astonished answer. "This old fellow, the Colonel, has pampered and indulged his slaves, it is true, and they have slipped through our fingers whenever we have attempted to chastise them; but they are not such fools as to dare resistance! Those niggers know as well as we, that it is *death*, by the law of the State, for a slave to strike a white man."

"Very true," said the other, "but it is dark and long past midnight, and beside they have been indulging their appetites, and we cannot tell what they may attempt to do."

"Pshaw!" he answered, contemptuously, "they are unarmed, and I should not fear in the least, to go in among them *alone*, armed only with my cowhide!"

"As you please, then," he said, rather dubiously, "but look well to your weapons; are they in order?"

"In prime order, Sir." And putting spurs to their horses, were soon at the house, where they dismounted and requested one of the party to remain with the horses.

"What," said he, "are you so chicken-hearted as to suppose those d——d cowardly niggers are going to get up an insurrection?"

"Oh no," he replied, carelessly, but would not consent to have the horses left alone. "Besides," said he, "they may forget themselves at this late hour; but if they do, a few lashes of the cowhide will quicken their memory, I reckon."

The slaves were aware of their movements, and prepared to receive them.

They stepped up to the door boldly, and demanded admittance, but all was silent; they tried to open it, but it was fastened. Those inside, ranged on each side of the door, and stood perfectly still.

The patrol finding the slaves not disposed to obey, burst off the slight fastening that secured the door, and the chief of the patrol bounded into their midst, followed by several of his companions, all in total darkness!

Vain is the attempt to describe the tumultuous scene which followed. Hand to hand they fought and struggled with each other, amid the terrific explosion of firearms,—oaths and curses, mingled with the prayers of the wounded, and the groans of the dying! Two of the patrol were killed on the spot, and lay drenched in the warm blood that so lately flowed through their veins. Another with his arm broken and otherwise wounded, lay groaning and helpless, beside the fallen slaves, who had sold their lives so dearly. Another of his fellows was found at a short distance, mortally wounded and about to bid adieu to life. In the yard lay the keeper of the horses, a stiffened corpse. Six of the slaves were killed and two wounded.

It would be impossible to convey to the minds of northern people, the alarm and perfect consternation that the above circumstance occasioned in that community. The knowledge of its occurrence was carried from one plantation to another, as on the wings of the wind; exaggerated accounts were given, and prophecies of the probable result made, until the excitement became truly fearful. Every cheek was blanched and every frame trembled when listening to the tale, that "insurrection among the slaves had commenced on the plantation of Col. Alexander; that three or four of the patrol had been killed, &c." The day after, people flocked from every quarter, armed to the teeth, swearing vengeance on the defenceless slaves. Nothing can teach plainer than this, the constant and tormenting fear in which the slaveholder lives, and yet he repents not of his deeds.

The kind old Colonel was placed in the most difficult and unenviable position. His warm heart was filled with sorrow for the loss of his slaves, but not alone, as is generally the case in such instances, because he had lost so much property. He truly regretted the death of his faithful servants, and boldly rebuked the occasion of their sudden decease. When beset and harrassed by his neighbors to give up his slaves to be tried for insurrection and murder, he boldly resisted, contending for the natural right of the slaves, to act in their own defence, and especially when on his own plantation and in their own quarters. They contended, however, that as his slaves had got up a dance, and had invited those of the adjoining plantations, the patrol was only discharging their duty in looking after them; but the gallant old Colonel defended his slaves, and told them plainly that he should continue to do so to the extent of his ability and means.

The poor slaves were sad enough, on the morning after their merry meeting, and they might be seen standing in groups, conversing with a very different air from the one they had worn the day before.

Their business was now to prepare the bodies of their late associates for the grave. Robert, the brave African, who had so boldly led them on the night before, and who had so judiciously provided for their escape, was calmly sleeping in death's cold embrace. He left a wife and five slave children. Two of the other slaves left families, whose pitiful cries it was painful to hear.

The Colonel's family, deeply afflicted by what was passing around them, attended the funeral. One of the slaves, who sometimes officiated as a minister, read a portion of Scripture, and gave out two hymns;—one of which commences with

"Hark! from the tomb a doleful sound."

Both were sung with great solemnity by the congregation, and then the good old man offered a prayer; after which he addressed the slaves on the shortness of human life and the certainty of death, and more than once hinted at the hardness of their lot, assuring, however, his fellow-slaves, that if they were good and faithful, all would be right hereafter. His master, Col. Alexander, was deeply affected by this simple faith and sincere regard for the best interests of all, both master and slave.

When the last look at their fellow-servants had been taken, the procession was formed in the following manner: First, the old slave minister, then the remains of the dead, followed by their weeping relatives; then came the master and his family; next the slaves belonging to the plantation; and last, friends and strangers, black and white; all moved on solemnly to the final resting-place of those brave men, whose descendants may yet be heard from, in defence of right and freedom.

# CHAPTER III.

### HORSE-RACING AND ITS CONSEQUENCES.

CAPT. Helm had a race-course on his plantation, on which he trained young horses for the fall races. One very fine horse he owned, called *Mark Anthony*, which he trained in the most careful manner for several months previous to the races. He would put him on the course every morning, sometimes covering him with a blanket, and then put him to his utmost speed, which he called "sweating him." Mark Anthony was to be put on the race-course in October following, as a competitor for the purse of ten thousand dollars, which was the amount to be lost or gained on the first day of the fall races. Capt. H. had also another young horse, called *Buffer*, under a course of training, which he designed to enter the lists for the second day. His course of training had been about the same as Mark Anthony's, but being a year or two younger, it was thought that he had not sufficient "bottom" to risk so much money on, as was at stake on the first day.

"Away they go, sweeping round the course with lightning speed, while every spectator's eye is strained, and every countenance flushed with intense anxiety."

page 41.

When the time for the races to commence came, all was bustle and excitement in the house and on the plantation. It was a fine October morning, and the sun shed a mellow radiance on all around, when people began to throng the race-course. Some came with magnificent equipages, attended by their numerous train of black servants, dressed in livery,—some in less splendid array,—and others on foot, all hurrying on to the exciting scene. There the noblest blood of Old Virginia, of which many are wont to boast, was fully represented, as was also the wealth and fashion of the country for many miles around.

All were in high spirits, and none seemed to fear that they would be the losers in the amount of money about to change hands. And for what, pray, is all this grand outlay—this vast expenditure? Merely the pleasure and gratification of witnessing the speed of a fine horse, and the vanity of prejudging concerning it.

The arrangements were at length completed,—the horses regularly entered, Mark Anthony among the rest,—and then the word "go!" was given, when each horse sprang as if for his life, each striving to take the lead. Away they go, sweeping round the course with lightning speed, while every spectator's eye is strained, and every countenance flushed with intense anxiety.

Some of the noble animals were distanced the first heat, and others were taken away by their owners.

The judges allowed twenty minutes to prepare the

horses for the second trial of their speed—a trial which must enrich or empoverish many of the thousands present. Already there were sad countenances to be seen in the crowd.

The horses were again in readiness, and the word given,—away they flew with the fleetness of the wind, to come in the second time.

But who can describe the anxiety written on every face, as they prepared for the third and last trial? I cannot. Many had already lost all they had staked, and others who had bet high began to fear for the result. Soon, however, all was again prepared and those foaming steeds, after having exerted their animal power to the utmost, have accomplished their task and come in for the last time. The purse was won, *but not by Mark Anthony.* Capt. Helm was more fortunate the second day. Buffer won the smaller purse, but the Captain came from the races, a much poorer man than when they commenced. These repeated failures and heavy losses had the effect to arouse him to a sense of his pecuniary position, and he soon after began to think and talk about going to some new country.

He resolved at last to visit the far-off "Genesee Country," which he shortly after put in practice, and after an absence of about three weeks he returned in good health, and delighted with the country; the more so, doubtless, because he said, "the more slaves a man possessed in that country the more he would be respected, and the higher would be his position in society."

Capt. Helm finally concluded to sell his plantation and stock, except the slaves, and remove to the Genesee Country, where he designed to locate his future residence.

The plantation and stock (retaining the slaves) were advertised for sale, and on a certain day named, all would be disposed of at a public sale, or to the highest bidder.

When the day of sale arrived, there flocked from all parts of the surrounding country the largest assemblage of people I ever saw in that place. A large number of wealthy and respectable planters were present, whose gentlemanly behavior should have been an example to others.

The majority of that vast crowd, however, were a rough, quarrelsome, fighting set, just such as might be expected from slave-holding districts. There were several regularly fought battles during the first day of the sale.

One Thomas Ford, a large, muscular, ferocious-looking fellow, a good specimen of a southern bully and woman-whipper, had been victorious through the day in numerous fights and brawls; but he had to pay dear for it when night came. Some one or more of the vanquished party, took advantage of the dark night to stab him in both sides. The knife of the assassin had been thrust into his thigh, tearing the flesh upward, leaving a frightful and dangerous wound; but what is most singular, both sides were wounded in nearly the same manner, and at the same time, for so quickly was the deed committed that the offenders made their escape, before an alarm could be raised for their detection; nor have I ever heard of any one being arrested for the crime.

Ford's groans and cries were painful to hear, but his brother acted like a madman; rushing hither and thither, with a heavy bludgeon in his hand, with which he indiscriminately beat the fences and whatever came in his way, crying "Oh my brother, my poor brother! Who has murdered my poor brother?"

Physicians came to the aid of the wounded man who at first thought he might recover, but in a climate like that of Virginia it was impossible. His friends did all they could to save him, but the poor wretch lingered a few days and died. Thus ended the life of a bad man and a hard master.

And who will wonder, if his slaves rejoiced to hear of his death? If they must be sold to pay his debts, they could not fall into the hands of a more heartless tyrant. Who then can blame those feeble women and helpless children, long held as chattels in his iron grasp, if they are grateful that the man-stealer is no more?

This Ford was a fair specimen of that class, known in more modern parlance as a "Border Ruffian." Such as are at this time endeavoring, by their swaggering and bullying, to cast on the fair fields of Kansas the deep curse of Slavery—a curse which, like the poison of the deadly Upas, blights all within its influence: the colored and the white man, the slave and the master. We were thankful, however, that no more lives were lost during the vendue, which was commenced with the stock; this occupied two days.

The reader will see that we had cause to be grateful, when he takes into consideration that drinking and fighting was the order of the day, and drunkenness and carousing the order of the night.

Then too, the practice of dueling was carried on in all its hideous barbarity. If a gentleman thought himself insulted, he would immediately challenge the offender to mortal combat, and if he refused to do so, then the insulted gentleman felt bound by that barbarous code of honor, to take his life, whenever or wherever he might meet him, though it might be in a crowded assembly, where the lives of innocent persons were endangered.

A case of this kind happened in Kentucky, where the belligerent parties met in a large concourse of people, the majority of them women and children; but the combat ensued, regardless of consequences. One woman was shot through the face, but that was not worthy of notice, for she was only a *colored woman;* and in that, as in other slave States, the laws give to the white population the liberty to trample under foot the claims of all such persons to justice. Justly indignant ladies present remonstrated, but all to no purpose. The Governor of the State was there and was in danger of being wounded by their flying bullets, and it is possible that if he had been in the place of the poor African, some action would have been taken, and laws made to protect the people against such inhuman practices. But I must return to Capt. Helm and the vendue.

The sale continued for several days, during which there was no such thing as rest or sleep or one quiet moment on the premises. As was customary in that State, Capt. Helm provided the food and drink for all who came, and of course a great many came to drink and revel and not to buy; and that class generally took the night time for their hideous outbreaks, when the more respectable class had retired to their beds or to their homes. And many foul deeds and cruel outrages were committed; nor could the perpetrators be detected or brought to justice. Nothing could be done but to submit quietly to their depredations.

One peaceable old slave was killed by having his head split open with an ax. He was found in the morning lying in the yard, with the bloody instrument of death by his side. This occaisoned some excitement among the slaves, but as the white people paid but little attention to it, it soon passed off, and the sorrowful slaves put the old man's remains in a rough box, and conveyed them to their last resting-place.

After the sale was over, the slaves were allowed a holiday, with permission to go and visit their friends and relatives previous to their departure for their new home in a strange land.

The slaves generally on Capt. Helm's plantation looked upon this removal as the greatest hardship they had ever met; the severest trial they had ever endured; and the separation from our old home and fellow-slaves, from our relatives and the old State of Virginia, was to us a contemplation of sorrowful interest. Those who remained, thought us the most unfortunate of human beings to be taken away off into the State of New York, and, as they believed, beyond the bounds of civilization, where we should in all probability be destroyed by wild beasts, devoured by cannibals, or scalped by the Indians. We never expected to meet again in this life, hence our parting interviews were as solemn as though we were committing our friends to the grave. But He whose tender mercies are over all his creatures, knew best what was for our good.

Little did Capt. Helm think when bringing his slaves to New York that in a few short years, they would be singing the song of deliverance from Slavery's thralldom; and as little thought he of the great and painful change, to be brought about in his own circumstances. Could any one have looked into futurity and traced the difficult path, my master was to tread,—could any one have foreseen the end to which he must soon come, and related it to him in the days of his greatness and prosperity, he would, I am certain, have turned from such a narrator of misfortune in a greater rage than did Namaan when the man of God told him "to go and dip seven times in the Jordan."

He could not have believed, nor could I, that in a few years the powerful, wealthy slaveholder, living in luxury and extravagance, would be so reduced that the *necessaries* of life even, were beyond his means, and that he must be supported by the town!

But I anticipate. Let us return to the old plantation which seems dearer than ever, now that we are about to leave it forever.

We thought Capt. Helm's prospects pretty fair, and yet we shuddered when we realized our condition as slaves. This change in our circumstances was calculated to awaken all our fears that had been slumbering, and bring all the perilous changes to which we might be subjected most vividly to mind.

We were about to leave the land of our birth, the home of our childhood, and we felt that untried scenes were before us. We were slaves, it is true, but we had heart-felt emotions to suppress, when we thought of leaving all that was so familar to us, and chose rather to "bear the ills we had, than to fly to those we knew not of." And oh, the terrible uncertainty of the future, that ever rests on the slave, even the most favored, was now felt with a crushing weight. To-day, they are in the old familiar cabin surrounded by their family, relatives and friends; to-morrow, they may be scattered, parted forever. The master's circumstances, not their own, may have assigned one to the dreadful slave-pen, and another to the distant rice-swamp; and it is this continual dread of some perilous future that holds in check every joyous emotion, every lofty aspiration, of the most favored slave at the South. They know that their owners indulge in high living, and they are well aware also that their continual indulgences engender disease, which make them very liable to sudden death; or their master may be killed in a duel, or at a horse-race, or in a drunken brawl; then his creditors are active in looking after the estate; and next, the blow of the auctioneer's hammer separates them perhaps for life.

Now, after the lapse of so many years, when my thoughts wander back, as they often do, to my native State, I confess that painful recollections drive from my mind those joyful emotions that should ever arise in the heart of man, when contemplating the familiar scenes of his youth, and especially when recurring to the venerable shades and the sheltering roof under which he was born. True, around the well-remembered spot where our childhood's years were spent, recollection still loves to linger; yet memory, ever ready with its garnered store, paints in glowing colors, Virginia's crouching slaves in the foreground. Her loathsome slave-pens and slave markets — chains, whips and instruments of torture; and back of all this is as truthfully recorded the certain doom, the retributive justice, that will sooner or later overtake her; and with a despairing sigh I turn away from the imaginary view of my native State.

What though she may have been justly styled, "The Mother of Presidents?" What avails the honor of being the birth-place of the brave and excellent Washington, while the prayers and groans of the down-trodden African daily ascend to heaven for redress? What though her soil be fertile, yielding a yearly product of wealth to its possessors? And what matter is it, that their lordly mansions are embowered in the shade of trees of a century's growth, if, through their lofty and tangled branches, we espy the rough cabin of the mangled bondman, and know that the soil on which he labors has drunk his heart's blood?

Ah! to me, life's sweetest memories are all embittered. Slavery had cast its dark and fearful shadow over my childhood, youth, and early manhood, and I went out from the land of my birth, a fettered slave.

A land which I can regard only as "the house of bondage and the grave of freedom." But God forgive me for having envied my master his fair prospects at this time.

After the sale of the plantation, Capt. Helm was in possession of quite a large sum of money, and having never paid much attention to his pecuniary interests, he acted as if there could be no end of it. He realized about forty thousand dollars from the sale of his estate in Virginia, which would have been a pretty sum in the hands of a man who had been accustomed to look after his own interests; but under the management of one who had all his life lived and prospered on the unrequited toil of slaves, it was of little account. He bought largely of every thing he thought necessary for himself or the comfort of his family, for which he always paid the most extravagant prices. The Captain was not as well qualified to take care of himself and family as some of his slaves were; but he thought differently, and so the preparations for leaving the old plantation for a home in the wilds of New York, went on under his direction, and at last we bade a final adieu to our friends and all we held dear in the State of Virginia.

## CHAPTER IV.

JOURNEY TO OUR NEW HOME IN NEW YORK.

ALL things having been prepared for our departure, our last "Good-bye" spoken, and our last look taken of the old plantation, we started, amid the sobs and prolonged cries of separating families, in company with our master, the overseer and another white man named Davis, who went with us to take back the five-horse "Pennsylvania team," which was provided for the conveyance of the food for the slaves, and what little baggage they might have, and also that of the overseer.

Capt. Helm had determined to leave his family until he could get his slaves settled in their future quarters, and a home provided for himself, when they were expected to join him.

We traveled northward, through Maryland, Pennsylvania, and a portion of New York, to Sodus Bay, where we halted for some time. We made about twenty miles per day, camping out every night, and reached that place after a march of twenty days. Every morning the overseer called the roll, when every slave must answer to his or her name, felling to the ground with his cowhide, any delinquent who failed to speak out in quick time. After the roll had been called, and our scanty breakfast eaten, we marched on again, our company presenting the appearance of some numerous caravan crossing the desert of Sahara. When we pitched our tents for the night, the slaves must immediately set about cooking not their supper only, but their breakfast, so as to be ready to start early the next morning, when the tents were struck; and we proceeded on our journey in this way to the end.

At Sodus Bay there was then one small tavern, kept by a man named Sill.

The bay is ten miles in length and from a half to two miles in breadth, and makes an excellent harbor. The surrounding country then was almost an unbroken wilderness.

After Capt. Helm had rested a few days at Sodus, he went six miles up the bay and purchased a large tract of land lying on both sides of that beautiful sheet of water, and put his slaves on to clear and cultivate it. Then came the "tug of war." Neither the overseer nor the slaves had the least knowledge of *clearing* land, and that was the first thing to be done.

It was useless to consult the Captain, for he knew still less about matters of that kind. To obviate this difficulty, our master bought out a Mr. Cummings, who had some cleared land on the west side of the bay. On this he put the overseer and a part of the slaves, and then hired a Mr. Herrington to take charge of the remainder. Herrington and his gang of slaves was sent to the east side to chop down the heavy timber and clear the land for cultivation, all of which had first to be learned, for we knew nothing of felling trees, and the poor slaves had rather a hard time of it.

Provisions were scarce and could not be procured for cash in that section. There was no corn to be had, and we had but little left. We had no neighbors to assist us in this trying time, and we came near starvation. True, the wild, romantic region in which we were located abounded in game,— elk, deer, bear, panther, and wolves, roamed abroad through the dense forest, in great abundance, but the business of the slaves was not hunting or fishing, but clearing the land, preparatory to raising crops of grain the coming season.

At last Capt. Helm chartered a boat, and manned it to go to the mouth of the Genesee River to buy corn. They embarked under favorable auspices, but soon there came on such a tremendous storm, that the boat could no longer be managed, and the crew in despair threw themselves on the bottom of the boat to await their inevitable destruction, when one of their number, a colored man named Dunbar, sprang to the helm, and with great difficulty succeeded in running her safely into a Canadian port, where they were obliged to part with every thing in their possession to obtain the means to return to their families in Sodus, who had given them up as lost. But, to the great joy of all, they came back at last with their lives, but with nothing for the famishing slaves. Before another boat could be sent for our relief, we were reduced to the last extremity. We became so weak we could not work, and it was difficult to drag ourselves about, as we were now obliged to do, to gather up all the old bones we could find, break them up fine and then boil them; which made a sort of broth sufficient barely to sustain life. This we drank, and merely existed, until at last, the long looked for boat returned, loaded with porvision, which saved us from starvation and gave us strength to pursue our labor.

chastisement, and the overseer was obliged to content himself with threatening what he would do if he caught him on the west side of the bay.

A short time after, the overseer called at the cabin of one of the slaves, and was not a little surprised to find there the refractory slave, Williams, in company with three other men. He immediately walked up to him and asked him some question, to which Williams made no reply. Attended, as he always was, by his ferocious bull-dog, he flourished his cowhide in great wrath and demanded an instant reply, but he received none, whereupon he struck the slave a blow with the cowhide. Instantly Williams sprang and caught him by the throat and held him writhing in his viselike grasp, until he succeeded in getting possession of the cowhide, with which he gave the overseer such a flogging as slaves seldom get. Williams was seized at once by the dog who endeavored to defend his brutal master, but the other slaves came to the rescue, and threw the dog into a huge fire which was near by, from which, after a singeing, he ran off, howling worse than his master when in the hands of Williams. He foamed and swore and still the blows descended; then he commanded the slaves to assist him, but as none obeyed, he commenced begging in the most humble manner, and at last entreated them as "gentlemen" to spare him; but all to no purpose. When Williams thought he had thrashed him sufficiently, he let him

"Instantly Williams sprang and caught him by the throat and held him writhing in his vice-like grasp, until he succeeded in getting possession of the cow-hide, with which he gave the overseer such a flogging as slaves seldom get."

go and hurried to his boat and rowed down the bay, instead of crossing it. The overseer no sooner found himself at liberty than he ran out, calling to a servant girl to bring his rifle, which was loaded. The rifle was brought, but before he could get to the bay, Williams had gone beyond his reach; but unfortunately another boat was at this moment crossing the bay, which he, mad with rage, fired into. The men in the boat immediately cried out to him not to repeat the shot, but he was so angry that he swore he would shoot somebody, and sent another bullet after them. No one was hurt, however, but the brave overseer was vanquished. Crest-fallen and unrevenged, he shortly after called on Capt. Helm for a settlement, which was granted, and bidding a final adieu to the "Genesee Country," he departed for Virginia, where he could beat slaves without himself receiving a cowhiding. No one regretted his absence, nor do I think any but the most heartless would cordially welcome his return to the land of Slavery.

# CHAPTER VI.

### REMOVAL FROM SODUS TO BATH.

CAPT. Helm went to Virginia for his family, and returning with them, concluded to locate his future residence in the village of Bath, Steuben County. He purchased a large tract of land near the village, a large grist mill, and two saw mills; also, two farms; one called the "Maringo," east of the village; and the other, called "Epsam," north of it; and a fine house and lot in the village. He also kept a distillery, which in those days was well patronized, for nearly every body drank whisky; and with Capt. Helm it was a favorite beverage.

The slaves were removed to Bath, where our master was well suited, and was everywhere noted for his hospitality. He had a great deal of land to cultivate, and carried on a multiplicity of business.

Soon after we were settled at Bath, Capt. Helm's eldest daughter, Jenny, was married to Mr. John

Fitzhugh, her cousin, who had come from Virginia to claim his bride.

The wedding was a splendid affair. No pains were spared to make it more imposing than any thing that had ever happened in that country. Never before had the quiet village of Bath seen such splendor. All that wealth, power and ambition could do, was done to make the event one of great brilliancy. Europe contributed her full proportion; Turkey, the Indias, East and West, were heavily taxed to produce their finest fabrics to adorn the bride and bridal guests; and contribute delicacies to add elegance to the festal scene. Two days previous to the wedding, the invited guests began to arrive with their retinue of servants, and on the evening of the marriage the large mansion was thrown open, and there was the most magnificent assemblage I ever beheld. In the drawing-room, where the ceremony took place, every thing was surpassingly elegant. Costly chandeliers shed their light on the rich tapestry, and beautiful dresses glittering with diamonds, and the large mirrors everywhere reflecting the gay concourse. While the servants were preparing supper it was announced that the hour had arrived for the ceremony to commence. The bridal pair took their place in the center of the apartment. Pearls, diamonds, and jewelry glittered on the bride with such luster, that it was almost painful to the eye to look upon her.

The minister, after asking God to bless the assembled guests, and those he was about to unite in the holy bonds of wedlock, proceeded in a very solemn and impressive manner with the marriage service. The ceremony concluded, and good wishes having been expressed over the sparkling wine, the man of God took his leave, two hundred dollars richer than when he came. The company were all very happy, or appeared so; mirth reigned supreme, and every countenance wore a smile. They were seated at tables loaded with luxuries of every description, and while partaking, a band of music enlivened the scene.

All business was suspended for several days, the wedding party making a tour of ten days to Niagara Falls. After a while, however, affairs assumed their usual aspect, and business took its regular routine.

The grist mill belonging to the Captain was the only one for many miles around, and was a source of great profit to him; the saw mills also, were turning out a large quantity of lumber, which was in good demand; and the distillery kept up a *steaming* business. It yielded, however, a handsome income to Capt. Helm, who was now, for the first time since I knew him, overseeing his affairs himself, dispensing altogether with the service of a regularly installed overseer.

The oldest son of our master had been absent from home for sometime, nor did he return to attend his sister's grand wedding. He had sought and obtained a commission in the United States service as a Lieutenant. This had been his own choice; he had preferred the service and hardships of a soldier, to a plantation well stocked with slaves, and the quietude of domestic life. He had cheerfully given up his friends and prospects as a planter, and entered the service of his country. Frank Helm, the second son, soon followed the example of his older brother, Lina. He obtained a like commission, but he did not, like his brother, get along quietly. His prospects as an officer were soon blighted, and all hope of being serviceable to his country vanished forever.

# CHAPTER VII.

### DUELING.

LINA Helm was an easy, good-natured, clever fellow; but his brother Frank was his opposite in nearly every thing; proud, fractious and unyielding. As might be expected, Frank, soon after entering the army, got into an "affair of honor," according to the duelist's code of laws. He was not, however, the principal in the difficulty. One of his friends and a brother officer, had a quarrel with a gentleman whom he challenged to mortal combat. Frank was the bearer of his friend's challenge, and on presenting it, the gentleman refused to accept it, saying that the challenger "was no gentleman." Then, according to the rules of dueling, no alternative was left for Frank, but to take his brother officer's place, and fight. This he did and came from the bloody field disabled for life. In consequence of his lameness, he was under the necessity of resigning his commission in the army, which he did, and came home a cripple, and nearly unfitted for any kind of business whatever

While on the subject of dueling, permit me to record some of the incidents of another "affair of honor," which occurred in the District of Columbia, between Gen. Mason and Mr. M'Carter, two antagonistic politicians.

M'Carter offered his vote to the inspectors, and Mason challenged it. M'Carter offered to swear it in, when Mason said if he did so he would perjure himself. This blew what appeared to be but a spark into an angry blaze, and a duel was momentarily expected; but their warlike propensities subsided into a newspaper combat, which was kept up for several weeks, each party supposing they had the advantage of their adversary. In this stage of the quarrel, Gen. Jackson, with one of his aid-de-camps, Dr. Bruno, visited Washington. Dr. Bruno was a friend of Gen. Mason's, and to him the General submitted the correspondence, desiring his opinion relative to the advantage one had obtained over the other. Dr. Bruno decided against his friend, which probably exasperated him still more, and the General expressed his determination to fight his antagonist. Dr. Bruno wrote to M'Carter to come to Washington, and he came immediately, and was as readily waited upon by the Doctor, who inquired if he would receive a communication from his friend, Gen. Mason. M'Carter replied, that he "would receive no communication from Gen. Mason, except a challenge to fight." The challenge was therefore sent, and accepted, and the Doctor appointed to make the necessary arrangements for the duel. He proposed the weapons to be pistols, and the distance, ten paces; to which M'Carter objected, because he said, "the General was a dead shot with the pistol, while he hardly knew how to use one." Then it was left to M'Carter to choose the mode of warfare. He proposed muskets and ten paces distance. This was agreed upon, and finally the morning arrived for the conflict, and people began to assemble in great numbers to witness this murderous scene.

The belligerent parties unflinchingly took their place, each with his loaded musket at his shoulder, and gazing in each other's face, with feelings of the most bitter hatred, while their eyes flashed vengeance.

Oh! what a state of mind was this in which to meet inevitable death? How could intelligent men, or gentlemen, if you please so to term them, look placidly on such a horrid scene? Was there no heart of humanity to interfere and arrest the murderous designs of these madmen? Alas, no! The slaveholder's "code of honor" must be acknowledged, though it outrage the laws of God and his country.

Dr. Bruno asks, "Gentlemen, are you ready?" and the duelists take their deadly aim at each other. The signal to fire is given, and both weapons are discharged, and when the smoke had cleared away, what a spectacle was there presented to the duellist and spectator? Gen. Mason, a husband, a father, a statesman, and a kind friend, lies bleeding, and gasping for breath. He is no more! Who will bear to his loving and unsuspecting wife, the sad intelligence of her sudden bereavement? Who will convey his lifeless body to his late residence, and throw grief and consternation into the bosom of his family, and drape in sadness his whole household? And yet this painful task must be performed. The family of General Mason remained entirely ignorant of what was transpiring regarding the duel, until his mangled corps was brought into his dwelling, from which he had so recently gone forth in all the vigor of life and manhood. And here let us drop the curtain, nor intrude on that scene of domestic affliction around the deserted hearth-stone of the bereaved family of General Mason.

But where is Mr. McCarter, the more fortunate party in the duel? Hurrying away from the frightful scene, his hands dripping with the blood of his fellow-man, he skulks about, until an opportunity is given him to step on board a vessel bound to a foreign port; he leaves home, friends and country, in the vain hope of finding peace of mind, and ridding himself of that guilt and censure which must attach itself to a crime so heinous as that of taking the life of another. I can but regard the inhuman practice of dueling as the legitimate fruit of Slavery.

Men who have been raised in the Slave States, where, if the laws do not give them the power, they do not restrain them from cruelly punishing every offender with personal violence, even unto death, if their insulted dignity seems to demand it. It is, however, encouraging to know that for a few years past the practice of dueling has somewhat fallen into disrepute among the more humane and candid class of community.

# CHAPTER VIII.

### HORSE-RACING AND GENERAL TRAINING.

AFTER the return of the wedding party, Mr. Fitzhugh purchased a tract of land near that of Capt. Helm, on which the newly-married couple commenced keeping house. They, however, became dissatisfied with their location, and soon after sold their possessions and returned to the South.

Capt. Helm still continued to take the oversight of his slaves, and was out every day, superintending his business, just as his overseer used to do.

About this time a man named Henry Tower came to Bath to hire "slave boys," as we were called. The Captain hired to him Simon and myself, and a Mr. Baker also hired to him one slave named Vol. McKenzie. We three started for Dresden, Ontario County, where we arrived in due time.

Mr. Tower had just bought a tract of land, three miles this side of the village of Lyons, on the Canandaigua outlet. Here Mr. Tower contemplated making great improvements, building mills, opening stores &c. This tract of land was comparatively wild, there being but a small frame house for a dwelling, one for a store, and another for a blacksmith shop. Mr. Tower had two brothers; James, the eldest, who took charge of the store, and John, the younger, who took charge of the hands who worked on the farm; Henry himself superintending the building of the mills. This firm had a great number of men in their employ that year. I was kept busy helping the women about the cooking and house-work. And here, for the first time in my life, I had a comfortable bed to sleep on, and plenty of wholesome food to eat; which was something both new and strange to me.

The Towers were thorough-going business-men; they built a large grist mill, with four run of stone, and also a distillery. In those days it was customary for nearly all classes to drink spirituous liquors; hence, the distilleries were sources of great pecuniary interest to those who owned them. But having lived to see the dreadful evils which the drinking of alcoholic beverages have produced on community, I can hardly speak of distilleries in the favorable light in which they were then regarded.

The Towers, with commendable enterprize, cleared a great number of acres of land during the first year I lived with them, besides doing a heavy business in the mill, store and distillery.

It was customary then for men to assemble at some public place for the purpose of drinking whisky and racing horses.

One Saturday afternoon there was to be a race, and all was excitement. Being young, I wished to go with the rest. I hurried through my work as fast as possible, and then, with a trembling heart, set off in search of my master, fearing lest he would refuse me the simple request. But he happened to be in uncommon good humor, and readily gave his consent; and away I went, "as happy as a lark." When I reached the race-ground, they were just preparing to run the horses. Seeing me, they knew me to be a poor friendless little slave boy, helpless and unprotected, and they could therefore do with me as they pleased, and have some fine sport at my expense.

When I was asked to ride one of the fast horses, I felt proud of the honor conferred, and was assisted to mount, feeling highly elated with the lofty position I had gained.

The word "go," was shouted, and the horse whirled off, and it seemed to me as if he flew with the speed of lightning. My hat fell off the first thing; and there I was, clinging with might and main to the neck of the fiery animal, my head bare, my feet bootless, and my old stripped shirt blown from my back, and streaming out behind, and fluttering like a banner in the breeze; my ragged pants off at the knees, and my long legs dangling down some length below; and at the same time crying "Whoa! whoa!" as loud as I could. Nor was this all; frightened as I was, nearly to death, I cast a despairing look behind me, and the loud, derisive laugh of the bystanders rung in my ears.

Ludicrous as I must have appeared, this was too much,—I felt a giddiness coming over me, my brain reeled, my hold relaxed, and the next instant I had fallen to the ground, where all consciousness left me. When I came to my senses I was lying in bed, surrounded by all the appurtenances of a dying person.

The first thing I heard was Mr. Tower scolding the men who put me on the horse, and threatening them with a law-suit for presuming to do such a thing without his permission. Mr. Tower considered himself holden to Capt. Helm for my safe return, and was therefore justly indignant at their placing my life in such peril. It was indeed a narrow escape, for the horse was running with all his speed when I fell. My bones were unbroken, however, and I suppose it must have been the tremendous jar I got when I fell that rendered me unconscious; nor do I think it impossible that the fright may not have contributed somewhat to the catastrophe.

It was while I was living with that gentleman that the greatest "general training" ever known in Western New York, came off at "Oak's Corners," in the town of Phelps. It really seemed to me that the whole world were going to the training, and I, of course, felt a great curiosity to go where "all creation" appeared to be going. Mr. Tower permitted me to go, and I started off in high spirits. When I arrived within two or three miles of the place the road was almost blocked up with people, and when I got to Oak's Corners the crowd beggared all description; carriages of all sorts were there, containing eatables of all kinds, and tents of all dimensions were on the road-side, for the houses could not begin to accommodate the people. The entire brigade was to meet at that place, and Gov. Lewis was expected to review the different companies, and all were anxious to see the Governor, for, in those days, it was a rare thing to see so high a dignitary in Western New York; the eastern portion of the State having had every thing of that kind their own way.

Nor was the means and mode of traveling brought to such perfection as now. The roads were new and rough, and our best public conveyances only the slow lumbering stage-coach; yet, notwithstanding these inconveniences, there was an innumerable crowd gathered at that place. I spent the day in walking about the encampment, and seeing what was to be seen, for it was all new to me.

Officers were riding over the ground, dressed in uniform, and mounted on their splendid steeds; their plumes waving over their cocked-hats in true military

D

array. A band of music, as is usual, accompanied the soldiers. There was also a "sham-fight," before the breaking up of the encampment, and it was really terrifying to me, who had never seen a battle fought, to witness two columns of troops drawn up, and, at the roll of the drum, behold them engage in deadly conflict, to all appearance, and the smoke curling up in a blackened mass toward heaven; and, above all, the neighing of horses, with the feigned groans of the wounded and dying. I inwardly prayed to God that those men might ever draw their weapons in a feigned encounter.

The first night I spent at the encampment was one long to be remembered; it was like the confusion of Babel. Of all the hideous noises I ever heard none could exceed those made there that night. They fired guns, quarreled, drank, and swore, till daylight. There was such a crowd at the tavern that I did not suppose I could get a bed, so I threw myself down upon a door-step, and began to compose myself to sleep, when a man came and wakened me, inquiring at the same time whose boy I was. I replied that I lived with Mr. Tower. "Follow me," said he; I arose and followed him into the house, where he procured for me a bed, to be shared with another "boy," who had already occupied it.

I had just began to dose, when the explosion of firearms startled all in the house. The keeper of the tavern ran up stairs in great alarm, and when an examination was made, we found that a drunken fellow had discharged his musket in the room below the one where we were sleeping, and that the ball had passed up through the second floor and completely through the bed on which I slept, to the roof, where, having passed through that also, rolled from thence to the ground! And yet, strange as it may appear, no one was injured, though the house was filled to overflowing with guests.

There were groups of disorderly and drunken men continually roaming over the camp-ground at night, who seemed to have no other object than to annoy others, and torment any one they might find sleeping, by shaking them, or, if soundly asleep, dragging them out of their beds by their feet. Among these thus annoyed by them was a physician from Canandaigua. Being a passionate man, they seemed to think it fine sport to arouse him from sleep and hear him scold. The first time they dragged him from his tent he merely remonstrated in a very gentlemanly manner, and quietly crept back again. The rowdies were disappointed; they had expected a "scene." As soon as he was asleep they attacked him again, dragging him out by the heels; then he was angry, and told them if they repeated the offence it would be at the peril of their lives, and a third time retired to his tent; but a third party soon came, and one, more bold than the military spirit, and sighed for the liberty to go out "on the lines" and fight the British.

The martial music, the waving plumes, and magnificent uniform, had driven from my mind entirely the bloodshed and carnage of the battle field; beside, I was sick and tired of being a slave, and felt ready to do almost any thing to get where I could act and feel like a free man.

I became acquainted with a Mr. McClure, a merchant in Bath, who, while on a journey to Philadelphia, to purchase goods, was taken suddenly ill and died; when his brother, George McClure, came on to attend to his diseased brother's business. He was a fine, persevering kind of man, and very soon got to be General McClure, and commanded the brigade in Steuben County, and, as such, was liable to be called at any time when his services were required, to go to the frontier and guard our lines from the invasion of the English army.

To him I applied for a situation as waiter, which he readily agreed to give me if I could get the consent of Captain Helm. I thought there would be no trouble about that; and oh! how I dreamed of and anticipated the happiness of being *something* beside a slave, for a *little while at least*. Almost every day I went to the store to talk to Gen. McClure of this greatest happiness imaginable, "going to the lines!" and was impatient for the chance to arrive that would send me there.

At last Gen. McClure wrote to Gen. Armstrong, to say that he was ready to obey any order that he might send him, and march to "the lines," if his services were needed; and, to *my* inexpressible joy, marching orders were returned. I nearly flew in search of Capt. Helm, never once suspecting that he would object; because I knew that he did not then require my services himself, and the pay would be quite as good as he had been receiving for my time; besides I had so completely set my heart on going, that it was impossible for me to dream of a disappointment so bitter as that of being denied going "to the lines."

Oh! how then were my high hopes fallen, and how much more hateful appeared that slavery which had blighted all my military prospects? Nor was Capt. Helm's heartless and mercenary reply to my humble pleading any antidote to my disappointed feelings and desire for freedom. He said, "you shall not go; I will permit nothing of the kind, so let there be an end to it. The *pay* is all well enough, I know, but if you get killed your wages will stop; and then who, do you suppose, will indemnify me for the loss? Go about your business, and let me hear no more of such nonsense!"

There was an emergency I had not provided for; and, as I then believed, the master could make no demand on or for the slaves beyond the grave, I was silent; but both master and myself were mistaken on that point; for I have since learned numerous instances where slaves have fought and died in the service of their master's country, and the slave-owner received his wages up to the hour of his death, and then recovered of the United States the full value of his person as property!

Gen. McClure left soon after for the frontier; my saddened heart followed him, and that was all; my body was in slavery still, and painful though it was, I must quietly submit.

The General, however, reaped but few if any laurels in that campaign; he burned the small village of Newark, in Canada, for which he got very little credit on either side of the lake; so I comforted myself as well as I could with the reflection, that all who "went to the wars" did not return covered with glory and laurels of victory.

I continued to live with the Towers; and in the fall of that year, I had the misfortune to cut my foot badly. While chopping fire wood at the door, I accidentally struck my ax against a post, which glanced the blow in such a manner that it came down with sufficient force to nearly sever my great toe from my left foot, gashing upward completely through the large joint, which made a terrible wound. Dr. Taylor was immediately called, and sewed the flesh together, taking two stitches on the upper, and one on the under, side of the foot, before it began to swell;

but when the swelling came on, the stitches on the upper side gave way, which occasioned the toe to fall over so much, that I have been slightly lame from that day to this. For several weeks I was unable to be moved, and was regularly attended by Dr. Taylor, but as soon as it could be done without danger, I was taken back to Capt. Helm's, where I found things in much the same condition as when I left them over a year before.

On leaving the family of Mr. Tower, I endeavored to express to them as well in my power the gratitude I felt for their kindness, and the attention I had received during my lameness.

We returned to Bath in a sleigh, and arrived without accident or any great suffering. But the kind treatment I had always received from the Messrs. Tower and family, made it very hard for me to reconcile myself to my former mode of living; especially now that I was lame and weak, from sickness and long confinement; besides, it was cold weather. Oh! how hard it did seem to me, after having a good bed and plenty of bed clothes every night for so long time, to now throw myself down, like a dog, on the "*softest side*" of a rough board, without a pillow, and without a particle of bedding to cover me during the long cold nights of winter. To be reduced from a plentiful supply of good, wholesome food, to the mere pittance which the Captain allowed his slaves, seemed to me beyond endurance.

And yet I had always lived and fared thus, but I never felt so bitterly these hardships and the cruelties of Slavery as I did at that time; making a virtue of necessity, however, I turned my thoughts in another direction.

I managed to purchase a spelling book, and set about teaching myself to read, as best I could. Every spare moment I could find was devoted to that employment, and when about my work I could catch now and then a stolen glance at my book, just to refresh my memory with the simple lesson I was trying to learn. But here Slavery showed its cloven foot in all its hideous deformity. It finally reached the ears of my master that I was learning to read; and then, if he saw me with a book or a paper in my hand, oh, how he would swear at me, sending me off in a hurry, about some employment. Still I persevered, but was more careful about being seen making any attempt to learn to read. At last, however, I was discovered, and had to pay the penalty of my determination.

I had been set to work in the sugar bush, and I took my spelling book with me. When a spare moment occurred I sat down to study, and so absorbed was I in the attempt to blunder through my lesson, that I did not hear the Captain's son-in-law coming until he was fairly upon me. He sprang forward, caught my poor old spelling book, and threw it into the fire, where it was burned to ashes; and then came my turn. He gave me first a severe flogging, and then swore if he ever caught me with another book, he would "whip every inch of skin off my back," &c.

This treatment, however, instead of giving me the least idea of giving it up, only made me look upon it as a more valuable attainment. Else, why should my oppressors feel so unwilling that their slaves should possess that which they thought so essential to themselves? Even then, with my back bleeding and smarting from the punishment I had received, I determined to learn to read and write, at all hazards, if my life was only spared. About this time Capt. Helm began to sell off his slaves to different persons, as he could find opportunity, and sometimes at a great sacrifice. It became apparent that the Captain, instead of prospering in business, was getting poorer every day.

# CHAPTER IX.

### DEATH BED AND BRIDAL SCENES.

NEITHER Capt. Helm nor his wife made any religious pretensions. I hardly know whether or not they were avowed infidels; but they alike ridiculed all religious professions and possessed some very singular notions regarding life and death.

I have often heard the Captain say, that no person need die unless they choose to do so; and his wife was of the same belief. I have frequently heard her remark that if mankind would firmly resist death it would flee from them.

An opportunity, however, was soon after given to test the truth of this strange dogma. Mrs. Helm's health began to decline, but she would pay no attention to it, following her usual course and regular routine of household duties; but all in vain; she was taken down, alarmingly ill, and it became apparent to all, that the "king of terrors" had chosen his victim.

"If any one had ever envied Mrs. Helm in her drawing-room, richly attired and sparkling with jewels, or as she moved with the stately step of a queen among her trembling slaves, they should have beheld her on her death-bed!"   page 85.

She tried with all her natural energy of character, to baffle his pursuit and escape his steady approach, but all to no purpose. "The valley and the shadow of death" were before her, and she had no assurance that the "rod and staff" of the Almighty would sustain and comfort her through the dark passage. She shrank with perfect horror from the untried scenes of the future.

If any one had ever envied Mrs. Helm in her drawing-room, richly attired and sparkling with jewels, or as she moved with the stately step of a queen among her trembling slaves, they should have beheld her on her death bed! They should have listened to her groans and cries for help, while one piercing shriek after another rang through the princely mansion of which she had been the absolute mistress!

Surrounded as she was with every elegance and luxury that wealth could procure, she lay shrieking out her prayers for a short respite, a short lengthening out of the life she had spent so unprofitably; her eyes wandering restlessly about the apartment, and her hands continually clinching the air, as if to grasp something that would prevent her from sinking into the embrace of death! There was not a slave present, who would have exchanged places with her. Not one of those over whom she had ruled so arbitrarily would have exchanged their rough, lowly cabin and quiet conscience, for all the wealth and power she had ever possessed.

Nothing of all she had enjoyed in life, nor all that she yet called her own, could give her one hour of life or one peaceful moment in death!

Oh! what a scene was that! The wind blew, and great drops of rain fell on the casements. The room lighted only with a single taper; the wretched wife mingles her dying groans with the howling of the storm, until, as the clock struck the hour of midnight she fell back upon her pillow and expired, amid the tears and cries of her family and friends, who not only deplored the loss of a wife and mother, but were grieved by the manner in which she died.

The slaves were all deeply affected by the scene; some doubtless truly lamented the death of their mistress; others rejoiced that she was no more, and all were more or less frightened. One of them I remember went to the pump and wet his face, so as to appear to weep with the rest.

What a field was opened for reflection, by the agonizing death of Mrs. Helm? Born and reared in affluence; well educated and highly accomplished, possessed of every means to become a useful woman and an ornament to her sex; which she most likely would have been, had she been instructed in the Christian religion, and had lived under a different influence. As infidelity ever deteriorates from the female character, so Slavery transforms more than one, otherwise excellent woman, into a feminine monster.

Of Mrs. Helm, with her active intellect and great force of character, it made a tyrannical demon. Her race, however, is ended; her sun gone down in darkness, and her soul we must leave in the keeping of a righteous God, to whom we must all give an account for the deeds done in the body. But in view of the transitory pleasures of this life; the unsatisfactory realization of wealth, and the certainty of death, we may well inquire, "What shall it profit a man to gain the whole world and lose his own soul?"

Some little time after the scene just recorded, there came to Bath a young physician named Henry, who commenced practice under very flattering prospects. He was an accomplished young man, well educated and very skillful in his profession. He was affable and gay in his manners, and very fond of company. An intimate acquaintance was soon formed with Capt. Helm and family, and he called almost daily to chat and drink wine with the Captain,—both being quite fond of a social glass.

One night in the depth of winter, the Doctor was called to see a patient who lived six miles down the Conhocton river. Previous, however, to the call, he had accepted an invitation to attend a party at Capt. Helm's, and there he was found. They had music and dancing, while the wine passed around very freely. None seemed to join in the dance and other amusements of the evening with more enjoyment than did

Dr. Henry; but after he was sent for, it being a most bitter cold night, he asked the Captain for a horse to ride to see his patient, to which he readily assented, and had his fine *race-horse* (for the Captain had not left off all his old habits), brought out from the stable, and the Doctor sprang lightly into the saddle. Unfortunately his way led by the race-course, and when the trained animal came to it he started with such speed as to throw the Doctor to the ground, where he lay all that terrible cold night. In the morning, some person going after wood, came in sight of the Doctor as he was trying to creep away on his frozen hands and feet. He was put into the sleigh and taken to the village with all possible speed. All was done for him that could be, but his feet and legs were frozen solid. His uncle, Dr. Henry, was brought as soon as possible, who decided that nothing could save his life but the amputation of both legs, just below the knee. This was done; but what a change in the prospects of this promising young man! Instead of stepping lightly about as he used to do, with a smiling countenance, he at last came forth after a tedious confinement, a cripple for life, hobbling about on his knees, sad and dejected. And what, think you, was the cause of this terrible calamity? What prevented the Doctor from an exertion to save his life? Wine, intoxicating wine, was undoubtedly the occasion of the heedless and reckless conduct of both himself and Capt. Helm.

And should not this circumstance be a warning to parents and guardians, to young men and children, "to look not upon the wine when it is red," and remember that at last "it will bite like a serpent and sting like an adder?" Should it not also remind those who have guests to entertain, of the sinfulness of putting the cup to their neighbor's lips? Certainly it should. But I must resume my story.

About this time Major Thornton of Bath, died. He had long been an intimate friend and acquaintance of Capt. Helm, and as the reader is already informed of the death of Mrs. Helm, they will not be surprised to know that he began to look earnestly after the widow of his late friend. It become apparent that his solicitude for the loneliness of Madam Thornton was not so much as a disconsolate widow, as that of making her the future Mrs. Helm; nor was it less observable that the new-made widow accepted the Captain's attentions with great favor, and more as a lover than a comforter.

The result was, after the Major had been dead six weeks, Capt. Helm was married to his widow, and brought her and her servants in great triumph to his house, giving her the charge of it. His own servants were discharged, and hers took their places.

All went on pleasantly for a while; then the slaves began to grow sullen and discontented; and two of them ran away. Capt. Helm started a man named

Morrison, a Scotchman, in pursuit, who hunted them ten days, and then returned without any tidings of the absconding slaves. They made good their escape and were never heard from afterwards, by those whose interest suffered by the loss.

I was one afternoon at a neighbor's house in the village, when I was suddenly taken so violently ill with pain in my head and side, that I had to be carried home. When we arrived there, I was allowed a pallet of straw to lie on, which was better than nothing. Day after day, my disease increased in violence, and my master employed a physician to attend me through my illness, which brought me very low indeed. I was constantly burning with fever, and so thirsty that I knew not what I would have given for a draught of cold water, which was denied me by the physician's direction. I daily grew weaker until I was reduced to helplessness, and was little else than "skin and bones." I really thought my time had come to die; and when I had strength to talk, I tried to arrange the few little business affairs I had, and give my father direction concerning them. And then I began to examine my own condition before God, and to determine how the case stood between Him and my poor soul. And "there was the rub." I had often excused myself, for frequent derelictions in duty, and often wild and passionate outbreaks, on account of the hardness of my lot, and the injustice with which I was treated, even in my best endeavors to do as well as I knew how. But now, with death staring me in the face, I could see that though I was a friendless "slave-boy," I had *not* always done as well as I knew how; that I had *not* served God as I knew I ought, nor had I always set a good example before my fellow-slaves, nor warned them as well as I might, "to flee the wrath to come." Then I prayed my Heavenly Father to spare me a little longer, that I might serve Him better; and in His mercy and gracious goodness, He did so; though when the fever was turning they gave me up; and I could hear them say, when they came to feel my pulse, "he is almost gone," "it will soon be over,' &c., and then inquire if I knew them. I did, but was too weak to say so. I recollect with gratitude, the kindness of Mrs. H. A. Townsend, who sent me many delicacies and cooling drinks to soften the rigor of my disease; and though I suppose she has long since "passed away" and gone to her reward, may the blessing of those who are ready to perish, rest upon the descendants of that excellent woman.

Capt. Helm was driving on in his milling, distillery and farming business. He now began to see the necessity of treating his slaves better by far than he had ever done before, and granted them greater privileges than he would have dared to do at the South. Many of the slaves he had sold, were getting their liberty and doing well.

# CHAPTER X.

### HIRED OUT TO A NEW MASTER.

WHILE I was staying with my master at Bath, he having little necessity for my services, hired me out to a man by the name of Joseph Robinson, for the purpose of learning me to drive a team. Robinson lived about three miles from the village of Bath, on a small farm, and was not only a poor man but a very mean one. He was cross and heartless in his family, as well as tyrannical and cruel to those in his employ; and having hired me as a "slave boy," he appeared to feel at full liberty to wreak his brutal passion on me at any time, whether I deserved rebuke or not; nor did his terrible outbreaks of anger vent themselves in oaths, curses and threatenings only, but he would frequently draw from the cart-tongue a heavy iron pin, and beat me over the head with it, so unmercifully that he frequently sent the blood flowing over my scanty apparel, and from that to the ground, before he could feel satisfied.

These kind of beatings were not only excessively painful, but they always reminded me of the blows I had so often received from the key, in the hand of Mrs. Helm, when I was but a little waiter lad; and in truth I must say that the effect of these heavy blows on the head, have followed me thus far through life; subjecting me to frequent and violent head-aches, from which I never expect to be entirely free. Even to this day I shudder at the thought, when I think how Robinson used to fly at me, swearing, foaming, and seeming to think there was no weapon too large or too heavy to strike me with.

He and I were at one time logging with a yoke of oxen, which it was my business to drive. At that time rattle-snakes were numerous, and a great terror to the inhabitants. To be bitten by one of these poisonous reptiles was certain and almost instant death; hence, the greatest caution and constant vigilance was necessary to avoid them while at work. I had been sent with the oxen to draw a log to the pile, and when I came up to it, I observed that it appeared to be hollow; but stepping forward, with the chain in my hand, ready to attach it to the log, when, oh, horror! the warning rattle of a snake sounded like a death-knell in my ears, proceeding from the log I was about to lay hold of. I was so much frightened by the sound, that I dropped the chain as though it were red hot, left my team, and ran with all the speed in my power, screaming "murder, murder!" as loud as I could.

This proceeding, which was the fearful impulse of the moment, offended Robinson, and gave him another opportunity to beat me most cruelly. He was himself as much afraid of rattle-snakes as I; but he was the master and I the "slave boy," which made a vast difference. He caught hold of me, and, with horrid oaths, beat me with his fist again and again; threatening me with awful punishment if I did not instantly return and bring the log to the desired spot. I never can forget the mortal agony I was in, while compelled by his kicks and blows to return and fasten the chain around the log containing the deadly serpent. I, however, succeeded with trembling hands, and drove the oxen, but keeping myself at the far therest possible distance from them and the log When I finally arrived at the pile, Mr. Robinson and some other men, cut a hole with an ax in the log, and killed the large, venomous rattle-snake that had occasioned me so much alarm and such a cruel beating. Nor was the uncontrolable and brutal passion of Robinson his only deficiency; he was mean as he was brutal.

He had, at one time, borrowed a wagon of a neighbor living two miles distant, through a dense forest. On the day of the total eclipse of the sun, it entered his head that it would be fine sport, knowing my ignorance and superstition, to send me, just as the darkness was coming on, to return the borrowed wagon. I accordingly hitched the ox-team to it and started. As I proceeded through the wood, I saw, with astonishment and some alarm, that it was growing very dark, and thought it singular at that hour of the day. When I reached the place of my destination it was almost total darkness, and some persons, ignorant as myself, were running about, wringing their hands, and declaring that they believed the Day of Judgment had come, and such like expressions.

The effect of all this was, however, very different from what my master had expected. I thought, of course, if the judgment day had come, I should be no longer a slave in the power of a heartless tyrant. I recollect well of thinking, that if indeed all things earthly were coming to an end, I should be free from Robinson's brutal force, and as to meeting my Creator, I felt far less dread of that than of meeting my cross, unmerciful master. I felt that, sinful as I had been, and unworthy as I was, I should be far better off than I then was; driven to labor all day, without compensation; half starved and poorly clad, and above all, subjected to the whims and caprices of any heartless tyrant to whom my master might give the power to rule over me. But I had not much time for reflection, I hurried home; my mind filled with the calm anticipation that the end of all things was at hand; which greatly disappointed my expectant master, who was looking for me to return in a great fright, making some very ludicrous demonstration of fear and alarm. But after a few months more of hardship I was permitted to return to Capt. Helm's, where I was treated much better than at Robinson's, and much better than the Captain used to treat his slaves.

Capt. Helm, not having demand for slave labor as much as formerly, was in the practice of hiring out his slaves to different persons, both in and out of the village; and among others, my only sister was hired out to a *professed* gentleman living in Bath. She had become the mother of two or three children, and was considered a good servant.

One pleasant Sabbath morning, as I was passing the house where she lived, on my way to the Presbyterian church, where I was sent to ring the bell as usual, I heard the most piteous cries and earnest pleadings issuing from the dwelling. To my horror and the astonishment of those with me, my poor sister made her appearance, weeping bitterly, and followed by her inhuman master, who was polluting the air of that clear Sabbath morning, with the most horrid imprecations and threatenings, and at the same time flourishing a large raw-hide. Very soon his bottled wrath burst forth, and the blows, aimed with all his strength, descended upon the unprotected head, shoulders and back of the helpless woman, until she was literally cut to pieces. She writhed in his powerful grasp, while shriek after shriek died away in heart-rending moanings; and yet the inhuman demon continued to beat her, though her pleading cries had ceased, until obliged to desist from the exhaustion of his own strength.

What a spectacle was that, for the sight of a brother? The God of heaven only knows the conflict of feeling I then endured; He alone witnessed the tumult of my heart, at this outrage of manhood and kindred affection. God knows that my will was good enough to have wrung his neck; or to have drained from his heartless system its last drop of blood! And yet I was obliged to turn a deaf ear to her cries for assistance, which to this day ring in my ears. Strong and athletic as I was, no hand of mine could be raised in her defence, but at the peril of both our lives;—nor could her husband, had he been a witness of the scene, be allowed any thing more than unresisting submission to any cruelty, any indignity which the master saw fit to inflict on *his wife*, but the other's *slave*.

Does any indignant reader feel that I was wanting in courage or brotherly affection, and say that he would have interfered, and, at all hazards, rescued his sister from the power of her master; let him remember that he is a *freeman;* that he has not from his infancy been taught to cower beneath the white man's frown, and bow at his bidding, or suffer all the rigor

E

of the slave laws. Had the gentlemanly woman-whipper been seen beating his horse, or his ox, in the manner he beat my poor sister, and that too for no fault which the law could recognize as an offence, he would have been complained of most likely; but as it was, she was but a "slave girl,"—with whom the slave law allowed her master to do what he pleased.

Well, I finally passed on, with a clinched fist and contracted brow, to the church, and rung the bell, I think rather furiously, to notify the inhabitants of Bath, that it was time to assemble for the worship of that God who has declared himself to be "no respecter of persons." With my own heart beating wildly with indignation and sorrow, the kind reader may imagine my feelings when I saw the smooth-faced hypocrite, the inhuman slave-whipper, enter the church, pass quietly on to his accustomed seat, and then meekly bow his hypocritical face on the damask cushion, in the reverent acknowledgment of that religion which teaches its adherents "to do unto others as they would be done by," just as if nothing unusual had happened on that Sabbath morning. Can any one wonder that I, and other slaves, often doubted the sincerity of every white man's religion? Can it be a matter of astonishment, that slaves often feel that there is no just God for the poor African? Nay, verily; and were it not for the comforting and sustaining influence that these poor, illiterate and suffering creatures feel as coming from an unearthly source, they would in their ignorance all become infidels. To me, that beautiful Sabbath morning was clouded in midnight darkness, and I retired to ponder on what could be done.

For some reason or other, Capt. Helm had supplied every lawyer in that section of country with slaves, either by purchase or hire; so when I thought of seeking legal redress for my poor, mangled sister, I saw at once it would be all in vain. The laws were in favor of the slave owner, and besides, every legal gentleman in the village had one or more of the Captain's slaves, who were treated with more or less rigor; and of course they would do nothing toward censuring one of their own number, so nothing could be done to give the slave even the few privileges which the laws of the State allowed them.

The Captain sold my aunt Betsy Bristol to a distinguished lawyer in the village, retaining her husband, Aaron Bristol, in his own employ; and two of her children he sold to another legal gentleman named Cruger. One day Captain Helm came out where the slaves were at work, and finding Aaron was not there, he fell into a great rage and swore terribly. He finally started off to a beach tree, from which he cut a stout limb, and trimmed it so as to leave a knot on the but end of the stick, or bludgeon rather, which was about two and a half feet in length. With this formidable weapon he started for Aaron's lonely cabin. When the solitary husband saw him coming he suspected that he was angry, and went forth to meet him in the street. They had no sooner met than my master seized Aaron by the collar, and taking the limb he had prepared by the smaller end, commenced beating him with it, over the head and face, and struck him some thirty or more terrible blows in quick succession; after which Aaron begged to know for what he was so unmercifully flogged.

"Because you deserve it," was the angry reply. Aaron said that he had ever endeavored to discharge his duty, and had done so to the best of his ability; and that he thought it very hard to be treated in that manner for no offence at all. Capt. Helm was astonished at his audacity; but the reader will perceive that the slaves were not blind to the political condition of the country, and were beginning to feel that they had some rights, and meant to claim them.

Poor Aaron's face and head, however, was left in a pitiable condition after such a pummelling with a knotty stick. His face, covered with blood, was so swollen that he could hardly see for some time; but what of that? Did he not belong to Capt. Helm, soul and body; and if his brutal owner chose to destroy his own property, certainly had he not a right to do so, without let or hindrance? Of course; such is the power that Slavery gives one human being over another.

And yet it must be confessed that among the poor, degraded and ignorant slaves there exists a foolish pride, which loves to boast of their master's wealth and influence. A white person, too poor to own slaves, is as often looked upon with as much disdain by the miserable slave as by his wealthy owner. This disposition seems to be instilled into the mind of every slave at the South, and indeed, I have heard slaves object to being sent in very small companies to labor in the field, lest that some passer-by should think that they belonged to a poor man, who was unable to keep a large gang. Nor is this ridiculous sentiment maintained by the slaves only; the rich planter feels such a contempt for all white persons without slaves, that he does not want them for his neighbors. I know of many instances where such persons have been under the necessity of buying or hiring slaves, just to preserve their reputation and keep up appearances; and even among a class of people who profess to be opposed to Slavery, have I known instances of the same kind, and have heard them apologize for their conduct by saying that "when in Rome, we must do as the Romans do."

Uncle Aaron Bristol was one of Capt. Helm's slaves who had a large amount of this miserable pride; and for him to be associated with a white man in the same humble occupation, seemed to give him ideas of great superiority, and full liberty to treat him with all the scorn and sarcasm he was capable of, in which my uncle was by no means deficient.

At this time the Captain owned a fine and valuable horse, by the name of *Speculator*. This horse, groomed by uncle Aaron, stood sometimes at Bath and sometimes at Geneva; and at the latter village another horse was kept, groomed by a white man. The white groom was not very well pleased with Aaron's continual disparagement of the clumsy animal which my uncle called "a great, awkward plow-horse;" and then he would fling out some of his proud nonsense about "*poor white people* who were obliged to groom their own old dumpy horses," &c.

Well, things went on in this unpleasant manner for several weeks, when at last the white groom and Aaron met at Geneva, and the horse belonging to the former, designedly or accidentally, escaped from his keeper, and came with full speed, with his mouth wide open, after Speculator. When the fiery fellow had overtaken uncle Aaron he attempted to grasp the wethers of Speculator with his teeth, instead of which he caught Aaron on the inside of his thigh, near the groin, from whence he bit a large piece of flesh, laying the bone entirely bare; at the same moment flinging Aaron to the ground, some rods off; and the next instant he kicked Speculator down a steep embankment. Aaron was taken up for dead, and Dr. Henry sent for, who dressed his wounds; and after several months' confinement he finally recovered. It is probable that the biting and overthrow of Aaron saved his life, as he must have otherwise been killed in the encounter of the two horses.

A while after his recovery, uncle Aaron succeeded in procuring a team and some kind of vehicle, in which he put his wife and children, and between two days, took "French leave" of his master as well as of the lawyer to whom his wife belonged.

The lawyer, however, was far from being pleased when he missed his property, and immediately set his wits to work to reclaim her. All was kept secret as possible, but it was whispered about that it was to be done by a State's warrant, for removing the clothing and furniture they had taken, and so, being thus arrested, "Madam Bristol" would be glad to return to her work in the lawyer's kitchen. But Aaron was a smart, shrewd man, and kept out of their reach, where he soon found friends and employment, and could go where he pleased, without having an infuriated master to beat and disfigure him with a knotted stick, until his clothes were bespattered with blood. They appreciated their liberty, and lived and died in peace and freedom.

Capt. Helm continued his old manner of treating slaves, dealing out their weekly allowance of corn or meal; but living as we now did, so much more intimately with white inhabitants, our condition was materially improved. The slaves became more refined in manners and in possession of far greater opportunities to provide for themselves, than they had ever before enjoyed, and yet it was *Slavery*. Any reverse in the fortunes of our master would be disadvantageous to us. Oh, how this fearful uncertainty weighed upon us as we saw that our master was not prospering and increasing in wealth; but we had not the dismal fears of the loathsome slave-pen, rice swamps, and many other things we should have to fear in Virginia. We were still *slaves*, and yet we had so much greater chance to learn from the kind, intelligent people about us, so many things which we never knew before, that I think a slave-trader would have found it a difficult task to take any one of us to a Southern slave market, if our master had so ordered it.

The village of Bath is rather an out-of-the-way place, hemmed in on all sides by mountains of considerable height, leaving an opening on the north, through a pleasant valley, to the head of Crooked Lake. Produce of every kind, when once there, met a ready sale for the New York market.

In the first settlement of the country this was the only outlet for the country produce, which was transported in rude boats or vessels called *arks*, built during the winter season to await the spring freshet; then they loaded them with wheat or other produce, and sent them to Baltimore or elsewhere. They used also to obtain great quantities of fine lumber, and floated it through the same rivers every spring; but it was attended with great loss of life and property.

Bath assumed a warlike appearance during the last war with Great Britain; the public square was dotted all over with officers, marquees, and soldiers' tents. Some of these soldiers were unprincipled and reckless men, who seemed to care very little what they did.

One evening I was walking around the encampment in company with a Mr. James Morrison, a clerk in the land office, looking at the soldiers, until we came near a sentinel on duty. He kept his gun to his shoulder until we came near enough, and then he attempted to run me through with his bayonet. Young Morrison sprang forward, and seizing the musket, told me to run; I did so, which probably saved my life.

E*

## CHAPTER XI.

#### THOUGHTS ON FREEDOM.

AFTER living sometime in Bath, and having the privilege of more enlightened society, I began to think that it was possible for me to become a free man in some way besides going into the army or running away, as I had often thought of doing. I had listened to the conversation of others, and determined to ask legal counsel on the subject the first opportunity I could find. Very soon after, as I was drawing wood, I met on the river bridge, Mr. D. Cruger, the eminent lawyer before mentioned, and I asked him to tell me if I was not free, by the laws of New York. He started, and looked around him as if afraid to answer my question, but after a while told me I was *not* free. I passed on, but the answer to my question by no means satisfied me, especially when I remembered the hesitancy with which it was given.

I sought another opportunity to speak with Mr.

Cruger, and at last found him in his office alone; then he conversed freely on the subject of Slavery, telling me that Capt. Helm could not hold me as a slave in that State, if I chose to leave him, and then directed me to D. Comstock and J. Moore; the first being at the head of a manumission society, and the last named gentleman one of its directors.

Our condition, as I have said before, was greatly improved; and yet the more we knew of freedom the more we desired it, and the less willing were we to remain in bondage. The slaves that Capt. Helm had sold or hired out, were continually leaving him and the country, for a place of freedom; and I determined to become my own possessor.

There is no one, I care not how favorable his condition, who desires to be a slave, to labor for nothing all his life for the benefit of others. I have often heard fugitive slaves say, that it was not so much the cruel beatings and floggings that they received which induced them to leave the South, as the idea of dragging out a whole life of unrequited toil to enrich their masters.

Everywhere that Slavery exists, it is nothing but *slavery*. I found it just as hard to be beaten over the head with a piece of iron in New York as it was in Virginia. Whips and chains are everywhere necessary to degrade and brutalize the slave, in order to reduce him to that abject and humble state which Slavery requires. Nor is the effect much less disastrous on the man who holds supreme control over the soul and body of his fellow beings. Such unlimited power, in almost every instance transforms the man into a tyrant; the brother into a demon.

When the first of our persecuted race were brought to this country it was to teach them to reverence the only true and living God; or such was the answer of Her Majesty Queen Elizabeth of England, when her subjects desired the liberty to bring from their native land the poor, ignorant African. "Let them," said the Queen, "be brought away only by their own consent, otherwise the act will be detestable, and bring down the vengeance of heaven upon us." A very different position truly, from the one assumed at the present day by apologists for the traffic in human flesh. But, to return to myself.

I had determined to make an effort to own myself, and as a preliminary step, I obtained permission of Capt. Helm to visit some friends living in Canandaigua and Geneva. This was in the winter of 1814. I went first to Geneva; from there to Canandaigua. Between the two villages I met a company of United States' troops, returning from Buffalo, where they had been to repel an invasion of the British.

The two villages above named, were small but very pretty, having been laid out with taste and great care. Some wealthy and enterprising gentlemen had come from the East into this great Western country, who were making every improvement in their power. The dense forest had long since fallen under the stroke of the woodman's ax, and in that section, flourishing villages were springing up as if by magic, where so lately roamed wild beasts and rude savages, both having fallen back before the march of civilization.

I called on James Moore, as directed by Mr. Cruger, and found he was one of the directors of the "Manumission Society," as it was then called. This was an association of humane and intelligent gentlemen whose object it was to aid any one who was illegally held in bondage. The funds of the society were ample; and able counsel was employed to assist those who needed it. The late lamented John C. Spencer, one of the most eminent lawyers in Western New York, was then counsel for that society.

I soon got an interview with Mr. Moore, to whom I related the history of my life,—the story of my wrongs and hardships. I told him about my having been hired out by Capt. Helm, which he said was sufficient to insure my freedom! Oh! how my heart leaped at the thought! The tears started, my breast heaved with a mighty throb of gratitude, and I could hardly refrain from grasping his hand or falling down at his feet; and perhaps should have made some ludicrous demonstration of my feelings, had not the kind gentleman continued his conversation in another direction.

He said that indispensable business called him to Albany, where he must go immediately, but assured me that he would return in March following; then I must come to him and he would see that I had what justly belonged to me—my freedom from Slavery. He advised me to return to Bath and go on with my work as usual until March, but to say nothing of my intentions and prospects. I returned according to his directions, with a heart so light, that I could not realize that my bonds were not yet broken, nor the yoke removed from off my neck. I was already free in spirit, and I silently exulted in the bright prospect of liberty.

Could my master have felt what it was to be relieved of such a crushing weight, as the one which was but partially lifted from my mind, he would have been a happier man than he had been for a long time.

I went cheerfully back to my labor, and worked with alacrity, impatient only for March to come; and as the time drew near I began to consider what kind of an excuse I could make to get away. I could think of none, but I determined to go without one, rather than to remain.

Just before the time appointed for me to meet Mr. Moore, a slave girl named Milly, came secretly to Bath. She had been one of Capt. Helm's slaves, and he had a while before sold her to a man who lived some distance west of the village. Milly had now taken the matter into her own hands. She had left her master to take care of himself, and was in short, "running away," determined as myself, that she would be a slave no longer; resolved on death, or freedom from the power of the slaveholder.

The time I had set for my departure was so near at hand, that I concluded to accompany her in her flight. When the dark night came on, we started together, and traveled all night, and just as the day dawned we arrived at Manchester, where we stopped a short time with one Thomas Watkins.

But I was not to be let go so easily. I had been missed at Capt. Helm's, and several men started in immediate pursuit. I was weary, and so intent on getting a little rest that I did not see my pursuers until they had well nigh reached the house where I was; but I *did* see them in time to spring from the house with the agility of a deer, and to run for the woods as for life. And indeed, I so considered it. I was unarmed to be sure, and not prepared to defend myself against two or three men, armed to the teeth; but it would have gone hard with me before I surrendered myself to them, after having dreamed as I had, and anticipated the blessings of a free man. I escaped them, thank God, and reached the woods, where I concealed myself for some time, and where I had ample opportunity to reflect on the injustice and cruelty of my oppressors, and to ask myself why it was that I was obliged to fly from my home. Why was I there panting and weary, hungry and destitute—skulking in the woods like a thief, and concealing myself like a murderer? What had I done? For what fault, or for what crime was I pursued by armed men, and hunted like a beast of prey? God only knows how these inquiries harrowed up my very soul, and made me well nigh doubt the justice and mercy of the Almighty, until I remembered my narrow escape, when my doubts dissolved in grateful tears.

But why, oh why, had I been forced to flee thus from my fellow men? I was guilty of no crime; I had committed no violence; I had broken no law of the land; I was not charged even with a fault, except of *the love of liberty* and a desire to be *free!* I had claimed the right to possess my own person, and remove it from oppression. Oh my God, thought I, can the American People, who at this very hour are pouring out their blood in defence of their country's liberty; offering up as a sacrifice on the battle field their promising young men, to preserve their land and hearthstones from English oppression; can they, will they, continue to hunt the poor African slave from their soil because he desires that same liberty, so dear to the heart of every American citizen? Will they not blot out from their fair escutcheon the foul stain which Slavery has cast upon it? Will they not remember the Southern bondman, in whom the love of freedom is as inherent as in themselves; and will they not, when contending for equal rights, use their mighty forces "to break *every yoke*, and let the oppressed go free?" God grant that it may be so!

As soon as I thought it prudent, I pursued my journey, and finally came out into the open country, near the dwelling of Mr. Dennis Comstock, who, as I have said, was president of the Manumission Society. To him I freely described my situation, and found him a friend indeed. He expressed his readiness to assist me, and wrote a line for me to take to his brother, Otis Comstock, who took me into his family at once. I hired to Mr. Comstock for the season, and from that time onward lived with him nearly four years.

When I arrived there I was about twenty-two years of age, and felt for the first time in my life, that I was my own master. I cannot describe to a free man, what a proud manly feeling came over me when I hired to Mr. C. and made my first bargain, nor when I assumed the dignity of collecting my own earnings. Notwithstanding I was very happy in my freedom from Slavery, and had a good home, where for the first time in my life I was allowed to sit at table with others, yet I found myself very deficient in almost every thing which I should have learned when a boy.

These and other recollections of the past often saddened my spirit; but *hope*,—cheering and bright, was now mine, and it lighted up the future and gave me patience to persevere.

In the autumn when the farm work was done, I called on Mr. Comstock for some money, and the first thing I did after receiving it I went to Canandaigua where I found a book-store kept by a man named J. D. Bemis, and of him I purchased some school books.

No king on his throne could feel prouder or grander than I did that day. With my books under my arm, and money of my own earning in my pocket, I stepped loftily along toward Farmington, where I determined to attend the Academy. The thought, however, that though I was twenty-three years old, I had yet to learn what most boys of eight years knew, was rather a damper on my spirits. The school was conducted by Mr. J. Comstock, who was a pleasant young man and an excellent teacher. He showed me every kindness and consideration my position and ignorance demanded; and I attended his school three winters, with pleasure and profit to myself at least.

When I had been with Mr. Comstock about a year, we received a visit from my old master, Capt. Helm, who had spared no pains to find me, and when he learned where I was he came to claim me as "his boy," who, he said he "wanted and must have."

Mr. Comstock told him I was *not* "his boy," and as such he would not give me up; and further, that I was free by the laws of the State. He assured the Captain that his hiring me out in the first instance, to Mr. Tower, forfeited his claim to me, and gave me a right to freedom,—but if he chose to join issue, they would have the case tried in the Supreme Court; but this proposition the Captain declined: he knew well enough that it would result in my favor; and after some flattery and coaxing, he left me with my friend, Mr. Comstock, in liberty and peace!

## CHAPTER XII.

#### CAPT. HELM—DIVORCE—KIDNAPPING.

THE business affairs of Capt. Helm had for some time been far from prosperous; and now he was quite poor. His slave property proved a bad investment, and Madam Thornton a far worse one. She had already applied for a divorce, and a good share of the estate as alimony; both of which she succeeded in getting, the Captain allowing her to take pretty much her own course. These troubles, with costs of lawsuits, bad management, &c., had now emptied the coffers of my old master almost to the last farthing; and he began to cast about him for some way to replenish his purse, and retrieve his fallen fortunes.

Had Capt. Helm been brought up to honorable industry, and accustomed to look after his own pecuniary interests, he doubtless would have sustained his position; or if reverses were unadvoidable, he would have by persevering industry, regained what he had lost. But he had been raised in a slave State, and Southern principles were as deeply instilled into his mind, as Southern manners were impressed on his life and conduct.

He had no partiality for labor of any kind; horse-racing and card-playing were far more congenial to his tastes; reduced as he now was, he would deny himself no luxury that his means or credit would procure. His few remaining slaves were given into the hands of an idle, brutal overseer—while they, half fed, half clothed, grew more and more discontented, and ran away on every opportunity that offered.

The Captain at last hit upon a method of making money, which, if it had been carried into operation on the high seas, would in all probability have been called by its right name, and incurred the penalty of the gallows—as piracy. Ought it then to be deemed less criminal because transpiring on the free soil of the American Republic? I think not. Nor was it less censurable on account of its failure.

The Captain's plan was to collect all the slaves he had once owned, many of whom had escaped to the surrounding villages, and when once in his grasp, to run them speedily into a slave State, and there sell them for the Southern market. To carry forward this hellish design, it was necessary to have recourse to stratagem. Some person must be found to lure the unsuspecting slaves into the net he was spreading for them. At last he found a scoundrel named Simon Watkins, who for the consideration of fifty dollars, was to collect as many of the slaves as he could at one place; and when he had done so, he was to receive the money, leaving Capt. Helm to do the rest.

Simon set immediately about the business, which was first to go to Palmyra, and in great kindness and generosity, give a large party to the colored people,—. desiring that all Capt. Helm's former slaves, *in particular*, should be present to have a joyous re-union, and celebrate their freedom in having a fine time generally.

Invitations were sent to all, and extensive preparation made for a large "social party," at Palmyra, at the house of Mrs. Bristol. My parents were invited; and Simon took the pains to come to Farmington to give me a special invitation. When the time arrived for the party, I went to Palmyra with the intention of attending. I had not the least suspicion of any thing wrong; yet, by some mysterious providence, or something for which I can not account, a presentiment took possession of my mind that all was not right. I knew not what I feared, and could in no way define my apprehensions; but I grew so uneasy, that I finally gave up the party and returned home, before the guests were assembled.

Capt. Helm and his assistants came on to Palmyra

in disguise, before evening, and secreted themselves in one of the hotels to await the arrival of their victims.

At the appointed hour the slaves began to assemble in large numbers and great glee, without the least suspicion of danger. They soon began their amusements, and in the midst of their mirth, Capt. Helm and party stealthily crept from their hiding place and surrounded the house; then bursting in suddenly upon the revelers, began to make arrests. Such a tumult, such an affray as ensued would be hard to describe.

The slaves fought for their lives and their liberty, and the Captain's party for their property and power. Fists, clubs, chairs, and any thing they could get hold of, was freely used with a strength and will of men who had tasted the joys of freedom. Cries and curses were mingled, while blows fell like hail on both sides. Commands from our old master were met with shouts of bold defiance on the part of the negroes, until the miserable kidnappers were glad to desist, and were driven off—not stealthily as they came, but in quick time and in the best way they could, to escape the threatened vengeance of the slaves, who drove them like "feathers before the wind." But it was a terrible battle and many were severely wounded; among them was my father. He was taken to his home, mangled and bleeding, and from the effects of that night's affray he never recovered. He lingered on in feeble health until death finally released him from suffering, and placed him beyond the reach of kidnappers and tyrants.

The Captain and his party, enraged and disappointed in their plans at Palmyra, returned to Bath to see what could be done there toward success, in getting up a gang of slaves for the Southern market. When they came among the colored people of Bath, it was like a hawk alighting among a flock of chickens at noon-day. They scattered and ran in every direction, some to the woods, some hid themselves in cellars, and others in their terror plunged into the Conhocton River. In this manner the majority of the negroes escaped, but not all; and those were so unfortunate as to get caught were instantly thrown into a large covered "Pennsylvania wagon," and hurried off, closely guarded, to Olean Point. Among those taken were Harry Lucas, his wife, Lucinda, and seven children; Mrs. Jane Cooper and four children, with some others, were also taken.

When Capt. Helm arrived at Olean Point with his stolen freight of human beings, he was unexpectedly detained until he could build a boat,—which, to his great dismay took him several days.

The sorrow and fearful apprehension of those wretched recaptured slaves can not be described nor imagined by any one except those who have experienced a like affliction. They had basked for a short season in the sunshine of liberty, and thought themselves secure from the iron grasp of Slavery, and the heel of the oppressor, when in the height of their exultation, they had been thrust down to the lowest depths of misery and despair, with the oppressor's heel again upon their necks. To be snatched without a moment's warning from their homes and friends,— hurried and crowded into the close slave wagon, regardless of age or sex, like sheep for the slaughter, to be carried they knew not whither; but, doubtless to the dismal rice swamp of the South,—was to them an agony too great for endurance. The adult portion of the miserable company determined at last to go no farther with their heartless master, but to resist unto death if need be, before they surrendered themselves to the galling chains they had so recently broken, or writhed again under the torturing lash of the slave-driver.

Harry Lucas and wife, and Jane Cooper, silently prepared themselves for the conflict, determined to sell their lives as dearly as possible. When they were nearly ready to start, Jane Cooper sent her oldest daughter and younger sister, (she who is now our worthy friend Mrs. P. of Bath), into the woods, and then when the men undertook to get Lucas and the two women on board the boat the struggle commenced. The women fought the Captain and his confederates like a lioness robbed of her whelps! They ran and dodged about, making the woods ring with their

F

screams and shouts of "Murder! Murder! Help! Help! Murder!" until the Captain's party, seeing they could do nothing to quell them, became so exceedingly alarmed lest they should be detected in their illegal proceedings, that they ran off at full speed, as if they thought an officer at their heels. In their hurry and fright they caught two of Harry's children, and throwing them into the boat, pushed off as quick as possible, amid the redoubled cries of the agonized parents and sympathizing friends, all trying in every way possible, to recover from the merciless grasp of the man-stealer, the two frightened and screaming children. Guns were fired and horns sounded, but all to no purpose—they held tightly the innocent victims of their cupidity, and made good their escape.

Mr. D. C———, a gentleman of wealth and high standing in Steuben County, became responsible for the fifty dollars which Capt. Helm promised to pay Simon Watkins for his villany in betraying, Judas-like, those unsuspecting persons whom it should have been his pleasure to protect and defend against their common oppressor,—his own as well as theirs.

In addition to this rascality, it can not appear very creditable to the citizens of Steuben County, that Capt. Helm and Thomas McBirney should both hold high and important offices at the time, and *after* they had been tried and convicted of the crime of kidnapping. Both of these gentlemen, guilty of a State's prison offence, were judges of the common pleas. T. McBirney was first judge in the county, and Capt. Helm was side judge; and notwithstanding their participation in, and conviction of, a flagrant outrage on the laws of God and man, they managed not only to escape the penalty, but to retain their offices and their respectable standing in community for years after.

# CHAPTER XIII.

LOCATE IN THE VILLAGE OF ROCHESTER.

I CONTINUED to labor in the employ of Mr. O. Comstock, whose son, Zeno, was married during the year 1816, and purchased a farm on the site of the present flourishing village of Lockport, to which he moved his family and effects; but from a mistaken supposition that the Erie Canal, which was then under contemplation, would take a more southern route, he was induced to sell his farm in Hartland, which has proved a mine of wealth to the more fortunate purchaser.

In the winter of that year, I was sent by my employer to Hartland with a sleigh-load of produce, and passed through the village of Rochester, which I had never before seen. It was a very small, forbidding looking place at first sight, with few inhabitants, and surrounded by a dense forest.

I recollect that while pursuing my journey, I overtook a white man driving a span of horses, who contended that I had not a right to travel the public highway as other men did, but that it was my place to keep behind him and his team. Being in haste I endeavored to pass him quietly, but he would not permit it and hindered me several hours, very much to my annoyance and indignation. This was, however, but a slight incident indicating the bitter prejudice which every man seemed to feel against the negro. No matter how industrious he might be, no matter how honorable in his dealings, or respectful in his manners,—he was a "nigger," and as such he must be treated, with a few honorable exceptions.

This year also, my father died in the village of Palmyra, where, as I have before mentioned, he received injuries from which he never entirely recovered. After about six months severe illness which he bore with commendable patience and resignation, his spirit returned to God who gave it; and his sorrowing friends and bereaved family followed his remains to their final abode, where we laid him down to rest from unrequited labor and dire oppression, until "all they who are in their graves shall hear the voice of the Son of God, and they that hear shall live forever," where the "tears shall be wiped from off all faces"— and where the righteous bondman shall no longer fear the driver's lash or master's frown, but freely join in the song of "Alleluia! The Lord God Omnipotent reigneth!"

My father had a good reputation for honesty and uprightness of character among his employers and acquaintances, and was a kind, affectionate husband and a fond, indulgent parent. His, I believe was the life and death of a good man. "Peace be to his ashes."

The following season I commenced a new business— that of peddling in the village of Rochester such articles as my employer, Mr. Comstock, desired to sell: the products of his farm,—wheat, corn, oats, butter, cheese, meat, and poultry—all of which met a ready sale, generally for cash at liberal prices. That market was then but little known to the generality of farmers, and the enterprising gentlemen of that place, were desirous of encouraging commerce with the surrounding country, offered every encouragement in their power. Hence, we found it a profitable business, which I continued in for several months.

The present flourishing city of Rochester was then, as I have said, but a village in its infancy, situated near the upper falls of the Genesee River, and about seven miles from its mouth. Here, some time previously, three gentlemen from Maryland bought a large tract of land, and as no business man could fail to observe and appreciate its rare advantages they commenced laying out a village. Sirs Fitzhugh, Carroll, and Rochester, composed the company; but the management of the business devolved almost wholly on Col. Rochester, whose wealth, enterprise, and intelligence well qualified him for the undertaking; and as it had been assigned him to cognominate the new village, I have heard it said that he jocularly gave his reason for selecting its present title, as follows: "Should he call it *Fitzhugh* or *Carroll*, the slighted gentleman would certainly feel offended with the other; but if he called it by his own name, they would most likely *both* be angry with him; so it was best to serve them alike."

There was then two grist mills,—one owned by Mr. Ely, and the other by Mr. Brown; one small building for religious worship, occupied by the Presbyterians on Carroll street (now State street); and but two stone buildings within what now comprises that beautiful city. There were then no brick buildings at all, but business was good; merchants and mechanics from the East soon began to settle there and give it a thriving aspect.

About this time another company was formed, whose moving spirit was Mr. E. Stone, a man of worth and talent; the object of which was to locate another village at the head of navigation and about half way between the mouth of the river and Rochester, which they called *Carthage.*

The company commenced building and improving the place so rapidly, that many who came to purchase residences and business stations were at a loss to decide which of the two places would finally become the center of business. It, however, was soon perceivable that the advantage of water privileges, stone, and access to both, was greatly in favor of Rochester. At Carthage the Genesee is narrow and its banks steep and abrupt, rising in many places three hundred feet above the bed of the river, which of course render the privileges and business on it far less easy of access for building purposes. I may have occasion to speak hereafter of the expensive and magnificent bridge at Carthage, which was the wonder and admiration of the times.

The following year I concluded to go into business for myself, and was as much at loss as others, whether to locate at Rochester or Carthage; but after considering the matter in all its bearings, and closely watching the progress of events, my choice preponderated in favor of Rochester, and to that place I went, designing to enter into business on my own account.

It was indeed painful to my feelings to leave the home and family of Mr. Comstock, where I had experienced so much real comfort and happiness, where I had ever been treated with uniform kindness, where resided those kind friends to whom I felt under the greatest obligation for the freedom and quietude I then enjoyed, as well as for the little knowledge of business and of the world that I then possessed.

Thinking, however, that I could better my condition, I subdued, as well as I could, my rising emotions, and after sincerely thanking them for their goodness and favors—wishing them long life and prosperity,—I took my departure for the chosen place of my destination.

Soon after I left Mr. Comstock's, that gentleman sent his hired man, named John Cline, to Rochester with a wagon load of produce to sell, as had been his custom for some time. In vain the family looked for his return at the usual hour in the evening, and began to wonder what had detained him; but what was their horror and surprise to find, when they arose the next morning, the horses standing at the door, and the poor unfortunate man lying in the wagon, *dead!* How long they had been there nobody knew; no one had heard them come in; and how the man had been killed was a matter of mere conjecture. The coroner was sent for and an inquest held, and yet it was difficult to solve the whole mystery.

The most probable explanation was, that he was sitting in the back part of the wagon, and fell over on his left side, striking his neck on the edge of the wagon box, breaking it instantly.

The verdict of the jury was, in accordance with these facts, "accidental death," &c.

When I left Mr. Comstock's I had acquired quite a knowledge of reading, writing, arithmetic, and had made a small beginning in English grammar.

F*

It had been for some time a question which I found hard to decide, whether or not I should pursue my studies as I had done. If I went into business as I contemplated, I knew it would end my proficiency in the sciences; and yet I felt a desire to accumulate more of the wealth that perisheth. Considering too that I was advancing in age, and had no means of support but by my own labor, I finally concluded to do what I have from that time to this deeply regretted,—give up the pursuit of an education, and turn my attention wholly to business. I do not regret having desired a competency, nor for having labored to obtain it, but I *do* regret not having spared myself sufficient leisure to pursue some regular system of reading and study; to have cultivated my mind and stored it with useful knowledge.

Truly has it been said, "knowledge is power." But it is not like the withering curse of a tyrant's power; not like the degrading and brutalizing power of the slave-driver's lash, chains, and thumb-screws; not like the beastly, demonical power of rum, nor like the brazen, shameless power of lust; but a power that elevates and refines the intellect; directs the affections; controls unholy passions; a power so God-like in its character, that it enables its possessor to feel for the oppressed of every clime, and prepares him to defend the weak and down-trodden.

What but ignorance renders the poor slave so weak

and inefficient in claiming his right to liberty, and the possession of his own being! Nor will that God who is "no respecter of persons," hold him guiltless who assumes unlimited control over his fellow. The chain of Slavery which fetters every slave south of Mason and Dixon's Line, is as closely linked arounb the master as the slave. The time has passed by when African blood alone is enslaved. In Virginia as well as in some other slave States, there is as much European blood in the veins of the enslaved as there is African; and the increase is constantly in favor of the white population. This fact alone speaks volumes, and should remind the slave-breeding Southerner of that fearful retribution which must sooner or later overtake him.

In September, 1817, I commenced business in Rochester. Having rented a room of Mr. A. Wakely, I established a meat market, which was supplied mostly by my former employer, Mr. Comstock, and was liberally patronized by the citizens; but there were butchers in the village who appeared to be unwilling that I should have any share in public patronage. Sometimes they tore down my sign, at others painted it black, and so continued to annoy me until after I had one of their number arrested, which put a stop to their unmanly proceedings.

The village was now rapidly increasing, and yet the surrounding country was mostly a wilderness. Mr.

E. Stone, who then owned the land on the east side of the river, thought his farm a very poor one; he, however, commenced clearing it in the midst of wild beasts and rattlesnakes, both of which were abundant, and in a few years was richly rewarded for his labor, in the sale of village lots, which commanded high prices.

In the summer of 1818, I commenced teaching a Sabbath School for the neglected children of our oppressed race. For a while it was well attended, and I hoped to be able to benefit in some measure the poor and despised colored children, but the parents interested themselves very little in the undertaking, and it shortly came to nought. So strong was the prejudice then existing against the colored people, that very few of the negroes seemed to have any courage or ambition to rise from the abject degradation in which the estimation of the white man had placed him.

This year, also, I purchased a lot of land, eighteen by fifty feet, situated on Main street, for which I was to pay five hundred dollars. Having secured my land, I began making preparations for building, and soon had a good two story dwelling and store, into which I moved my effects, and commenced a more extensive business.

Some disadvantage as well as sport was occasioned On business men, who resided on the confines of Ontario and Genesee Counties. It was indeed laughable to witness the races and manouvering of parties in those days when men were imprisoned for debt. If a man in Ontario County had a suspicion that an officer was on his track, he had only to step over the line into Genesee, to be beyond the power of an officer's precept.

A great deal of trouble as well as unpleasant feeling was engendered by the exercise of that law, which allowed the creditor so great advantage over the debtor. This, together with the fact that very many of the citizens of Rochester were men of small means, the more wealthy portion felt called upon to protect their interests, by forming themselves into what was called a "Shylock Society," the object of which was to obtain a list of all the names of persons who had been, or were then, on "the limits" for debt. This list of names was printed, and each member of the society furnished with a copy, which enabled him to decide whether or not to trust a man when he came to trade. The formation of this society gave rise to another, whose members pledged themselves to have no dealing with a member of the "Shylock Society," and also to publish all defaulters in "high life," which served to check these oppressive measures and restore harmony.

Among others who came to settle in the thriving village of Rochester, was a colored man named Daniel Furr, who came from the East. He soon became acquainted with a very respectable young white lady, of good family, who after a short acquaintance appeared to be perfectly enamored of her dusky swain; and notwithstanding the existing prejudice, she did not scruple to avow her affection for him,— a devotion which appeared to be as sincerely returned by the young "Othello." They resolved to marry; but to this, serious objections arose, and all that the lady's family and friends could do to break off the match was done, but without effect. They could, however, prevail on no one to perform the marriage ceremony in the village, and finally concluded to go to a magistrate in the town of Brighton, four miles distant. At this stage of the proceedings I was appealed to, to accompany them. I took the matter into consideration and came to the conclusion that I could take no active part in the affair, nor bear any responsible station in the unpleasant occurrence. Is it no sin in the sight of the Almighty, for Southern gentlemen (?) to mix blood and amalgamate the races? And if allowed to them, is it not equally justifiable when the commerce is prompted by affection rather than that of lust and force? But I at length consented to accompany them, after learning that all the mischief was already done that could be feared, and that the gallant lover desired to marry the lady as the only atonement he could make for the loss of her reputation.

We arrived at the house of the magistrate about one o'clock at night, and all were soundly sleeping. They were, however, aroused, and when our business was made known, an exciting scene followed. The magistrate refused at first to marry them; and the lady of the house took aside the intended bride, spending two hours in endeavoring to dissuade her from the contemplated union; assuring her that her house should be freely opened to her, that no attention should be spared during her expected confinement, &c.; but all to no purpose. They returned to the parlor where the magistrate again tried his power of persuasion, but with as little success as his lady had met: and then he reluctantly married them. The newly-made husband paid a liberal fee, and we took our leave. I returned to my home to reflect on the scenes of the past night, and Mr. and Mrs. Furr to the house of a friend of the bride in Penfield.

The report soon reached the village that the marriage had been consummated, which produced a great excitement. Threats of an alarming character were openly made against the "nigger" who had dared to marry a white woman, although at her own request. And there was also a class of persons who associated together, professing great friendship for the persecuted husband, and often drew him into their company, pretending to defend his cause while they were undoubtedly plotting his destruction.

One day, after Furr had been drinking rather freely with his pretended friends, he was taken so violently ill, that a physician was immediately called. I was with him when the doctor arrived. He gazed upon the suffering man with an angry expression, and inquired in a tone of command, "Daniel, what have you been doing?" In vain the poor creature begged for relief, the doctor merely repeating his question. After looking at him for some time, he finally administered a potion and hastily left the room, saying as he did so, "that Furr was as sure to die as though his head had been cut off." And so it proved, though not so speedily as the medical man had predicted; nor did he ever visit him again, notwithstanding he lingered for several days in the most intense agony. It was a strong man grappling with disease and death, and the strife was a fearful one. But death at last ended the scene, with none of all his professed friends, except his faithful but heart-broken wife, to admmister to his necessities. No sound save that of the moaning widow broke the stillness of his death-chamber. A few friends collected, who prepared the emaciated body for the grave; enclosing it in a rude board coffin it was conveyed to its last resting place, followed by three or four men, just as the shades of evening had fallen upon this sin-cursed world; there in darkness and silence we lowered his remains, and left the gloomy spot to return to his disconsolate wife, who had been too ill to join the meager procession.

It has ever been my conviction that Furr was poisoned, most likely by some of his false friends who must have mingled some deadly drug with his drinks or food; nor do I believe that the medicine administered by the physician was designed to save his life. But to Him who knoweth all things, we leave the matter.

His despised, forsaken, and bereaved wife soon followed him to the grave, where she sleeps quietly with her innocent babe by her side; and where probably this second Desdemonia finds the only refuge which would have been granted her by a heartless and persecuting world.

Oh, when will this nation "cease to do evil and learn to do well?" When will they judge character in accordance with its moral excellence, instead of the complexion a man unavoidably bears to the world?

# CHAPTER XIV.

### INCIDENTS IN ROCHESTER AND VICINITY.

AFTER long petitioning, the inhabitants of that section succeeded in having the new county of Monroe set off from Genesee and Ontario Counties, in 1821, which gave a new impulse to the business interests of the already flourishing town, which had heretofore labored under some disadvantages in consequence of having all public business done at Canandaigua or Batavia.

About this time, too, was the Carthage bridge built by a company of enterprising gentlemen of that village, which at that day was considered one of the wonders of the age; but as its history is well known to all interested in the enterprises of those days, it is only necessary to say, that the magnificent structure, so grand in its appearance, such a pattern of mechanical ingenuity, exhibiting in all its vast proportions, both strength and beauty, combined with utility and grandeur; and erected at such an enormous expense of time, labor, and cash, was destined soon to fall. It had cost some ten thousand dollars; and had been warranted by the builders to stand one year. How great then must have been the loss and disappointment when in a little more than twenty-four hours after the time specified, the ruins of that beautiful structure were found floating on the broad bosom of the Genesee! And yet when we take into consideration the vast amount of human life which hourly passed over its solid surface, we can but wonder at the intervention of a kind Providence which prevented any loss of life at the time of its fall. A child had but just passed over it, when with one general crash it sank to the waters below; mocking in its rapid flight, the wisdom of the architect and foresight of frail humanity. The fall of Carthage bridge was indeed a calamity felt by the public generally, and sounded the death-knell of all future greatness to Carthage, or at least for some years to come.

About this time the village was thrown into a state of excitement by the arrest of a colored woman named Ellen, who it was charged had escaped from service due to a Mr. D., south of Mason and Dixon's Line. She had been arrested in accordance with a law passed by Congress in 1793, which forbids persons owing service in one State to flee to another; and which also obliges those receiving such service, to render to the claimant any fugitive from labor due, &c. Poor Ellen! She had many friends and able counsel, but nothing short of an open violation of the law of the land, could prevent her return to the house of bondage. She was tried and given up to him who claimed dominion over her. Hopeless and heart-broken, she was escorted from the boasted land and village of freedom, by a company of the "Light Horse," under the command of Capt. Curtis. One poor, persecuted slave woman, upon whose heart had fallen a shadow darker than death's; driving every earthly hope of liberty from her wounded spirit; helpless and forlorn! She indeed must have required this military parade—this show of power! And that too, by men who throw up their caps with a shout for freedom and equal rights! Oh, "consistency, thou art a jewel!"

As I recollect but one other incident of the kind occurring in Rochester, I will now name it.

A colored man named Davis, generally known as "Doctor Davis," with a reputation unsullied for industry, truth and sobriety, was arrested as a fugitive from slave labor in Kentucky. Two men came on from that State, acting in the double capacity of agents for the claimant and witnesses against the slave. They employed Mr. L. as counsel, and hastened on the trial of the afflicted African. When it became generally known that Davis was arrested, and about to be tried, the excitement grew intense among all classes; but more particularly among the colored people. When the trial came on, the Court room was crowded to overflowing, and every avenue leading to it densely thronged with deeply anxious persons, assembled to witness the result. It became evident, however, that the poor man must be given up to his grasping master, unless some means were devised to rescue him from the power of an unjust law. His friends were on the alert, and as the trial proceeded, the colored men found an opportunity to get him into a corner of the crowded apartment; where, while the officers stood at the door, they dressed him in disguise, and otherwise so completely changed his personal appearance, that he passed out of the Court room, undetected by the officers, and as all supposed was safely pursuing his way to Canada.

The hawk-eyed counsel for the Kentuckians, however, too soon observed exultation written on every dusky countenance, to keep quiet. Starting to his feet in great alarm, he cried out "Where is Davis?" And oh, how that question startled every one present. Every eye gazed hither and thither, and every ear intently listened for the answer. After a moment of breathless silence, the excited counsellor was assured that the "bird had flown," which announcement was received with a rapturous shout of joy by the audience, greatly, however, to the discomfiture of the gentlemen from Kentucky, who had thought themselves so sure of their prize. Nor would they be thwarted now. It was not yet too late to overtake their victim, and slavery required at their hands a sacrifice which they were ready to make. Hand-bills were in immediate circulation, offering a reward of fifty dollars for the apprehension of the flying fugitive. Fifty dollars, for the body and soul of a man to plunge into the degradation of Slavery! Fifty dollars for the ruin of a fellow being, for whom Christ gave his precious life! Yes, fifty dollars are offered to any human blood-hound who will hunt and worry the poor slave, who must fly from this boasted land of liberty, to seek protection in the dominion of England's Queen!

Unfortunately for Davis, some of these hand-bills were thrown on board the very packet on which he had embarked for Buffalo; nor was this all. The bills would have left him uninjured, but a scoundrel—an apology for a man—was there also, who, for the consideration of fifty dollars was willing to compromise all pretensions to manhood and humanity, and drag from the boat the panting slave, whom he cast beneath the heel of his oppressor. When Davis was finally retaken, those Kentucky dealers in human chattels, held him with a grasp that banished all hope of escape by flight; and then in his sorrow and despair the wretched, hopeless man cried out "Oh, my God, must I return to the hell of Slavery? Save me, Oh, dear

Lord, save this, thy helpless, friendless servant, from a fate so dreadful! Oh, Christian friends and neighbors, I appeal to you to rescue me from a life far more terrible than death in any form! Oh, God, is there no protection for me in the laws of New York? I claim it, by all that is sacred in her past history! Give me liberty or death! or death!" he repeated, with a shudder; then casting one glance of hopeless agony on his persecutors, he secretly drew from his pocket a razor, and before he could be prevented he drew it across his throat, and fell gasping in the midst of his slave-hunting tormentors, while a collection of bystanders cried "Shame! shame! on the institution of Slavery!"

Poor Davis was not dead, but supposing he soon would be, these gentlemen were requested to give security, and indemnify the town for all expenses it might incur on Davis' account. But instead of giving their bond as requested, they took a sudden start for Kentucky, where it was very generally desired they might remain.

With good treatment, Davis, after a long time, recovered sufficiently to be removed by his friends to a place of safety; and when so far restored as to be able he returned to Rochester, where he received assistance which enabled him to reach Canada. I have often heard from him during his residence in that country, where no slaves exist and he has done well, having quite an extensive practice in medicine, and lives in the quiet enjoyment of that liberty which he struggled so hard to obtain and came so near losing; yet, to this day he prefers death to Slavery. And who does not? None, who have breathed the air of freedom after an experience of unrequited toil to enrich a brutal and selfish master. Truly is it said, "a contented slave is a degraded being."

# CHAPTER XV.

SAD REVERSES OF CAPT. HELM.

I MUST again introduce to the kind reader my old master, Capt. Helm, who we left residing in Bath, several years ago. And as I have before intimated he had now become a very poor man; indeed so reduced was he now that he lived with one of his slave women, and was supported by public charity! Learning, too, that I had saved by my industry a few hundred dollars, it seemed very congenial with his avaricious habits to endeavor to obtain what I possessed. In accordance with his plan he employed a lawyer named Lewland to come to my place of business, which he did, and demanded of me to pay Capt. Helm two hundred dollars. He also left a notice, forbidding all persons to take or destroy any property in my possession; and then impudently inquired how I expected to gain my freedom; if I thought of applying for a writ of *habæus corpus;* and many

G

other questions; to which I replied that I should pay no money on the order of Capt. Helm; apply for no writ; but should continue to maintain my personal rights and enjoy the freedom which was already mine, and which I designed to keep, assuring him that the Captain had forfeited his claim, if he had any, to me or my services, when he hired me to Mr. Tower.

He hung about me for a day or two, and then left me to pursue my business—I saw no more of him. Some time afterward Mr. H. E. Rochester informed me that he had a *subpœna* for me, which I found was issued by the direction of Capt. Helm. By Mr. Rochester's counsel, I took it to Mr. A. Sampson, who assured me that my old master had commenced a suit against me in the Court of Equity, and the case would be tried before Wm. B. Rochester, Esq., who was one of the circuit judges. Capt. Helm claimed every particle of property I possessed; a claim that occasioned me great anxiety and some cost.

Mr. Sampson encouraged me to hope, however, that the case would be dismissed as two other cases of that kind had been.

I labored to the best of my ability to prepare myself for the trial, which was to decide whether I had a right to possess myself and command my own services and earnings, or whether all belonged to Capt. Helm. As I looked forward with anxious forebodings to the day appointed for the suit to commence, I was startled by the announcement of my old master's *death!* Yes, Capt. Helm was dead; and with him died the law suit. He who had so wronged me, who had occasioned me so much suffering and sorrow had gone to his account. He who had once been thought to be one of the wealthiest as well as one of the greatest men in the county, died a pauper—neglected and despised, and scarcely awarded a decent burial. Like his wife, who died such a horrid death, he had been reared in affluence and was an inheritor of vast possessions, but his home was in a slave State; he was raised on a plantation, and nurtured in the atmosphere of Slavery.

In his youth he had contracted the habit of drinking to excess, beside that of gambling, horse-racing and the like, which followed him through life. Forgotten and scorned in his poverty by many who had partaken of his abundance, sipped his wine, and rode his fast horses.

During the last war his princely mansion was ever open to the officers of the army, and many a wounded soldier has been cheered and comforted by his hospitality. But now he is regarded as no better than his poorest slave, and lies as lowly as they, in the narrow house appointed for all the living.

My old master had two brothers: the oldest, Thomas Helm, was a Captain in the United States Army, and had been in many hard-fought battles. His younger brother, William, was a Captain also; but Thomas was the man to awaken curiosity. I have lived with him, but never knew of his going unarmed for an hour, until he left Virginia and came to Steuben County, where he died. When at the South, I have seen strangers approach him, but they were invariably commanded to "stand" and to "approach him at their peril." He finally came to the State of New York, bringing with him his "woman" with whom he lived, and two children, with whom he settled on a piece of land given him by my old master, where the old soldier lived, died, and was buried on one of his small "clearings" under an old apple tree. He owned a few slaves, but at his death his "woman" collected every thing she could, and among the rest, two or three slave children, to whom she had no right or claim whatever, and made her way to Kentucky. About a year ago I visited the spot where the brave old defender of his country had been buried, but found very little to mark the resting place of the brother of my old master. They had passed away. Their wealth, power and bravery had come to nought; and no tribute was now paid to the memory of one of "Old Virginia's best families." The *blood* of which they were wont to boast, was now no more revered than that which commingled with the African and circulated in the veins of his despised and down-trodden slaves.

# CHAPTER XVI.

### BRITISH EMANCIPATION OF SLAVERY.

AS time passed on I found myself progressing in a profitable business. I had paid for my house and lot, and purchased another adjoining, on which I had erected a valuable brick building. The Lord prospered all my undertakings and I felt grateful for my good fortune. I kept all kinds of groceries and grain, which met a ready sale; and now I began to look about me for a partner in life, to share my joys and sorrows, and to assist me on through the tempestuous scenes of a life-long voyage. Such a companion I found in the intelligent and amiable Miss B———, to whom I was married on the eleventh of May, 1825. She was the youngest daughter of a particular friend, who had traveled extensively and was noted for his honesty and intelligence.

About this time, too, "Sam Patch" made his last and fatal leap from a scaffold twenty five feet above the falls of Genesee, which are ninety-six feet in height. From thence he plunged into the foaming river to rise no more in life. The following spring the body of the foolish man was found and buried, after having lain several months in the turbulent waters of the Genesee.

This year was also rendered memorable by the efficient labors of Professor Finney, through whose faithful preaching of the gospel, many were brought to a saving knowledge of the truth.

The "Emancipation Act" had now been passed, and the happy time for it to take effect was drawing nigh. Slavery could no longer exist in the Empire State nor receive the protection of her laws. Would to God it had so continued to be what it professed—the refuge of the bondman and the home of the free. But alas! Now the flying fugitive from Slavery finds no security within her borders; he must flee onward, to the dominion of Queen Victoria, ere he rests, lest the exaction of the odious "Fugitive Slave Law" return him to the house of bondage.

But the Emancipation Bill had been passed, and the colored people felt it to be a time fit for rejoicing. They met in different places and determined to evince their gratitude by a general celebration. In Rochester they convened in large numbers, and resolved to celebrate the glorious day of freedom at Johnson's Square, on the *fifth* day of July. This arrangement was made so as not to interfere with the white population who were everywhere celebrating the day of their independence—" the Glorious Fourth,"—for amid the general and joyous shout of liberty, prejudice had sneeringly raised the finger of scorn at the poor African, whose iron bands were loosed, not only from English oppression, but the more cruel and oppressive power of Slavery.

They met according to previous appointment, Mr. A. H———, having been chosen president, Mr. H. E———, marshal, and Mr. H. D———, reader of the "Act of Emancipation," and "The Declaration of Independence." A large audience of both white and colored people assembled, and the day which had been ushered in by the booming cannon, passed by in the joyous realization that we were indeed free men. To the music of the band the large procession marched from the square to the hotel, where ample provision was made for dinner, after listening to the following oration; which I had been requested to deliver.

I must not omit to mention that on the morning of that happy day, a committee of colored men waited upon the Hon. Matthew Brown, and in behalf of the citizens of Monroe County, presented their thanks for his noble exertions in the Legislature, in favor of the Act by which thousands were made free men.

They were received by that worthy gentlemen

with grateful and pleasing assurances of his continued labor in behalf of freedom.

Now I will lay before the reader my address to the audience on that eventful day.

# CHAPTER XVII.

ORATION—TERMINATION OF SLAVERY.

THE age in which we live is characterised in no ordinary degree, by a certain boldness and rapidity in the march of intellectual and political improvements. Inventions the most surprising; revolutions the most extraordinary, are springing forth, and passing in quick succession before us,—all tending most clearly to the advancement of mankind towards that state of earthly perfection and happiness, from which they are yet so far distant, but of which their nature and that of the world they inhabit, are most certainly capable. It is at all times pleasing and instructive to look backward by the light of history, and forward by the light of analogical reasoning, to behold the gradual advancement of man from barbarism to civilization, from civilization toward the higher perfections of his nature; and to hope—nay, confidently believe, that the time is not far distant when liberty and equal rights being everywhere established, morality and the religion of the gospel everywhere diffused,—man shall no longer lift his hand for the oppression of his fellow man; but all, mutually assisting and assited, shall move onward throughout the journey of human life, like the peaceful caravan across the burning sands of Arabia. And never, on this glorious anniversary, so often and so deservedly celebrated by millions of free men, but which we are to-day for the first time called to celebrate—never before, has the eye been able to survey the past with so much satisaction, or the future with hopes and expectations so brilliant and so flattering; it is to us a day of two-fold joy. We are men, though the strong hand of prejudice and oppression is upon us; we can, and we will rejoice in the advancement of the rapidly increasing happiness of mankind, and especially of our own race. We can, and we will rejoice in the growing power and glory of the country we inhabit. Although Almighty God has not permitted us to remain in the land of our forefathers and our own, the glories of national independence, and the sweets of civil and religious liberty, to their full extent; but the strong hand of the spoiler has borne us into a strange land, yet has He of His great goodness given us to behold those best and noblest of his gifts to man, in their fairest and loveliest forms; and not only have we beheld them, but we have already felt much of their benignant influence. Most of us have hitherto enjoyed many, very many of the dearest rights of freemen. Our lives and personal liberties have been held as sacred and inviolable; the rights of property have been extended to us, in this land of freedom; our industry has been, and still is, liberally rewarded; and so long as we live under a free and happy government which denies us not the protection of its laws, why should we fret and vex ourselves because we have had no part in framing them, nor anything to do with their administration. When the fruits of the earth are fully afforded us, we do not wantonly refuse them, nor ungratefully repine because we have done nothing towards the cultivation of the tree which produces them. No, we accept them with lively gratitude; and their sweetness is not embittered by reflecting upon he manner in which they were obtained. It is the dictate of sound wisdom, then, to enjoy without repining, the freedom, privileges, and immunities which wise and equal laws have awarded us—nay, proudly to rejoice and glory in their production, and stand ready at all times to defend them at the hazard of our lives, and of all that is most dear to us.

But are we alone shut out and excluded from any share in the administration of government? Are not the clergy, a class of men equally ineligible to office? A class of men almost idolized by their countrymen, ineligible to office! And are we alone excluded from what the world chooses to denominate polite society? And are not a vast majority of the polar race excluded? I know not why, but mankind of every age, nation, and complexion have had lower classes; and, as a distinction, they have chosen to arrange themselves in the grand spectacle of human life, like seats in a theater—rank above rank, with intervals between them. But if any suppose that happiness or contentment is confined to any single class, or that the high or more splendid order possesses any substantial advantage in those respects over their more lowly brethren, they must be wholly ignorant of all rational enjoyment. For what though the more humble orders cannot mingle with the higher on terms of equality. This, if rightly considered, is not a curse but a blessing. Look around you, my friends: what rational enjoyment is not within your reach? Your homes are in the noblest country in the world, and all of that country which your real happiness requires, may at any time be yours. Your industry can purchase it; and its righteous laws will secure you in its possession. But, to what, my friends, do you owe all these blessings? Let not the truth be concealed. You owe them to that curse, that bitter scourge of Africa, whose partial abolishment you are this day convened to celebrate. Slavery has been your curse, but it shall become your rejoicing. Like the people of God in Egypt, you have been afflicted; but like them too, you have been redeemed. You are henceforth free as the mountain winds. Why should we, on this day of congratulation and joy, turn our view upon the origin of African Slavery? Why should we harrow up our minds by dwelling on the deceit, the forcible fraud and treachery that have been so long practised on your hospitable and unsuspecting countrymen? Why speak of fathers torn from the bosom of their families, wives from the embraces of their husbands, children from the protection of their parents; in fine, of all the tender and endearing relations of life dissolved and trampled under foot, by the accursed traffic in human flesh? Why should we remember, in joy and exultation, the thousands of our countrymen who are to-day, in this land of gospel light, this boasted land of civil and religious liberty, writhing under the lash and groaning beneath the grinding weight of Slavery's chain? I ask, Almighty God, are they who do such things thy chosen and favorite people? But, away with such thoughts as these; we will rejoice, though sobs interrupt the songs of our rejoicing, and tears mingle in the cup we pledge to Freedom; our harps though they have long hung neglected upon the willows, shall this day be strung full high to the notes of gladness. On this day, in one member at least of this mighty Republic, the Slavery of our race has ceased forever! No more shall the insolent voice of a master be the main-spring of our actions, the sole guide of our conduct; no more shall thers hands labor in degrading and profitless servitude. Their toils will henceforth be voluntary, and be crowned with the never failing reward of industry. Honors and dignities may perhaps never be ours; but wealth, virtue, and happiness are all within the compass of our moderate exertions. And how shall we employ a few moments better than in reflecting upon the means by which these are to be obtained. For what can be more proper and more profitable to one who has just gained an invaluable treasure, than to consider how he may use it to the best possible advantage? And here I need not tell you that a strict observance to all the precepts of the gospel ought to be your first and highest aim; for small will be the value of all that the present world can bestow, if the interests of the world to come are neglected and despised. None of you can be ignorant of what the gospel teaches. Bibles may easily be obtained; nor can there be a greater disgrace, or a more shameful neglect of duty than for a person of mature age, and much more, for any father of a family to be without that most precious of all books—the Bible. If, therefore, any of you are destitute of a Bible, hasten to procure one. Will any of you say that it can be of no use to you, or that you cannot read it? Look then to that noblest of all remedies for this evil, the Sunday School—that most useful of all institutions.

There you may learn without loss of time or money, that of which none should be ignorant—to read.

Let me exhort you with earnestness to give your most sincere attention to this matter. It is of the utmost importance to every one of you. Let your next object be to obtain as soon as may be, a competency of the good things of this world; immense wealth is not necessary for you, and would but diminish your real happiness. Abject poverty is and ought to be regarded as the greatest, most terrible of all possible evils. It should be shunned as a most deadly and damning sin. What then are the means by which so dreadful a calamity may be avoided? I will tell you, my friends, in these simple words—hear and ponder on them; write them upon the tablets of your memory; they are worthy to be inscribed in letters of gold upon every door-post—"industry, prudence, and economy." Oh! they are words of power to guide you to respectability and happiness. Attend, then, to some of the laws which industry impose, while you have health and strength. Let not the rising sun behold you sleeping or indolently lying upon your beds. Rise ever with the morning light; and, till sun-set, give not an hour to idleness. Say not human nature cannot endure it. It can—it almost requires it. Sober, diligent, and moderate labor does not diminish it, but on the contrary, greatly adds to the health, vigor, and duration of the human frame. Thousands of the human race have died prematurely of disease engendered by indolence and inactivity. Few, very few indeed, have suffered by the too long continuance of bodily exertion. As you give the day to labor, so devote the night to rest; for who that has drunk and reveled all night at a tippling shop, or wandered about in search of impious and stolen pleasures, has not by so doing not only committed a most heinous and damning sin in the sight of Heaven, but rendered himself wholly unfit for the proper discharge of the duties of the coming day. Nor think that industry or true happiness do not go hand in hand; and to him who is engaged in some useful avocation, time flies delightfully and rapidly away. He does not, like the idle and indolent man, number the slow hours with sighs—cursing both himself and them for the tardiness of their flight. Ah, my friends, it is utterly impossible for him who wastes time in idleness, ever to know anything of true happiness. Indolence, poverty, wretchedness, are inseparable companions,—fly them, shun idleness, as from eminent and inevitable destruction. In vain will you labor unless prudence and economy preside over and direct all your exertions. Remember at all times that money even in your own hands, is power; with it you may direct as you will the actions of your pale, proud brethren. Seek after and amass it then, by just and honorable means; and once in your hand never part with it but for a full and fair equivalent; nor let that equivalent be something which you do not want, and for which you cannot obtain more than it cost you. Be watchful and diligent and let your mind be fruitful in devises for the honest advancement of your worldly interest. So shall you continually rise in respectability, in rank and standing in this so late and so long the land of your captivity.

Above all things refrain from the excessive use of ardent spirits. There is no evil whose progress is so imperceptible; and at the same time so sure and deadly, as that of intemperance; and by slow degrees it undermines health, wealth, and happiness, till all at length tumble into one dreadful mass of ruin. If God has given you children, he has in so doing imposed upon you a most fearful responsibility; believe me, friends, you will answer to God for every misfortune suffered, and every crime committed by them which right education and example could have taught them to avoid. Teach them reverence and obedience to the laws both of God and man. Teach them sobriety, temperance, justice, and truth. Let their minds be rightly instructed—imbued with kindness and brotherly love, charity, and benevolence. Let them possess at least so much learning as is to be acquired in the common schools of the country. In short, let their welfare be dearer to you than any earthly enjoyment; so shall they be the richest of earthly blessings.

My countrymen, let us henceforth remember that we are men. Let us as one man, on this day resolve that henceforth, by continual endeavors to do good to all mankind, we will claim for ourselves the attention and respect which as men we should possess. So shall every good that can be the portion of man, be ours— this life shall be happy, and the life to come, glorious.

———

The opinion of the public regarding the celebration and performances of that day, together with the behavior of the colored people, will be seen by the following short extract from the *Rochester Daily Advertiser*, published soon after the occurrence of those events:

"ABOLITION OF SLAVERY.

"The extinction of that curse by the laws of our State, was marked with appropriate rejoicings on the part of the African race in this neighborhood. A procession of considerable length and respectable appearance, preceded by a band of music, moved from Brown's Island through the principal streets to the public square, yesterday forenoon, where a stage and seats were erected, for the speakers and audience. The throne of Grace was addressed by the Rev. Mr. Allen, a colored clergyman. The act declaring all slaves free in this State, on the fourth day of July, 1827, was read, which was succeeded by the reading of the Declaration of Independence and delivery of an oration by Mr. Steward. We have heard but one opinion from several gentlemen who were present, and that was highly complimentary to the composition and delivery of the same.

"The exercises were concluded by a short discourse from the Rev. Mr. Allen, and the procession moved off to partake of an entertainment prepared for the occasion. The thing was got up in good order, and passed off remarkably well. The conduct of the emancipated race was exemplary throughout, and if their future enjoyment of freedom be tinctured with the prudence that characterised their celebration of its attainment, the country will have no reason to mourn the philanthropy that set them free."

Thus ended our first public celebration of our own and our country's freedom. All conducted themselves with the strictest propriety and decorum, retiring to their homes soberly and in proper season.

## CHAPTER XVIII.

### CONDITION OF FREE COLORED PEOPLE.

PURSUANT to a call given in the summer of 1830, by the colored residents of Philadelphia, for a National Convention of their race, I started in company with a friend to attend it; having previously engaged seats inside Mr. Coe's stage-coach as far as Utica, N. Y., to which place we had paid our fare the same as other passengers.

We rode on to Auburn very pleasantly, but when at that place, we with others moved to resume our seats; we were met by a stern rebuke for presuming to seat ourselves on the inside, and were ordered to ride on the outside of the coach. In vain we expostulated in vain we reminded the driver of the agreement, and of our having paid for an inside seat; we were told to take the outside of the coach or remain behind.

Desiring to attend the convention, we concluded to go

on, submitting to this rank injustice and dishonesty, until our return, when we determined to sue the proprietor of that line of stages. An opportunity was offered soon after, when I commenced a suit for damages against Mr. Sherwood, who was the great stage proprietor of those days. He, however, cleared himself by declaring that he was in no way responsible for the failures of Mr. Coe, to whom I must look for remuneration. I never found it convenient to sue Mr. Coe, and so the matter ended.

We passed through New York City to the place of our destination, where we found many of our brethren already assembled.

Philadelphia, which I now saw for the first time, I thought the most beautiful and regularly laid out city I ever beheld. Here had lived the peaceable, just, and merciful William Penn; and here many of his adherents still reside. Here, too, was the place where the Rt. Rev. Bishop Allen, the first colored American bishop in the United States, had labored so successfully. When the Methodists sought to crush by cruel prejudice the poor African, he stepped boldly forward in defence of their cause, which he sustained with a zeal and talent ever to be revered.

Thousands were brought to a knowledge of the truth, and induced "to seek first the kingdom of heaven and its righteousness," through his instrumentality. Through the .benign influence of this good man, friends and means were raised for his poor brethren, to build houses of worship, where they would no more be dragged from their knees when in prayer, and told to seat themselves by the door. Oh, how much good can one good and faithful man do, when devoted to the cause of humanity—following in the footsteps of the blessed Christ; doing unto others as they would be done by; and remembering those in bonds as bound with them. What though his skin be black as ebony, if the heart of a brother beats in his bosom? Oh, that man could judge of character as does our Heavenly Father; then would he judge righteous judgment, and cease to look haughtily down upon his afflicted fellow, because "his skin is colored not like his own."

We convened at the specified time, and organized by appointing Rev. R. Allen, president, A. Steward, vice-president, and J. C. Morrell, secretary. The convention which continued in session three days, was largely attended by all classes of people, and many interesting subjects were ably discussed; but the most prominent object was the elevation of our race. Resolutions were passed calculated to encourage our brethren to take some action on the subjects of education and mechanism. Agricultural pursuits were also recommended;—and here allow me to give my opinion in favor of the latter, as a means of sustenance and real happiness.

I knew many colored farmers, all of whom are well respected in the neighborhood of their residence. I wish I could count them by hundreds; but our people mostly flock to cities where they allow themselves to be made "hewers of wood and drawers of water;" barbers and waiters,—when, if they would but retire to the country and purchase a piece of land, cultivate and improve it, they would be far richer and happier than they can be in the crowded city. It is a mistaken idea that there is more prejudice against color in the country. True, it exists everywhere, but I regard it less potent in the country, where a farmer can live less dependant on his oppressors. The sun will shine, the rains descend, and the earth bring forth her increase, just as readily for the colored agriculturist as for his pale face neighbor. Yes, and our common mother Earth will, when life is ended, as readily open her bosom to receive your remains in a last embrace, as that of the haughty scorner of our rights.

In the city, however, there is no escape from the crushing weight of prejudice, to ramble over fields of your own cultivation; to forget your sorrows in the refreshing air that waves the loaded branches of an orchard of your own planting; nor to solace yourself with a gambol over the green meadow with your little ones. It is all toil, toil, with a burthened heart until shadows fall across the hearth-stone, and dismal forebodings darken the fireside, from whence the weary wife retires to refresh herself in broken slumber for the renewed toil of another day. Will not my friends think of these and many other advantages in favor of a country life, and practice accordingly?

After the close of the convention, I returned to my business in Rochester.

Until the discussion, which commenced about this time on the subject of temperance, I had been engaged, as most other grocers were at that time, in the sale of spirituous liquors somewhat extensively. My attention had never before been called especially to the subject, though I had witnessed some of its direst evils; but now, when I saw the matter in its true light, I resolved to give it up. I was doing well and making handsome profits on the sale of alcoholic beverages. I had also experienced a good deal of trouble with it. My license allowed me to sell any quantity less than five gallons; but it was a fine of twenty-five dollars if drunk on the premises,—one half of the sum to go to the complainant. If a vicious man got out of funds it became both easy and common for him to give some person a sixpence, half of which was to be spent for whisky, which made him a witness for the other, who would make immediate complaint, and collect his share of the fine. Nor could I prevent men who came with bottles, and purchased whisky, from drinking it where they pleased; consequently I was often called to answer to such complaints.

One morning a man entered my store and called for liquor, which the clerk gave him. After drinking it, he went directly to the office of A. House, Esq., and entered a complaint against the clerk who had served him; then stepped out for consultation with his counsel. At that moment I arrived at the office of the magistrate to whom I immediately made complaint against myself, relating to him also just how the event happened. In a few minutes the original complainant returned, to whom 'Squire House explained that he should have arraigned the proprietor of the store, and not the clerk as he had done. Determined on making a speculation, however, he demanded a precept for myself. The 'Squire, laughing most heartily, informed him that he was too late,—that Mr. Steward had the start of him, having just entered a complaint against himself, by which he saves one half of the fine. The man walked out, looking rather "cheap," nor did he or others annoy me afterwards by making complaints of that kind.

But now I saw, as never before, the sin of selling that which would make beasts of men, and only stopped to inquire what was duty in the matter. All the arguments in favor of its sale were more forcible then than now. All classes of persons used and drank the article; and it required more moral courage, to relinquish the business than it does now. Nevertheless, it appeared plain to my mind, that duty to God and my fellow-men required it, and I cheerfully gave it up forever.

I could not conscientiously, nor do I see how any man can, continue to traffic in this most fruitful source of pauperism and crime. No benefit whatever arises from its use as a beverage or from its sale. It is a curse to the drinker, to the seller, and to the community. Those who are licensed venders take from the government fifty dollars for every one put into the treasury. The money paid for licenses is a very meager compensation for the beggary, crime, and bloodshed which rum produces. All who have any knowledge of the statistics of the State, or of our prison and police records know, that intemperance has done more to fill the prisons, work-houses, alms-houses, and asylums of the State than all other influences combined; and yet men uphold the traffic. Their favors are for those who love its use and sale, and their anathemas for him who is striving to save a nation of drunkards from swift destruction; yea, their own sires, sons, and brothers from the grave of the inebriate.

When in Rochester a short time since, soliciting subscribers for this work, I stepped into a distillery and asked a man to subscribe for it. He hesitated in his decision until he took a tumbler and filling it with brandy, invited me to drink. I thanked him, saying I never drink brandy. "Never drink!" he growled, "then I tell you, sir, that you stand a much better chance of being struck by lightning than of getting a subscriber here." Oh, very well: most likely had he agreed to take a copy, he would have been sorely displeased with my views of the liquor traffic, and perhaps with the compliment I have here paid him.

But in the foregoing remarks I have said but a tithe of what my heart feels, when I think of the sufferings occasioned by drunkenness.

Even the cup of the burthened slave, writhing in his chains and toiling under the lash, is not full of bitterness until the demon rum throws in its dregs and fills it to overflowing.

How often does it occur that a passionate master, heated with wine,—mad with himself and all about him, pours out his vengeful ire on the head and back of some helpless slave, and leaves him weltering in his blood! How often may be heard the agonized wail of the slave mother, deploring the departure of some innocent child that has been lost in gambling, while the master was intoxicated!

How often do the shrieks of the poor but virtuous slave girl, ring through the midnight air, as she, pleading for death rather than life, rushes screaming away from a brutal master, infuriated and drunk! If it is a fact, and certainly it is, that the master is thus affected by his costly wine; what, think you, will be the temper and condition of the coarse and heartless overseer who drinks his miserable whisky or bad brandy? It is horrible, beyond description. I have often myself seen a drunken overseer, after pouring down dram after dram, mount his horse and ride furiously among the slaves, beating, bruising, mangling with his heavy cowhide every one he chanced to meet, until the ground presented the appearance of a battlefield.

# CHAPTER XIX.

PERSECUTION OF THE COLORED PEOPLE.

WHILE the colored population of New York were rejoicing in the measure of freedom allowed them by the more wholesome laws of that State, our brethren in Ohio were being oppressed and maltreated by the unjust and odious "black laws" of that professedly free State, enacted with special reference to the disposition of the colored race.

In Cincinnati, O., within sight of the slave land of Kentucky, a terrible persecution had commenced, and an effort was made to drive all colored persons from the place.

Our people had settled there in large numbers, but now a mob had assembled in that city with the determination to drive them, not only from their homes and city, but from the State. A bloody conflict ensued, in which the white and black man's blood mingled freely. So great had been the loss of property; and

## 174    PERSECUTION OF THE COLORED PEOPLE.

so horrid and fearful had been the scene, that our people chose to leave, rather than remain under such untoward circumstances. They lived in constant fear of the mob which had so abused and terrified them. Families seated at the fireside started at every breath of wind, and trembled at the sound of every approaching footstep. The father left his family in fear, lest on his return from his daily labor, he should find his wife and children butchered, and his house left desolate.

Meetings were held to devise plans and means for leaving the place where they had been so cruelly treated. But where should they go? And why should they be compelled to leave the State of Ohio? The fact is, that the African race there, as in all parts of this nominally free Republic, was looked down upon by the white population as being little above the brute creation; or, as belonging to some separate class of degraded beings, too deficient in intellect to provide for their own wants, and must therefore depend on the superior ability of their oppressors, to take care of them. Indeed, both the time and talents of eminent men have been wasted in unsuccessful research for the line of demarkation, between the African and the highest order of animals,—such for instance as the monkey or the ourang-outang. Some even, have advanced the absurd idea, that wicked Cain transmitted to them the "mark" which the Almighty set upon him for the murder of his brother; and that he, (who then must have survived the deluge), is the progenitor of that despised and inferior race—the negro slave of the United States of America!

If it be true, that the natural inferiority of the black man, connects him so closely with the animal creation, it looks passing strange to me that he should be made responsible for the violation of laws which he has been declared too imbecile to aid in framing or of comprehending. Nor is it less strange to see him enslaved and compelled by his labor to maintain both his master and himself, after having declared him incapable of doing either. Why not let him go then? Why hold with an unyielding grasp, so miserable and useless a piece of property? Is it benevolence that binds him with his master's chain? Judge ye. Stranger still is the fact of attaching such vast influence to his presence and so much concern regarding his movements, when in a state of freedom, if indeed, he is of so little worth and consequence, and so nearly related to the brutes that perish.

Surely, the Legislature of Ohio, or of any other State, would never feel called upon to sit in grave counsel, for the purpose of framing laws which would impose fine and imprisonment on a monkey, should one chance to locate within its jurisdiction; nor would they think it advisable for the court to assemble, or a jury to be empanneled, to drive from their midst an ourang-outang. And yet this and more must be done to get rid of the hated negro, who has been born in that State, or has fled to it for protection from the manstealer.

When strangers pass hastily through this country, and after a careless glance at the colored population, report them to be "an indolent, improvident, and vicious class of persons," they should consider some of the many obstacles thrown in the way of the most favored of that race. Knowing as they do, the rigor of the law, and feeling as they do, the oppressive power of prejudice, it becomes almost impossible for them to rise to that station they were designed to fill, and for which their natural abilities as certainly qualify them, as though they had never been robbed of their God-given rights. But let us return to our tried friends in Cincinnati.

They finally resolved to collect what they could of their possessions and establish a colony in Canada. In accordance with this resolution, they agreed to first send an agent to obtain liberty to settle there, and if successful to select and purchase a large tract of land, making such arrangements as he thought best for their speedy removal to their new home. Israel Lewis was their appointed agent, who departed immediately for Upper Canada to perform his mission; and there for the present we will leave him and return to Rochester

Our more favored brethren in New York felt a deep sympathy for their outraged countrymen in Cincinnati; a sympathy equaled only by their indignation at the cause of such demand.

A meeting expressive of their views and feelings on that subject, was convened in the city of Rochester, during which, the following preamble and resolutions were read and unanimously adopted:

*Whereas,* The city of Cincinnati has again become the scene of another dreadful mob and bloodshed, where nothing but terror and confusion reigned for a number of hours together.

*And Whereas,* Our brethren and fellow citizens were left exposed to the fury of an ungovernable mob, made up of the base, the ignorant, and vile, the very dregs of society; and probably led on by slaveholders, who of all men are the most execrable; while boasting of liberty, he tramples on the dearest rights of men and is the greatest robber of it on earth.

*Resolved,* That we deprecate an appeal to arms by any class of our fellow citizens, except in extreme cases, and we think that such a case has been presented in the late outrage at Cincinnati.

*Resolved,* That when a class of men so far forget the duty they owe to God, their fellow men, and their country, as to trample under their feet the very laws they have made, and are in duty bound to obey and execute, we believe it to be the duty of our brethren and fellow citizens, to protect their lives against such lawless mobs; and if in the conflict, any of the mobocrats perish, every good citizen should say Amen.

*Resolved,* That we do truly sympathize with the friends of God's poor; the friends of the oppressed, throughout this boasted land of liberty, in the losses they have sustained in consequence of the mob.

*Resolved,* That we believe the time is not far distant, when the *Queen City of the West,* shall be redeemed from the hateful influence of the slaveholder; redeemed from that cruel prejudice of caste which hangs like a mill-stone around the neck of our people; redeemed from all those unequal laws, which have a tendency to make the

H*

strong stronger and the weak weaker; redeemed from their false-hearted friends, whose sarcastic smile is more to be feared than the frowns of an open enemy.

*Resolved*, That the untiring exertions of our friends, and the indefatigable industry of our brethren, are sure guarantees that the State of Ohio will not long be what she now is,—a hissing and by-word on account of her iniquitous laws; but that she will rise above every narrow minded prejudice, and raise up her sable sons and daughters and place them on an equality with the rest of her citizens.

*Resolved*, That we deeply deplore the loss our friends have sustained in the destruction of their printing press in Cincinati.

*Resolved*, That we as an oppressed people, feel it our duty to give our undivided support to the press and the laborers in our cause.

Mr. Israel Lewis made his way to Canada, and having obtained permission to establish a colony, he bargained with the Canada Company for one township of land, for which he agreed to pay the money demanded, in a few days, and then returned to Cincinnati, by way of Rochester. The poor, persecuted colored people, had in the mean time made ready for their flight from their homes, their native land, and from this boasted free Republic, to seek a residence in the cold and dreary wilds of Canada; to claim that protection from the English government which had been denied them in the land of their birth; and like the overtasked Israelites, "they went out with their wives and their little ones," but with smaller possessions.

During the stay of Mr. Lewis in Rochester, he

reported there and elsewhere, that eleven hundred persons were then in the dense woods of Canada in a state of actual starvation, and called upon the humane everywhere, to assist them in such extreme suffering.

To me he also told the story of their destitution, which affected me deeply. I had at that time just made a public profession of my faith in the christian religion and my determination to be governed by its holy precepts. I felt for the distressed and suffering everywhere; but particularly for those who had fled, poor and destitute, from cruel task-masters, choosing rather the sufferings of cold and hunger, with liberty, than the meager necessities of life and Slavery. I concluded to go to Canada and try to do some good; to be of some little service in the great cause of humanity.

As soon as practicable therefore, I left Rochester for Toronto, the capital of Upper Canada, which I found quite a thriving town, and containing some fine brick buildings, and some I saw were built of mud, dried in the sun, wearing rather a poor than pretty appearance. At Toronto we hired a team to take us on to Ancaster, fifty miles distant. We traveled now through a new country; the roads were very bad, and the inhabitants few. We, however, reached Ancaster, a small village, where we remained one night and next morning pursued our journey to the settlement of the poor fugitives from Cincinnati. After some hard traveling, we finally arrived at the place where we found our brethren, it is true, but in quite destitute circumstances. Our fare was poor indeed, but as good as they could get. The township was one unbroken wilderness when purchased for the colony, and of course their lands must be cleared of the heavy timber before crops could be got in, hence, there was a great deal of destitution and suffering before their harvest could ripen after the land was prepared for the seed.

The day after I arrived at the settlement, which consisted of a few rude log cabins, a meeting was called to give the township a name. Several were suggested, but I at length motioned to name it in honor of the great philanthropist, Wilberforce. This was carried, and the township from that time has been known by that name. It is situated on what is known as the Huron Tract, Kent County, London District, and is the next north of the township of London. Our neighbors on the south, were a company of Irish people, who owned the township, and on the west side were a township of Welshmen, a hardy, industrious and enterprising people.

In Wilberforce there were no white inhabitants; the land appeared level and handsome, with but one stream of any magnitude running through it; this was the Oxsable, which was dry during a part of the year. All was one vast forest of heavy timber, that would compare well with that of Western New York.

Beech, maple, ash, elm, oak, whitewood, bass, balm of gilead, &c. The soil was good for corn, wheat, rye, oats, and most kinds of the grain and vegetables raised in New York, and was a superior grazing country, about fifteen miles from London. This was a village containing perhaps thirty dwellings, and two hundred inhabitants; a court-house and jail all under one roof, built of stone and plastered; small doors and windows in the style of some of the old English castles. London was built in the forks, or between the east and west branches of the river Thames; hence, you would hear people speak of "going to the forks," instead of the village; it is about two hundred miles from Buffalo, and the nearest port between the two is Port Stanley, thirty miles from London.

I returned from Canada, where I had seen an oppressed people struggling with the hardships and privations of a new settlement; I had seen wretchedness in some places, but by no means sufficient to justify the report made by Mr. Lewis, and I determined I would remove there with my family, and do sll in my power to assist the colored people in Canada.

I had witnessed a disposition on the part of some to prevent our brethren from settling in Wilberforce, while the colonizationists made a grand argument of it in favor of their wicked policy. All must see that it became a necessity with those who fled to Canada to save themselves from constant abuse or from Slavery, and in some instances their lives; and not because they admitted the justice of one portion of American citizens driving another from their native land; nor their right to colonize them anywhere on the habitable globe.

All these things taken into consideration, determined me to join them in the enterprize of building up an asylum for the oppressed, where our colored friends could obtain a home, and where, by their industry they could obtain a competency for themselves, besides providing a safe retreat for the weary fugitive from Slavery; guiding by its beacon light of liberty, the destitute and oppressed everywhere, to home and plenty.

I felt willing to make any sacrifice in my power to serve my Lord, by administering to the necessities of my down-trodden countrymen. How far my desire has been accomplished God only knows, but I do know that the purest motives influenced me, and an honest purpose directed my steps in removing to Wilberforce. Not so with all, however. Some there were, Judas-like, who "cared not for the poor; but because he was a thief and had the bag, and bare what was put therein," made great exertions for a time in favor of the settlement. It too soon became apparent that to make money was the prominent object with by far too great a number of the colonists; hence, our future difficulties.

# CHAPTER XX.

### REMOVAL TO CANADA.

IN 1830, I closed my business in Rochester, preparatory to leaving for Canada. Some of my friends thought I had better remain in the States and direct emigrants to Wilberforce; while others were certain I could benefit them more by going myself at once,—the latter I had determined to do; but as the time drew near for me to start, an unaccountable gloominess and forebodings of evil took possession of my mind. Doubts of the practicability of the undertaking began to arise, though nothing unfavorable had occurred. To the throne of grace, I often bore the subject and besought my Heavenly Father to enlighten my mind, and direct my steps in duty's path regarding it; but to confess the truth, I never received any great encouragement from that source, though it occupied my mind constantly. During the hours of slumber I was continually being startled by frightful dreams,—

sometimes I thought I saw a monstrous serpent as large as a log stretched across the road between Rochester and the Genesee River; at another I thought myself in the air so high that I could have a full view of the shores of Lake Ontario, and they were alive with snakes; and then I saw a large bird like an eagle, rise up out of the water and fly toward the south.

Notwithstanding these omens, I turned my steps toward Wilberforce. In May, 1831, we bid adieu to our friends in Rochester, and taking passage to Buffalo on a canal boat, we arrived in due time, and from whence we sailed for Port Stanley, or as it is sometimes called, Kettle Creek. It took a week to make this trip, which, with favorable wind might have been made in two days. The mouth of the creek makes a safe harbor at that place, where there is also a dock, one ware-house and several farm houses. The place was then very wild and picturesque in its appearance; we did not stop long, however, to admire its beauty, but engaged a farmer to take us on to London. Ten miles on our way, and we came to a newly laid out village, called St. Thomas, from whence we pursued our journey through a new country to London, where we arrived tired and hungry, and put up for the night with a Mr. Faden. There I purchased a span of horses for one hundred and fifty dollars, and putting them before a new lumber wagon brought on

## ARRIVAL WITH FAMILY AT WILBERFORCE. 185

from Rochester, we started for our wild and new home in good spirits, at which we arrived in good time.

The colony was comprised of some fourteen or fifteen families, and numbered some over fifty persons in all. The first business done after my arrival, was to appoint a board of managers, to take the general oversight of all the public business of the colony. The board consisted of seven men, chosen by the settlers, and as I was now one of them, they gave me the office of President. It was also resolved by the board, to send out two agents for the purpose of soliciting aid for the erection of houses for worship, and for the maintenance of schools in the colony.

The Rev. N. Paul was chosen one of their agents, and he received from me a power of attorney, authorising him to collect funds for the above purposes in England, Ireland, and Scotland; the other, I. Lewis was empowered to solicit and collect funds for the same objects in the United States.

Preparations were immediately made to fit Mr. Paul out for his mission to England, from whence he was to remit any funds he might receive to Arthur Tappan, of New York City; first to pay for his outfit, and afterwards to the treasurer of the board of managers, for the support of schools in Wilberforce. Mr. Paul, however, still lacked money to proceed to England, and therefore went to Rochester, where he found my old and tried friend Everard Peck; who was ever known as the poor man's friend, and the support of the weak everywhere. To this good man, whose memory is still dear to thousands, Mr. Paul showed his power of attorney, at the same time informing him of the condition and wants of the colony; and as was ever his wont, when help was needed, his purse, (though not one of the heaviest), was at his service. Through the kind influence of Mr. Peck, and some of the colored friends in that city, a note for seven hundred dollars was drawn up, signed by Mr. P. and cashed at the Bank, which enabled the agent to make the voyage without further delay. He reached England, and collected quite large sums of money, but entirely failed in the remittance of any sums, either to Mr. Tappan or myself. When the note of seven hundred dollars became due, Mr. Peck was obliged to pay, and lose it. It was out of my power, nor had any of the friends the means to do any thing towards paying it, inasmuch as they had assisted Paul all they could and got nothing in return. There was one thing, however, that the reverend gentleman did do,— he wrote me from time to time, to keep me advised of the success of his mission, and once informed me that he had then twelve hundred dollars on hand; but not a farthing could we get. We wrote him again and again, reminding him of the bank debt, and the uneasiness of his friends on account of it, but all to no purpose,—the Atlantic was between us, and he was making money too easily, to like to be interrupted. He never paid one dollar.

Let us now look after the other agent, who had likewise been fitted out, to prosecute his mission in the States. That he collected money professedly for the assistance of the colony, is too well known to require proof, but how much, we could not determine; we had reason to believe, however, that he retained quite a large sum. He would neither pay it over to the board, nor give any account of his proceedings. Very little did he ever pay over to the aid of the colony as designed. He was frequently written to, and every means in our power used, to induce him to give some account of his mission, but in vain; he would do nothing of the kind. Things went on in this way for two years, when it became evident that he had no intention of satisfying the minds of the settlers; and farther, that he meant to collect what he could, and use it as he pleased. We learned too, that when abroad, he lived extravagantly,—putting up at the most expensive hotels, giving parties, and doing many things, not only beyond his means, but that brought dishonor on the cause and colony. When he returned to the settlement, he would, if he had funds, make presents to his particular friends instead of paying it to the treasurer, as he was pledged to do, until the majority of the colony became thoroughly disgusted with his heartlessness and dishonesty. It was also perceivable that Lewis and Paul both, were getting weary of the solicitations of the board and complaints of the settlers, and were anxious to be rid of them, and enjoy their ill gotten gains in their own way.

It was never intended by the managers, to send out agents to beg money to be divided among the colonists; but to support schools, &c. Most of the settlers were able to work and did so; and were now getting along quite pleasantly.

Finally, after we had tried every means in vain, to get a settlement with Lewis, and to obtain his papers, there was nothing more we could do, but to warn the public against him, by publishing the facts in the case; this we did in various newspapers of Canada and in the States. An article inserted in the "Rochester Observer," to that effect, was like throwing a lighted match into a keg of powder. The excitement was intense on the part of Lewis and his friends, who were joined by the friends of N. Paul, to destroy, if they could, the board of managers. I, however, being the only member of that devoted board, who happened to be extensively known in the States, their anathemas were all poured out on me, and all their energies brought forward to insure my destruction. They were few in number, it is true, but they had money, and I had little to spend in litigation; besides, Lewis was in debt, and his creditors did not like to see his

eans of paying them swept away. The Canadians
emed to think there was no harm done if Lewis did
:t money out of the "Yankees," as long as it came
to their hands at last, and so, on the whole, they
ised a tremendous storm, designed, however, to
reep nobody away but myself; and I have con-
iued to this day, notwithstanding all their artful
alignity. Nothing, I am persuaded, could have
ved me from imprisonment at that time, had I not
)ssessed a high reputation for truth and honesty
iring my previous sojourn in the colony.

Lewis had dealt somewhat extensively with Mr.
)nes, who was the principal agent for the Canada
)mpany; but failing to fulfil his agreement, regard-
g the payment for a large tract of land, it so
:asperated Mr. Jones, that he declared he would
ive nothing to do with any of the colored people;
id so when I wanted to buy a lot of land, he would
)t sell it to me because he so despised Lewis.

How much harm can one wicked man do! and yet
cannot be right to judge the character of a whole
ass or community by that of one person.

# CHAPTER XXI.

### ROUGHING IT IN THE WILDS OF CANADA.

THE "Canada Company," of which I have so frequently spoken, was an association of wealthy gentlemen, residing in England; something like the East India Company, especially regarding the title of lands. They had sent on their agent and purchased a large tract of land known as the "Huron Tract," extending from London to Lake Huron, where they laid out a village, named Goderich, sixty miles distant from Wilberforce. With this company, Mr. Lewis had contracted for a township of land, as agent for the Cincinnati refugees; but failing to meet the demand, the company kindly extended the time of payment; but when that time also passed without receiving any thing from Lewis, the general agent, Mr. Jones became so indignant, that he utterly refused to sell a foot of land to any colored person whatever. This proved to be one of the greatest detriments to the prosperity of the colony it ever met.

The Society of Friends at this time, however, with commendable sympathy for the oppressed and abused colored residents of Cincinnati, and with their proverbial liberality, raised a sum of money sufficient to purchase eight hundred acres of land of the Canada Company for the benefit of the colony. The funds were placed in the hands of one of their number, Frederick Stover, who went to Canada as their agent, purchased the land, and settled colored people upon it, which comprised nearly all of the Wilberforce settlement. This occurred before I settled in Canada, and the consequence was, when I desired to purchase land, none could be obtained. At the time, however, of which I am speaking, the Canada Company were constructing a road through their possessions, some seventy miles in length, and the principal contractor, Mr. Ingersoll, had agreed to take land in part payment for his services on the road. In accordance with this agreement, he accepted one lot of land situated within the Wilberforce settlement, which he agreed to sell to Mr. Lewis for twenty-five dollars. Mr. Lewis, knowing that I was anxious to purchase, accepted the offer, and then came and showed the contract, offering it to me on condition that I paid him the twenty-five dollars which he had just paid Mr. Ingersoll. This I was glad to do; I paid the demand; took an assignment on the back of the receipt, and passed into immediate possession of the land. He at the same time requested me to take up a note of twenty-five dollars for him; which I did, on his promising to refund the money in a short time.

I commenced laboring on the wild land I had purchased; cleared some ten acres, which in consequence of its being so heavily timbered, cost me at least twenty-five dollars per acre; built a house and barn—supposing myself its legal possessor,—until I chanced to meet Mr. Ingersoll, who informed me that Mr. Jones had refused to sell him the land to be disposed of to a colored person; that he had duly informed Lewis of the fact, and had returned to him the twenty-five dollars received. Not a word of this, had Lewis communicated to me, though he knew I was making expensive improvements, in the faith that I was its only owner. Instead of atoning for the wrong already done me, he made it the basis of a deeper injury.

After one year's residence in Wilberforce, I found it necessary to return to Rochester to settle some unfinished business; and when on my way thither I stopped at London, where I found Lewis, who had not only preceded me but had taken out a *capias*, for forty pounds currency. I was therefore obliged to get bail for my appearance at court, after which I pursued my journey.

On my arrival in Rochester, I found business at a stand; and the community in a state of excitement and alarm, on account of that fell destroyer, the cholera. This was its first visit to the United States, and the fearful havoc it was making, spread terror and consternation throughout the land. I returned to Canada; but found on my arrival at London, that "the pestilence that walketh at noon-day," had preceded me, and taken from that village my friend, Mr. Ingersoll, with several others. So great had been the alarm, that instead of my appearing at court as I expected to do, I found it adjourned, and the judge returned to his home.

I hastened on to Wilberforce, which had fortunately escaped the fearful scourge, with terrible apprehensions.

Having a little spare time, I went out with my rifle, in search of deer; but soon came upon a large wolf, which I wounded with the first shot; he, however, sprang aside and was gone. On looking about for him I espied another!—reloading my rifle, I fired, and he fell dead at my feet, while my dog at the same time I heard barking furiously. Having dispatched this second intruder, I saw that my dog had the first one, entangled in the branches of a fallen tree. I searched for my balls, and was vexed to find that I had left them at home. In this predicament I cut with my knife, a knot from a beech limb, put it in my

I

rifle, and took deadly aim at the enraged wolf. The wooden ball struck him between the eyes and killed him on the spot.

The two dead animals, with their skins, I sold for nine dollars and a half,—making pretty good wages for a few hours labor.

Hunting was very generally pursued by the settlers, with great earnestness and considerable skill. The forest abounded with deer, wolves, bears, and other wild animals. Bears were plenty, and very troublesome because so dangerously tame. One day, our children had built for themselves a play-house, a few rods from the door, and were enjoying their play when they were called in to dinner. A moment after, I observed one of the settlers gazing intently at the play-house; I called to know what so attracted his attention, and he informed me that an old bear, with three cubs, had just then taken possession of the play-house. And sure enough there they were! knocking about among the dishes, and munching the crumbs of bread which the children had left. The man was supplied with a loaded rifle and urged to shoot them, but he begged to be excused from a pitched battle with so many; and the bears leisurely took their departure for the woods without molestation. The play-house, however, was soon deserted by the children after these unbidden guests had made so free with it; and we were ourselves somewhat alarmed for the safety of our children, who were accustomed to roam in the edge of the forest, and make swings of the luxuriant grape vines.

But such incidents are common in a new country, surrounded as we were by a dense wilderness.

## CHAPTER XXII.

#### NARROW ESCAPE OF A SMUGGLER.

FROM the time I first settled in Wilberforce, my house had ever been open to travelers and strangers; but a conversation I happened to overhear, led me to take a course different from what I had at first intended. I was at a public house about twenty miles from home, when I heard the landlord advising his guest to eat heartily, for, said he, "you will find nothing more worthy of your attention, until you reach Wilberforce. When you arrive at that settlement, inquire for A. Steward, from the States, and he will give you a meal fit for a prince." I began to reflect on the subject and concluded, inasmuch as people would send company to me, it would be better to make some preparation for entertaining them. I had plenty of furniture, and all I needed was a larger supply of food, to commence keeping a tavern. This was easily obtained, and I opened a public house which was well patronized.

One day while I was absent from home, a man drove to the door the finest span of horses, I think I ever saw,—black as jet, with proudly arched necks, and glossy tails that nearly swept the ground. The gentleman sprang from his carriage, bounded through the open door, and in the most excited manner, began to inquire "who owns this establishment? When will he return? Can I be accommodated? Can I see your barn?" &c. The stable boy took him to the barn, from whence he soon returned; his face flushed, and breathing so heavily as to be heard all through the apartment; trembling so violently that he could scarcely speak at all,—but made out to inquire, "if there was not some place besides the barn where he could put his horses?" He was told that there was a small shelter built for cows, in bad weather, and the next moment he was examining it. In a very short time he had his horses and carriage stowed away in the cow-shed. He acted like a crazy man; but when he had secured his horses, he re-entered the house and frankly apologized for his conduct. "I may as well tell you the truth," said he; "I am suspected of smuggling goods; a reward is offered for my arrest, and the constables are on my track, in pursuit of me. My name is Cannouse, and I am from M———, in Ontario County."

But perhaps they can not prove you guilty of smuggling, said I, in an after conversation.

"Ah," said he, "there is for me no such hope or probability; I have been engaged for the last few months in the sale of dress-goods and broad-cloths, and my exposure and flight is the consequence of my own folly. While in the village of St. Catharines, I took a young girl out to ride, after she had engaged to accompany another young fellow, which of course offended him; and he being too well posted up on my affairs, went directly to the custom house officer and informed against me. I was sitting in the parlor, perfectly at ease, when a young man, a relative of the young lady in question, burst into the room, shouting, 'Fly! fly! for your life! The officers are upon you!' And I did fly; with barely time to reach the woods, for as I sprang through the back door, the officers entered through the front door. My horses were my first consideration; they had been raised by my father, and should I lose them, I should never dare to meet him again. In my hasty flight, I engaged the young man to conceal them till night, and then to drive them to a certain place where I would meet him. This he did, and I kept on my flight until I came to the house of a friend, where I halted to make inquiries. The gentleman had just come from London, and had seen handbills at every conspicuous place, describing me and my horses. I asked him what I should do?

He said, 'you are not safe a moment; there is no hope but in flight; avoid the main road, and get to the colony if you can; if you succeed, go to A. Steward; he is an upright man and will never betray you for money.' And here I am: if I am arrested, six months imprisonment, three hundred dollars fine, and the forfeiture of my father's valuable and favorite horses, will be my portion. I have had no regular meal for the last three days, and my head aches violently."

We gave him some refreshment, and conducted him to a room, assuring him that he should have it to himself. All remained quiet until midnight, when a man knocked cautiously at our door. I opened it myself, and a gentleman, looking carefully about the place, inquired,

"Are you full?"

"No," said I.

"Have you any travelers here to night?"

"Yes."

"How many?"

"Two."

"Where are they?"

"In this room; walk in, sir."

He took the light from my hand, and stepping lightly up to a bed, where two travelers were quietly sleeping, he closely examined their faces. He soon returned the light, and without further inquiry retired from the house. When his companions came up, I distinctly heard him tell them that the smuggler was not there.

"You may be mistaken," said the other, "and we must search the barn for his horses."

This they did thoroughly, after procuring a lantern but without finding any thing to reward their diligent search; and they finally drove off.

When they had gone, Cannouse groaned most bitterly, and trembled from head to foot at the thought of his narrow escape. The next day an officer rode up to where the children were playing, with a handbill which he read, and inquired if they had seen a person bearing that description, pass *that day?* They answered negatively, and he rode on. The poor frightened Cannouse stayed with us a week; and nearly every day during the time, the house and barn were searched for him. The children kept watch, and when they saw any one coming they would let him know, in time to take himself and horses into a thicket near by. When he thought pursuit was over, he started to leave; but when, in a half hour after, a *posse* of men drove up to my door, flourishing their handbills, I thought it all over with Cannouse. I told them that he was not there; but they chose to have another search, and when they found nothing, the officer sprang into his carriage, exclaiming, "come on, boys; we'll soon have him now; we have tracked him here, and he can't be far off."

Cannouse had left us, feeling quite secure; but he had traveled but a short distance, when he observed a horse shoe loose, and to get it fastened he drove down to a blacksmith's shop, which happened to stand at the foot of a hill; and between it and the highway there had been left standing a clump of trees which nearly hid it from view. While there, getting his horse shod, the officers passed him unobserved, and he finally escaped.

Some time after, a gentleman called on us who had seen Cannouse in Michigan, where he was doing well. He had succeeded in reaching Detroit, from whence he passed safely to his home; but probably learned a lesson not to be forgotten. He was a talented young man—one who would have felt deeply the disgrace of imprisonment,—and it was indeed a pleasure to me to do what I could, to effect his release from an unenviable position. I would never have betrayed him; but happily I was not asked directly for him, until he was gone from my house and protection.

## CHAPTER XXIII.

### NARRATIVE OF TWO FUGITIVES FROM VIRGINIA.

THE settlers in Wilberforce, were in general, industrious and thrifty farmers: they cleared their land, sowed grain, planted orchards, raised cattle, and in short, showed to the world that they were in no way inferior to the white population, when given an equal chance with them. In proof of this let me say, that it was uniformly the practice of persons traveling from London to Goderich, to remain in our settlement over night, in preference to going on to find entertainment among their own class of people. And we believe that the whites are bound to admit, that the experiment of the Wilberforce colony proves that the colored man can not only take care of himself, but is capable of improvement; as industrious and intelligent as themselves, when the yoke is taken from off their necks, and a chance given them to exercise their abilities. True, many of them had just escaped from cruel task-masters; ignorant of almost every thing but the lash,—but the air of freedom so invigorated and put new life into their weary bodies, that they soon became intelligent and thrifty.

Among the settlers might be gathered many a thrilling narrative, of suffering and hair-breadth escapes from the slave-land,—one of which I will tell as 'twas told to me.

In a small rude cabin, belonging to one of the large plantations in Virginia, sat at a late hour of the night, an afflicted slave-man and his devoted wife, sad and weeping. At length the husband repeated what he before had been saying:

"I tell you, wife, we must flee from this place, without delay. Oh, I cannot endure the idea of seeing you sold for the Southern market, to say nothing of myself; and we shall most likely be separated, which I can't bear! Oh, Rosa, the thought distracts me,— I can't bear it!"

"Are you sure," said Rosa, "that master thinks of such a frightful doom for us?"

"Oh yes, I know it; I heard master to-day making a bargain with the slave dealer that has been hanging about here so long; and when it was finished, I heard him reading over the list, and our names, wife, are the first on it."

"Oh, dear!" sobbed the wife, "we shall certainly

be retaken and whipped to death; or else we shall starve in the wilderness! Oh, it is very hard to be compelled to leave all our friends and the old plantation where we were born!"

"Yes; it is both hard and unjust," said Joe, and an indignant frown contracted his brow,—"here is our birth-place, and here, for forty years have I toiled early and late to enrich my master; and you, my poor wife, a few years less; and now we are to be sold, separated, and all without a choice of our own. We must go, Rosa. If we die, let us die together!"

"It shall be as you say, Joe," she replied, "but it frightens me to think of the hardships of the way, and the danger of being recaptured."

"Courage, wife: no fate can be worse than the one designed for us; and we have no time to lose To-morrow night, then, we must make the first effort to gain our liberty, and leave all that is dear to us except each other!" And they retired to rest, but not to sleep.

The following night was very dark; and as soon as all was quiet on the plantation, they stole out of their cabin and stealthily crept over the ground until they reached the highway; and then, guided only by the north star, they made their way to the nearest woods. So fearful had they been of being suspected, that they took no provision of any kind with them. All night they plunged forward through the tangled thicket and under-brush, sorrounded by thick darkness, glancing now and then upward to their only light,

> "Star of the North! though night winds drift the fleecy drapery of the sky,
> Between thy lamp and thee, I lift, yea, lift with hope my sleepless eye."

When day dawned they threw their weary bodies on the ground, famished and thirsty, and waited for the darkness to again conceal them while they pursued their journey. The second day of their flight, the pain of hunger became almost beyond endurance. They found a few roots which relieved them a little; but frequently they lost their way, and becoming bewildered, knew not which way to go; they pushed on, however, determined to keep as far from their pursuers as possible. Their shoes were soon worn out; but bare-footed, bare-headed, and famishing with hunger, they pressed forward, until the fourth day, when they found themselves too weak to proceed further. Hope, the anchor of the soul, had failed them! They were starving in a dense forest! No track or path could they find, and even had they seen a human being, they would have been more terrified than at the sight of a wild beast!

Poor Rosa, could go no farther—her strength was all gone—and as her emaciated husband laid her on the cold earth, he exclaimed, "Oh, dear God! *must* we, after all our efforts, starve in this dark wilderness! Beside his fainting wife, he finally stretched himself, sheltered only by a few bushes, and tried to compose himself to die! but resting a few moments revived him, and he aroused himself, to make one more effort for life! "Stay you here, wife, and I will try once more to find the highway; it cannot be far from here; and if I am taken, I will submit to my fate without a struggle; we can but die." So saying, he left her, and began to reconnoitre the country around them. Much sooner than he expected he emerged from the wood, and not far distant he saw a house in the direction from whence he came; being, however, as most of the slaves are, superstitious, he thought it would be a bad omen to turn backward, and so continued to look about him. It seemed, he said, that some unseen power held him, for though starving as he was, he could not take a step in that direction; and at last as he turned around, to his great joy, he saw another dwelling a little way off, and toward that he hastened his now lightened footsteps. With a palpitating heart, he approached the door and knocked cautiously. The man of the house opened it, and as soon as he saw him, he said, "You are a fugitive slave, but be not alarmed, come in; no harm shall befall you here; I shall not inquire from whence you came; it is enough for me to know that you are a human being in distress; consider me your friend, and let me know your wants."

"Bread! Oh, for a morsal of bread!" said the famished creature, while his hitherto wild and sunken eyes, began to distil grateful tears. The "good Samaritan" stepped to another apartment and brought him a piece of bread, which he expected to see him devour at once, but instead, he looked at it wistfully, literally devouring it with his eyes; turned it over and over, and at last stammered out, "my good master, without a piece of bread for my poor starving wife, I can never swallow this, tempting as it is."

"Poor man," said his benefactor, "can it be that you have a wife with you, wretched as yourself?" He brought out a loaf of bread, some cheese and meat, and while the fugitive was preparing to return, the kind gentleman said, "I am glad you came to me; had you called at the house you first saw, you would have been betrayed, and immediately arrested. You must remember," he continued, "that you are young and valuable slaves, and that your master will make every effort in his power to find you, especially since he has made a sale of you. To-day and to-night, remain in the woods, and the next morning you may come to me, if all is quiet; should I see danger approaching you, I will warn you of it by the crack my rifle. Go now, to your poor wife, and listen for the signal of danger; if you hear none, come to me at the appointed time." He returned, and after feeding his helpless Rosa, she revived, and soon felt quite comfortable and grateful.

When the morning came for them to leave their retreat, they listened intently, but hearing nothing, Joe started for the residence of his friend. He had been gone but a short time, when his wife, who lay in the bushes, thought she heard the tramp of horses,— she crept nearer the highway, and peeping through the bush—Oh, horror! what was her consternation and sickening fear, to find herself gazing upon the well-known features of her old master, and two of his neighbors, all armed to the teeth! Her heart seemed to stand still, and the blood to chill in her veins. Had she been discovered she would have been an easy prey, for she declared that she could not move a step. In the meantime her husband had got about half way to the residence of his preserver, when his quick ear detected the sound made by the feet of horses, and as he stopped to listen more intently, the sharp crack of a rifle sent him bounding back to his concealment in the forest.

The party of horsemen rode on to the dwelling of the kind hearted gentleman, and inquired whether he had seen any fugitive slaves pass that way.

"I saw," said he, "a man and woman passing rapidly along the road, but do not know whether they were fugitives, as I did not see their faces." The human blood-hound, thanked the gentleman for the information, and immediately set out in pursuit; but, just as the informant had intended, in a direction *opposite* to that the slaves had taken. That night, Joe and Rosa visited the house of their benefactor, where they were supplied with clothing and as much food as they could carry; and next day they went on their way rejoicing. They settled in Cincinnati, where they lived happily, until the mob drove them with others, to the Wilberforce settlement, where they are in no danger of the auction block, or of a Southern market; and are as much devoted to each other as ever.

# CHAPTER XXIV.

### PLEASANT RE-UNION OF OLD AND TRIED FRIENDS.

IT is well known to those who have assisted in clearing land in a new country, that bears, who are not Jews, are very troublesome, and levy a heavy tax on the settlers, to supply themselves with pork—their favorite food. One old bear in particular, had for a long time annoyed the colonists, by robbing their hog-stys almost every night. We failed in all our plans to destroy his life, until a woman saw him one day, walking at ease through the settlement. A half dozen of us gave chase immediately, and came up with him after traveling two miles. So anxious was I to kill him, that I fired at first sight and missed him, which gave us another two miles chase. When, however, we came up, he was seated on a branch of a tree, leisurely surveying us and the dogs, with great complacency. The contents of my rifle brought him to the ground, and stirred his blood for battle. One blow from his powerful paw, sent my fine greyhound some yards distant, sprawling upon the ground, and when he renewed the attack, Bruin met him with extended jaws, taking and munching his head in his mouth. My rifle was now reloaded, and the second shot killed him on the spot. We tied his legs together, and lifting him on a pole, marched in triumph into the settlement, where guns were discharged and cheers given, in approbation of our success.

One winter's evening we had drawn closely around the blazing fire, for the air was piercing cold without, and the snow four feet deep on a level. Now and then, a traveler might be seen on snow-shoes; but though our cabin was situated on the king's highway, we seldom saw company on such a night as this. While the wind whistled, and the snow drifted about our dwelling, we piled the wood higher in our ample fire-place, and seated ourselves again, to resume the conversation, when I was startled by a loud and furious knocking at the door. I opened it to what I supposed to be three Indians. Their costume was that of the red man; but the voice of him who addressed me was not that of an Indian. "Can you keep three poor devils here to night?" said he, and when I made further inquiry, he repeated the same question; "we can sleep," he continued, "on the soft side of a board; only give us poor devils a shelter."

I told him we were not accustomed to turn away

any one on such a night; that they were welcome to come in; and they were soon seated around our large and cheerful fire.

They had laid aside their snow-shoes and knapsacks, and the heat of the fire soon made their blankets uncomfortable; but as one of them made a move to throw it off, another was heard to whisper, "wait a little; we are among strangers, you know; so do not make a display of yourself." The fellow drew his blanket about him; but we had heard and seen enough to awaken curiosity, if not suspicion. In passing out of the room soon after, I heard one of these pretended Indians say to his companion, "I know these folks are from the States, for I smell coffee." When they finally sat down to table, and saw silver upon it, they cast surprised and knowing glances at each other, all of which we closely observed, and were convinced, that they were not red men of the forest, but belonged to that race who had so long looked haughtily down upon the colored people; that the least exhibition of comfort, or show of refinement astonished them beyond measure.

In the meantime, my wife had whispered to me that she was sure that the principal speaker was no other than the aristocratic Mr. G———, of Canandaigua. I could not believe it; I could not recognize in that savage costume, one who had been bred in affluence, and "the star" of genteel society. But my wife soon developed the affair to our mutual satisfaction: G———, on taking from her a cup of coffee, remarked, "this looks good; and I have had no good coffee since I left my mother's house."

"Does your mother still reside in C———?" asked Mrs. Steward.

"My mother! my mother! what do you know of my mother!" said he, looking sharply at her; but observing that they were recognized, they began to laugh, and we had a hearty congratulation all round; while G———, starting up from table, exclaimed, "Come, boys, off with this disguise; we are among friends now."

Our Indian guests, now appeared in costume more like "Broadway dandies," than savages. Dressed in the finest cloth, with gold chains and repeaters; and all that constituted the toilet of a gentleman. After tea they requested to dry some costly furs, which they took from their knapsacks and hung around the fire. The following day they took their leave, with many apologies and explanations, regarding their appearance and conduct. They were in the wilderness, they said, trading for very valuable furs; they had money, jewelry and rich goods, which they had taken that method to conceal.

During all this time, there had been another visitor in the house, who was sitting in a corner, absorbed in writing. Our mock Indians had noticed him, and not knowing who he was, expressed a determination "to quiz that deaf old devil," after supper. We all seated ourselves around the fire, and our Canandaigua friends, though no longer savages, had not forgotten the silent man in the corner; they began to question him, and he aroused himself for conversation; nor was it long before they forgot their design to quiz him, and found themselves charmed listeners to the brilliant conversation, of that world-renowned champion of humanity, Benjamin Lundy, for he it was.

On this particular evening, he gave us a sketch of his journey to Hayti; to accompany there and settle some emancipated slaves; which I thought very interesting, and as I have never seen it in print I will here relate it, as near as I can, in his own words:

In the State of Maryland, there lived a slaveholder, the proprietor of some sixty slaves, and being somewhat advanced in years, he determined to free them, in accordance with the laws of that State, which required that they be sent out of it.

He had thought the matter over, but being undecided where to send them, he sent for Mr. Lundy to assist him in his proposed plan; who was only too glad to comply with a request calculated to carry out his own plans of philanthropy and equal rights.

When he had listened to the suggestions and expressed desires of the planter, he offered his arguments in favor of the West India Islands; and it was decided to send them to Hayti, as their future place of residence.

Six weeks were allowed for preparations; then Mr. Lundy was to return and take charge of them on the voyage, and see them settled in their new homes.

When the appointed time arrived, Mr. Lundy was there to accompany them on board a vessel bound for Hayti; on which was furnished as comfortable quarters, as the kindness of their conscientious master and his own benevolent heart could suggest. When all was ready, the Christian master came on board, to take leave of those faithful servants,—many of whom had served him from their childhood, and all of whom he had bound to his heart by kindness and Christian benevolence. It was a sad parting; not because the slaves did not love liberty, but because they appreciated their master's kind forbearance, and solicitude for their future welfare. He had ever been a humane and indulgent master; one who lightened the burthen of the poor slave, all in his power. A moment's reflection will show, that it is invariably this conscientious kind of slaveholders, who are induced to emancipate their slaves; and not the avaricious, cruel tyrant, who neither fears God nor regards his fellow man.

The master of the slaves had kindly informed them of his intentions,—of the probable length of the voyage, and the unavoidable sickness they would experience, &c.; but now, they were gazing up into his kind face for the last time, as he knelt in prayer, commending that numerous flock—raised on his own plantation—to the care and protection of Almighty God, beseeching Him to protect them in the storm and dangers of the ocean; to guide them through this life, and save them in the world to come; until the sobs and cries of the poor slaves drowned his utterance. He at length took his final leave of them, and of Mr. Lundy; and the ship sailed immediately. They, however, met storms and adverse winds, which detained them; and then the poor, ignorant slaves began to believe what they had before suspected: that this was only some wicked plan of Mr. Lundy's, laid to entice them away from a kind master, and to plunge them into some dreadful degradation and suffering. "Master" had not told them of the adverse winds, and they were certain that some mischief was intended; they grew sullen and disobedient; and notwithstanding the kindness of Mr. Lundy, they murmured and complained, until his kind heart sank within him; still he pursued the even tenor of his way, trusting in God for deliverance. He watched over them in sickness, and administered to all their wants; but his tender solicitude for their health and comfort, only excited suspicion, and increased their ungrateful ill humor.

One pleasant evening, Mr. Lundy paced the deck in deep thought. He was sad, and well nigh hopeless. He had seen enough in the fierce look and sullen scowl; and had heard enough of the bitterness, and threatening anger of the negroes, to know that a storm was gathering, which must soon burst in all its wild fury over his devoted head. He was a small, feeble man, compared with those who watched his every movement, and gnashed their teeth upon him so fiercely. None but the Almighty could save him now; and to Him who "rides upon the wings of the wind, and maketh the clouds His chariot," he drew near in fervent prayer; after which he retired in peace and confidence to his berth. During the night, a fine breeze sprang up; and when he went on deck the next morning, they were in sight of the luxuriant shore of Hayti! The officers of the island boarded the ship; but their language was unintelligible to the negroes, who still looked daggers at every one who spoke. They landed; but the fearful, and ungrateful slaves continued sullen and forbidding. Mr. Lundy left them, however, and went into the country, where he selected their future residence; and made every preparation for their comfort and convenience in his power; saw them conveyed to their neat, pleasant homes, and all happily settled. This work was accomplished; and he merely called to bid adieu to his ungrateful charge, when he found that one of the slaves had been appointed to speak to him, in behalf of the whole number, and confess how deeply they had wronged him. While they were conversing, the

K

others gathered around, with tears and prayers for forgiveness; and finally fell at his feet, imploring pardon for themselves, and blessings on the kind, patient and humane Benjamin Lundy. He hurried from the affecting scene, and soon after returned to America.

Thus that cold evening passed more pleasantly away in our rude cabin; and our Canandaigua gentlemen, after an agreeable acquaintance, and pleasant chat with Mr. Lundy, retired for the night—not like savages, but like gentlemen as they were; and I doubt not, with a more exalted opinion of "the deaf old devil in the corner"

# CHAPTER XXV.

### PRIVATE LOSSES AND PRIVATE DIFFICULTIES.

SOON after settling in Wilberforce, I found that the rumor I had heard in the States, concerning the refusal to sell land to colored persons, was literally correct, and my farm being too small to yield a support for my family, and knowing it would be useless to apply for more land, I engaged to carry packages for different merchants in the adjoining villages, as well as to and from the settlement. Possessing a pair of excellent horses and a good wagon, I found it a profitable business, and the only one I could well do, to eke out the proceeds of my farm, and meet my expenses.

One day as I was returning from the village, one of my horses was taken suddenly ill. I took him to a tavern near by, and as I could discover no cause for his illness, I concluded to leave him a few days, supposing rest would soon restore him. I accordingly hired another horse, and returned to the colony. In a day or two after, I collected my packages as usual, and started on my route, designing to leave the hired horse and take my own; but when I arrived at the tavern, I found some Indians engaged in taking off the hide and shoes of my poor, dead horse. This was indeed, a great loss to me; but I consoled myself with the thought that I had one good horse left, yet he would hardly be sufficient to accomplish alone, the labor I had engaged to perform; nor had I the means to spare, to purchase another. I therefore hired one, and commenced business again, with the determination to make up my loss by renewed diligence and perseverance, I started in good spirits; but had procceded but a few miles, when my remaining horse, which I had supposed perfectly sound, reeled and fell in the harness! And before I could relieve him of it, my noble animal and faithful servant, had breathed his last! Without a struggle or a movement he lay lifeless on the cold earth. I was sad. I deplored the loss of my good, and valuable team; but more the mystery and suspicion that hung over the event. I returned home and sat down to devise some plan of procedure. What could I do? Half the means of our support had been suddenly and mysteriously snatched from us. What could I do next? While thus ruminating, I arose to answer a summons at the door, and who should enter but Mr. B. Paul, a brother to our foreign agent, who had so long absented himself from our house, that I was indeed surprised to see him at this time. He, however, seated himself, with great apparent concern for my recent loss, which he soon made the subject of conversation and the object of his visit.

"There has been," said he, "a great deal of unpleasant feeling, and injudicious speaking on both sides, for which I am heartily sorry. The colony is too weak to sustain a division of feelings; and now, that your recent losses have left you in a far less favorable condition to sustain yourself and family, I have called to make a settlement of our former difficulties, and to offer you two hundred and fifty dollars out of the collections for the colony."

I saw through the plan at once, and considered it only a bribe, to prevent my exposing the iniquity of others. Should I consent to take a part of the ill-gotten spoils, with what confidence could I attempt to stay the hand of the spoiler. I wanted money very much, it is true; but after a moment's reflection, not enough to sanction the manner in which it had been obtained; and though I confess, the offer presented to me a strong temptation, I am thankful that I was enabled to resist it. I refused to accept the money; and after sending away the tempter and his offered gain, I felt my heart lighter, and my conscience more peaceful than is often the lot of sinful, erring man in this world of trial and conflict; and yet I could but feel that the mystery in which the death of my horses was involved, was partially at least, explained.

# CHAPTER XXVI.

INCIDENTS AND PECULIARITIES OF THE INDIANS.

DURING our residence in Canada, we were often visited by the Indians, which gave us an opportunity to learn their character, habits and disposition; and some incidents illustrative of the peculiarities of that abused people, I will here mention.

I recollect one bitter cold night, about eleven o'clock, I happened to awake, and looking out toward the fire, I was surprised to see standing there, erect and quiet, a tall, brawny Indian, wrapped in his blanket; his long hunting knife and tomahawk dangling from his belt; and his rifle in his hand. Had he been in his own wigwam, he could not have looked about him with more satisfaction and independence. I instantly sprang to my feet, and demanded his errand.

"Me lost in the woods, and me come to stay all night," was his grave reply.

"Then," said I, "give me your weapons, and I will

make no objection." He disarmed himself, and gave his weapons to me, with an air of haughty disdain for my fears. I put them in a place of safety and then prepared his bed, which was nothing more than the floor, where they choose to sleep, with their head to the fire. My offer of anything different from this he proudly resented as an insult to his powers of endurance, and would say, "beds for pale faces and women; hard board for Indians." He threw himself down, drew his blanket about him, and was soon sleeping soundly. As soon as the day began to dawn, he was up, called for his arms, and after thanking me in the brief Indian style of politeness, departed for the forest. He had found our doors all fastened, save a low back door, through which he entered, passing through a back room so full of miscellaneous articles, that it was difficult to go through it in the day time without upsetting something; but the Indian understood all this, he made no noise, nor would he have spoken at all, had I not awakened; and yet, he would have scorned to injure any one beneath the roof that gave him shelter, unless he had been intoxicated.

One sabbath afternoon, one of my children was sitting in the door, when a tall, emaciated Indian came up and said, "Will my little lady please to give me a drink of water?" While she went for it, I invited him to a seat within. There was something dignified and commanding in his appearance, and something in his voice and countenance, that won my confidence and respect at once. He remained in the place some time, and I learned his history.

In his younger days he had been a great warrior; and even now, when recounting, as he often did, the scenes of the battle field, his eye would burn with savage fire, lighting up his whole countenance with the fiercest kind of bravery, and often with a hideous yell that would startle our very souls, he would burst from the room and bound over the fields and forest, with the fleetness of a deer—making the woods ring with his frightful war-cry, until the blood seemed ready to curdle in our veins. He had also been one of the famous Tecumseh's braves; and had stood by him when he fell on the fifth of October, 1813. This old brave, whenever he called the name of Tecumseh, bowed his head reverently; and would often try to tell us how very deeply they mourned when it could no longer be doubted that the brave heart of Tecumseh, brother of the celebrated Wabash prophet, had ceased to beat.

"Had an arrow pierced the sun and brought it to my feet," said the old warrior, "I could not have been more astounded than at the fall of Tecumseh. Then he told us that once, after a great and victorious battle, Tecumseh, in his war paint and feathers, stood in the midst of his braves, when a little pale faced girl made her way weeping to him and said, "My mother is

K*

very ill, and your men are abusing her, and refuse to go away." "Never," said the Indian, "did I see a frown so terrible on the face of Tecumseh, as at that moment; when he with one hand clutched his tomahawk, and with the other led the little girl to the scene of riot. He approached the unruly savages with uplifted tomahawk, its edge glittering like silver, and with one shout of 'begone!' they scattered as though a thunderbolt had fallen in their midst."

But the old warrior at Wilberforce fought no more battles, except in imagination those of the past. After peace was declared he bought a valuable piece of land, with the intention of spending the remainder of his life more quietly; but unfortunately there lived not far from him a man who had once been the possessor of that farm, and had lost it in some way, and was now in reduced circumstances.

He was both envious and vicious; and because he could not himself buy the land, he was determined that the old Indian should not have it. After having tried many ways to get it from him, he finally complained of him, for fighting for the British and against the country where he now resided. This was successful; he was arrested and thrown into prison, and without a trial, removed from one prison to another, until he, with several others, was sent South to be tried as traitors. While on the way, the keeper of this Indian wished to call on his mother, who lived in a little cottage by the roadside, to bid her farewell. She was an aged woman, and when her son left her to join his companions, she followed him to the door weeping, wringing her hands in great distress, and imploring the widow's God to protect her only son. She had had four; all of whom went forth, with an American mother's blessing, to fight in defence of their country; and this one alone, returned alive from the field of battle. Now as he took his final departure for the South, she clasped her hands, raised her tearful eyes to heaven, and while large drops rolled over her wrinkled cheeks, she cried, "Oh, God, protect my only one, and return him to me in safety, ere I die." This scene, the imprisoned, and as some supposed, heartless Indian. watched with interest; no part of it escaped his attention; but they passed on, and safely reached Detroit. The prisoners were conducted to a hotel and secured for the night; our Indian hero being consigned to an attic, which they supposed a safe place for him. There happened to be on that night, a company of showmen stopping at that hotel, and exhibiting wax-work; among the rest, was a figure of General Brock, who fell at Queenston Heights, and a costly cloak of fur, worn by the General previous to his death. Nothing of this escaped the eagle-eye and quick ear of the Indian. When all was quiet in the hotel, he commenced operations, for he had made up his mind to leave, which with the red man is paramount to an accomplishment of his design. He found no great difficulty in removing the window of his lofty apartment, out of which he clambered, and with the agility of a squirrel and the caution of a cat, he sprang for the conductor and on it he slid to the ground. He was now free to go where he pleased; but he had heard something about the cloak of Gen. Brock; he knew too, that the friends of the General had offered fifty guineas for it, and now he would just convey it to them.

With the sagacity of his race, he surveyed the hotel, and determined the exact location of the show-room. Stealthily and noiselessly, he entered it; found the cloak—took it and departed, chuckling at his good fortune. As he was creeping out of the apartment with his booty, a thought struck him, which not only arrested his footsteps, but nearly paralized his whole being. Would not his keeper be made to answer, and perhaps to suffer for his escape and theft? Of course he would. "Then in the darkness I saw again," said the old brave, "that old pale-faced mother, weeping for the loss of her only son," when he immediately returned the cloak to its place, and with far more difficulty than in his descent, he succeeded in reaching his attic prison, where he laid himself down, muttering to himself, "not yet,—poor old pale-face got but one."

They took him to Virginia, where, instead of a trial,

they gave him about the same liberty they do their slaves. He staid one winter; but when the spring opened, the fire of the red man took possession of him, and when sent to the forest to chop wood, he took a bee-line for his former residence. But what was he to do for food? With a rifle, he could live happily in the woods, but he had none; so after considering the matter, he said to himself, "Me *must* get a rifle," and instantly started for the highway. The first cabin he saw, he entered in great apparent excitement, and told the woman of the house, that he had seen a "big deer in the woods, and wanted a rifle to shoot it. When you hear my gun," he said, "then you come and get big deer." She gave him her husband's excellent rifle and a few bullets; he looked at them, and said he must have more, for "it was a big deer;" so she gave him the bullet-mould and a piece of lead, with which he departed, after repeating his former injunction, to come when she heard the rifle; but, said he, "she no hear it yet."

He at length arrived at his own farm, from which he had been so cruelly driven, and concealed himself behind a log in sight of his own house, to watch the inmates. He soon learned that it was occupied by the man who had persecuted him in order to obtain it, his wife and one child. All day until midnight, he watched them from his hiding place, then assuming all the savage ferocity of his nature, and giving himself the most frightful appearance possible, he entered the house, and noiselessly passed to their sleeping room, where he placed himself before them with a long knife in his hand. Having assumed this frightful attitude, he commanded them in a voice of thunder, to get up and give him some supper. They were awake now. Oh, horror! what a sight for a guilty man, and a timid woman! "Me come to kill you!" said the Indian, as he watched their blanched cheeks and quivering lips. They tottered about on their trembling limbs to get everything he asked for, imploring him for God's sake to take all, but spare their lives. "Me will have scalps," he answered fiercely; but when he had eaten all he desired, he adjusted his blanket, and putting on a savage look, he remarked as if to himself, "Me go now get my men and kill him, kill he wife, and kill he baby!" and left the house for his post of observation.

The frightened inmates lost no time, but hastily collecting some provisions, fled to the frontier, and were never heard of afterwards.

The Indian immediately took possession of his own and quite an addition left by the former tenants.

While the kind-hearted old Indian repeated to me the story of his wrongs, it reminded me of the injustice practised on myself, and the colored race generally. Does a colored man by hard labor and patient industry, acquire a good location, a fine farm, and comfortable dwelling, he is almost sure to be looked upon by the white man, as an usurper of *his* rights and territory; a robber of what he himself should possess, and too often does wrong the colored man out of,—yet, I am happy to acknowledge many honorable exceptions.

I have often wondered, when looking at the remnant of that once powerful race, whether the black man would become extinct and his race die out, as have the red men of the forest; whether they would wither in the presence of the enterprising Anglo-Saxon as have the natives of this country. But now I have no such wondering inquiries to make; being persuaded that the colored man has yet a prominent part to act in this highly-favored Republic,—of what description the future must determine.

# CHAPTER XXVII.

#### OUR DIFFICULTIES WITH ISRAEL LEWIS.

BEING under the necessity of referring again to the difficulties existing in the Wilberforce colony, I shall here introduce a circular, published in New York city, which will give the reader an understanding of the real cause of our embarrassments, and the character of our agent, Israel Lewis.

### CIRCULAR

*New York, May 9th,* 1836.

The committee of colored citizens of the city of New York, as servants of the public, sincerely regret the necessity of bringing the within subject before the public. Their duty to God, to society, and to themselves, only actuates them in this matter.

The fact that many individuals in different sections of the country, have long suspected the integrity of Israel Lewis, but possessing no authentic documentary evidence, they have been prevented from making an effort, to counteract his too successful attempts and those of his agents, in the collection of funds from the public, has induced us to transmit this circular.

<table>
<tr><td>THEODORE S. WRIGHT,</td><td>DAVID RUGGLES,</td></tr>
<tr><td>PETER OGDEN,</td><td>JOHN STANS,</td></tr>
<tr><td>THOMAS DOWNING,</td><td>WILLIAM P. JOHNSON,</td></tr>
<tr><td>GEORGE POTTS,</td><td>WILLIAM HAMILTON,</td></tr>
<tr><td>CHARLES B. RAY,</td><td>SAMUEL E. CORNISH.</td></tr>
</table>

ISRAEL LEWIS.

*Wilberforce, U. C., March 28th,* 1836.

The board of managers of the Wilberforce settlement, met and passed unanimously the following resolutions—Present, Austin Steward, Philip Harris, Peter Butler, William Bell, John Whitehead, Samuel Peters.

*Resolved,* 1st. That we deeply regret the manner in which our friends in the States have been imposed upon by Israel Lewis; and that we hereby inform them, as a board of managers or otherwise, that we have received less than one hundred dollars of all the money borrowed and collected in the States.

*Resolved,* 2d. That although we have not received one hundred dollars from said Lewis, yet, when we shall have received the funds collected by our agent, the Rev. Nathan Paul, in England, we will refund as far as our abilities will allow and our friends may require, the money contributed for our supposed benefit, by them in the States.

*Resolved,* 3d. That we tender our sincere thanks to our beloved friends, Arthur Tappan and others, who have taken such deep interest in the welfare of our little colony.

*Resolved,* 4th. That the foregoing resolutions be signed by the whole board, and se. t to the States to be published in the *New York Observer* and other papers.

AUSTIN STEWARD, *President*,<br>
PETER BUTLER, *Treasurer*,<br>
JOHN HALMES, *Secretary.*

PHILIP HARRIS,<br>
WILLIAM BELL,<br>
JOHN WHITEHEAD,  } *Managers.*<br>
SAMUEL PETERS,

*New York, April 25th,* 1836.

At a public meeting of the colored citizens of New York city, held in Phœnix Hall, Thomas L. Jennings in the Chair, and Charles B. Ray, Secretary, the following resolutions were passed unanimously:

*Resolved,* That the thanks of this meeting be tendered to the Rev. Samuel E. Cornish, for the able and satisfactory report of his mission to Upper Canada, especially to the Wilberforce settlement.

*Resolved,* That this meeting deem it their imperative duty, to announce to the public, that in view of facts before them, Israel Lewis* has abused their confidence, wasted their benevolence, and forfeited all claim to their countenance and respect.

*Resolved,* That a committee of ten, be appointed to give publicity to the foregoing resolutions; also, to the communication from the managers of the Wilberforce settlement, as they may deem necessary in the case.

THOMAS L. JENNINGS, *Chairman,*<br>
CHARLES B. RAY, *Secretary.*

It will now appear that I was not the only unfortunate individual who had difficulty with Mr. Lewis.

---

*It necessarily follows that the public should withhold their money from his subordinate agents.

Mr. Arthur Tappan made known through the press, about this time, that Israel Lewis was not a man to be fully relied upon in his statements regarding the Wilberforce colony; and also, if money was placed in his hands for the benefit of the sick and destitute among the settlers, it would be doubtful whether it was faithfully applied according to the wishes of the donors.

For this plain statement of facts, Mr. Lewis commenced a suit against Mr. Tappan, for defamation of character; laying the damages at the round sum of ten thousand dollars. It appeared that Lewis valued his reputation highly now that he had elevated himself sufficiently to commence a suit against one of the best and most respectable gentlemen in New York city; a whole souled abolitionist withal; one who had suffered his name to be cast out as evil, on account of his devotion to the colored man's cause—both of the enslaved and free; one who has, moreover, seen his own dwelling entered by an infuriated and pro-slavery mob; his expensive furniture thrown into the street as fuel for the torch of the black man's foe; and, amid the crackling flame which consumed it, to hear the vile vociferations of his base persecutors, whose only accusation was his defence of the colored man. This noble hearted, christian philanthropist, who took "joyfully the spoiling of his goods" for the cause of the oppressed, was the chosen victim of Lewis' wrath and violent vituperation; and that too, where he was well known as a'most honorable, humane gentleman; and all for naming facts which were quite generally known already.

Lewis returned to Wilberforce, flushed and swaggering with the idea of making his fortune in this speculation of a law-suit against Mr. Tappan; and to remove all obstacles, he sent a man to me, to say that if I would publish nothing, and would abandon the interests of the colonists, he would give me a handsome sum of money. I soon gave him to understand that he had applied to the wrong person for anything of that kind; and he then laid a plan to accomplish by fraud and perjury, what he had failed to do by bribery.

I have before mentioned the fact of my having taken up a note of twenty-five dollars for Mr. Lewis, on condition that he would soon refund the money. I did it as a favor, and kept the note in my possession, until about a year afterward, when I sued him to recover my just due on the note. We had then began to differ in our public business, which led to other differences in our transaction of both public and private matters relating to the colony. He of course gave bail for his appearance at court, and it ran along for some time until he found he could not bribe me to enter into his interests, and then for the first time, he declared that I had stolen the note! And finally succeeded in getting me indicted before the grand jury!

In this I suppose Lewis and his confederates had two objects: first, to get rid of me; secondly, that they might have a chance to account for my continued hostility, by saying that it arose in consequence of a private quarrel, and not for any true interest I had in their collecting money deceptively.

Lewis appeared so bent on my destruction, that he forgot it was in my power to show how I came by the note. The Court of King's Bench met, but in consequence of the cholera, was adjourned, and of course, the case must lie over until another year.

When the time for the trial drew near, I was, in the midst of my preparations to attend it, counselled and advised by different persons to flee from the country, which I had labored so hard and so conscientiously to benefit, and received in return nothing but detraction and slander. But conscious of my innocence, I declared I would not leave; I knew I had committed no crime; I had violated no law of the land,—and I would do nothing to imply guilt. He who hath formed the heart, knoweth its intent and purpose, and to Him I felt willing to commit my cause. True, the court might convict, imprison, and transport me away from my helpless family of five small children; if so, I was determined they should punish an innocent man. Nevertheless, it was a dark time; I was not only saddened and perplexed, but my spirit was grieved, and I felt like one " wounded in the house of his friends,"—ready to cry out, "had it been an enemy I could have borne it," but to be arraigned, for the *first* time in my life, as a *criminal*, by one of the very people I had spent my substance to benefit, was extremely trying. Guiltless as I knew myself to be, still, I was aware that many incidents had transpired, which my enemies could and would construe to my disadvantage; moreover, Lewis had money, which he would freely distribute to gain his point right or wrong, and to get me out of his way.

In due time the trial came on, and I was to be tried for *theft!* Lewis had reported all through the settlement that on a certain time I had called at his house, and from a bundle of papers which his wife showed me, I had purloined the note, which had caused me so much trouble. To prove this it was necessary to get his wife to corroborate the statement. This was not an easy matter. Mrs. Lewis, indignant and distressed by her husband's unkindness, had left him and taken up her abode in the family of a hospitable Englishman. After Lewis had been sent out as an agent for the colony, finding himself possessed of sufficient funds to cut a swell, he associated and was made a great deal of, by both ladies and gentlemen in high stations of life; the consequence of which was, he looked now with disdain upon his faithful, but illiterate wife, who like himself had been born a slave, and bred on a Southern plantation; and who had with him escaped from the cruel task-master, enduring with him the hardships and dangers of the flying fugitive.

Now her assistance was necessary to carry forward his plans, and he endeavored in various ways to induce her to return, but in vain. When he sent messengers to inform her how sorry he felt for his past abuse, she said she feared it was only some wicked plot to entice her away from the peaceable home she had found. Lewis saw that he must devise some other method to obtain her evidence. He therefore called on the brother of the Englishman in whose family Mrs. Lewis was, and in a threatening manner told him that he understood his brother was harboring his wife, and that he intended to make him pay dear for it. The brother, to save trouble, said he would assist him to get his wife, and that night conducted Lewis to her residence. No better proof can be given that Mrs. Lewis possessed the true heart of a woman, than that the moment her husband made humble concessions, and promised to love and protect her henceforth, she forgave him all his past infidelity and neglect, and looked with hope to a brighter future. In return Lewis presented her with a note, telling her to take it to a certain person and present it, and he would give her twenty dollars on it. This would, he doubtless thought, leave her in his power.

As Mrs. Lewis could not read, the unsuspecting wife presented the paper all in good faith. The gentleman looked at her sharply, suspiciously,—and then asked her, if she was not aware that she was presenting him a paper completely worthless! The poor woman was mortified and astonished; and instead of returning to her husband, fled to Wilberforce, and called at our house. Knowing how disastrous to me would be her false statement, and ignorant of her state of mind, I asked her if she had come to assist Mr. Lewis by swearing against me. I saw at once, that she had not yet been informed of her husband's design.

"Swear against you, Mr. Steward!" said she. "I know nothing to swear that would injure you; I have always known you as an honest, upright man, and you need not fear my turning against an innocent person, for the benefit of one I know to be guilty. Nor would I have left my place, had I known what I now do." So all help and fear was ended in that quarter.

When at length the appointed morning arrived, I arose early, but with a saddened heart. I looked upon my wife and helpless family, reflecting that possibly this might be the last time we should all assemble around the breakfast table in our hitherto quiet home, and I could scarcely refrain from weeping. I, however, took my leave, and a lad with me, to bring back a message of the result, if the court found sufficient cause to detain me for trial. But when I found that I must be tried, I felt too unhappy to make others so, and kept out of the lad's way. He returned without a message; and I took my seat in the prisoner's box. I had just taken a letter out of the post office, from Rochester, containing recommendations and attestations from the first men in the city, of my good character, which relieved my feelings somewhat; nevertheless, my heart was heavy, and especially when, soon after I took my seat, a trap-door was opened and a murderer was brought up and seated by my side!

Chief Justice Robinson, made his appearance in great pomp—dressed in the English court style—then the crier, in a shrill voice, announced the opening of the court, and finished by exclaiming, "God save the King!" His lordship then called the attention of the jury to the law of the land; particularly to that portion relating to their present duty; and the grand jury presented me to the court, for feloniously taking a certain promissory note from the house of Israel Lewis. The King's Attorney had but one witness, and that was Lewis. He was called to the stand, permitted to relate his story, and retire without any cross-examination on the part of my Attorney; but that gentleman called up three respectable white men, all of whom swore that they would not believe Israel Lewis under oath! Then submitted the case to the jury without remark or comment, and the jury, without leaving their seats, brought in a verdict of "NOT GUILTY." Thus ended my first and last trial for theft!

L

Oh, how my very soul revolted at the thought of being thus accused; but now that I stood justified before God and my fellow-men, I felt relieved and grateful; nor could I feel anything but pity for Lewis, who, like Haman, had been so industriously engaged in erecting "a gallows fifty cubits high" for me, but found himself dangling upon it. He raved like a madman, clutched the arm of the Judge and demanded a new trial, but he shook him off with contempt and indignation, as though he had been a viper. In his wild fury and reckless determination to destroy my character, he had cast a foul stain upon his own, never to be effaced. I had felt bound to preserve my reputation when unjustly assailed, but it had been to me a painful necessity to throw a fellow-being into the unenviable and disgraceful attitude in which Lewis now stood; and yet, he would not, and did not yield the point, notwithstanding his ignominious defeat.

He very soon began to gather his forces for another attack upon me, and followed the same direction for his accusation,—the land purchase.

The reader will recollect without further repetition, that as I could purchase no land of the Canada Company, because of their indignation against Lewis, I was glad to accept of the contract he had made with Mr. Ingersoll, for lot number four in the colony; that I paid the sum demanded, and took his assignment on the back of the contract, and as we then were on good terms, it never occurred to me that a witness was necessary to attest to the transaction. But after his failure to prove me a thief; his next effort was to convict me of forgery! It will be remembered that Lewis after selling out to me, returned the contract to Mr. Ingersoll, and that I had lost by the means, the land, and at least five hundred dollars' worth of improvements. Then I brought a suit against Lewis, to recover the money I had paid him for the contract; and then it was that he asserted and attempted to prove, that I had forged the assignment, and therefore, had no just claim on him for the amount paid. But in this, as in the other case, he met a defeat and made an entire failure. I recovered all that I claimed, which was only my just due. One would suppose that after so many unsuccessful attempts to ruin me, he would have left me alone,—but not so with Lewis: he had the ambition of a Bonaparte; and doubtless had he possessed the advantages of an education, instead of having been born and bred a slave, he might, like an Alexander or Napoleon, have astonished the world with his deeds of daring. I am, however, no admirer of what the world call "great men,"—one humble, self-sacrificing christian, like Benjamin Lundy, has far greater claim on my respect and reverence.

Lewis, failing in his second attack, backed up as he had been in all his wicked course, by a friend wearing the sacred garb of a minister of the gospel, cooled off, and it became evident to all, that he was meditating some different mode of warfare. To this concealed confederate, I must attach great blame, on account of the influence his station and superior learning gave him, not only over Mr. Lewis, but the colonists generally, and which should have been exerted for the good of all, in truth and honesty.

# CHAPTER XXVIII.

### DESPERATION OF A FUGITIVE SLAVE.

WE had as yet received no funds from our foreign agent, N. Paul, and the board of managers had resolved to send a man after him. An Englishman and a white man named Nell, would gladly undertake the mission, leaving his wife and five children among the settlers. Again was I under the necessity of returning to New York, to obtain the funds required to send out Mr. Nell after our agent in England.

The night before I left home, I had a singular dream which I will briefly relate. I dreamed of journeying on a boat to Albany, and of stopping at a house to take tea. Several persons, I thought, were at the table, and as a cup of tea was handed me, I saw a woman slyly drop something into it. I, however, drank the tea, and dreamed that it made me very sick.

I found it difficult to drive from my mind th unpleasant impression this dream had made upon it, but finally succeeded in doing so, attributing it to the many and malicious threatenings which had been made by Lewis and his associates. They had boldly asserted, that "if I went to the States, I would never return alive," and several other threats equally malignant. I, however, started with Mr. Nell for Rochester, where we made an effort to raise money to aid in defraying the expenses of the voyage, and succeeded in collecting about a hundred dollars. From thence we passed on to Albany, where we fell in company with a number of Mr. Paul's friends, who appeared to be terribly indignant, and accused me of coming there to expose their friends,—Paul and Lewis. We had some warm words and unpleasant conversation, after which they left me very unceremoniously, and appeared to be very angry. A short time after, one of them returned, and in the most friendly manner invited me to his house to tea. I was glad of an opportunity to show that I harbored no unpleasant feelings toward them, and immediately accompanied him home. The moment that we were all seated at the table, an unpleasant suspicion flashed through my mind. The table, the company—all seemed familiar to me, and connected with some unpleasant occurrence which I could not then recall. But when the lady of the house poured out a cup of tea, and another was

DEATH PREFERRED TO SLAVERY. 247

about to pass it, I heard her whisper, "I intended that for Mr. Steward," my dream for the first time, flashed through my mind, with all the vivid distinctness of a real incident. I endeavored to drive it from my thoughts, and did so. Pshaw! I said to myself; I will not be suspicious nor whimsical, and I swallowed the tea; then took my leave for the steamboat, on our way to New York city.

When we had passed a few miles out of Albany, the boat hove to, and there came on board four men— one of the number a colored man. The white men repaired to their state-rooms, leaving the colored man on deck, after the boat had returned to the channel. He attracted my attention, by his dejected appearance and apparent hopeless despair. He was, I judged, about forty years of age; his clothing coarse and very ragged; and the most friendless, sorrowful looking being I ever saw. He spake to no one, but silently paced the deck; his breast heaving with inaudible sighs; his brow contracted with a most terrible frown; his eyes dreamily fastened on the floor, and he appeared to be considering on some hopeless undertaking. I watched him attentively, as I walked to and fro on the same deck, and could clearly discover that some fearful conflict was taking place in his mind; but as I afterwards repassed him he looked up with a happy, patient smile, that lighted up his whole countenance, which seemed to say plainly, I see a way of escape, and have decided on my course of action. His whole appearance was changed; his heart that before had beat so wildly was quiet now as the broad bosom of the Hudson, and he gazed after me with a look of calm deliberation, indicative of a settled, but desperate purpose. I walked hastily forward and turned around, when, Oh, my God! what a sight was there! Holding still the dripping knife, with which he had cut his throat! and while his life-blood oozed from the gaping wound and flowed over his tattered garments to the deck, the same exultant smile beamed on his ghastly features!

The history of the poor, dejected creature was now revealed: he had escaped from his cruel task-master in Maryland; but in the midst of his security and delightful enjoyment, he had been overtaken by the human blood-hound, and returned to his avaricious and tyrannical master, now conducting him back to a life of Slavery, to which he rightly thought death was far preferable.

The horrors of slave life, which he had so long endured, arose in all their hideous deformity in his mind, hence the conflict of feeling which I had observed,—and hence the change in his whole appearance, when he had resolved to endure a momentary pain, and escape a life-long scene of unrequited toil and degradation.

There happened to be on the boat at the time, several

"I walked hastily forward and turned around, when, Oh, my God! what a sight was there! He still held the dripping knife, with which he had cut his throat."

page 248.

companies of citizen soldiers, who, shocked by the awful spectacle, expressed their decided abhorrence of the institution of Slavery, declaring that it was not for such peculiar villainy, that their fathers fought and bled on the battle field. So determined were they in their indignation; so loudly demanded they a cessation of such occurrences on board our boats, and the soil of a free State, that the slaveholders became greatly alarmed, and with all possible dispatch they hurriedly dragged the poor bleeding slave into a closet, and securely locked the door; nor have I ever been able to learn his final doom. Whether the kindly messenger of death released him from the clutches of the man-stealer, or whether he recovered to serve his brutal master, I have never been informed.

After this exciting scene had passed, I began to realize that I was feeling quite ill; an unusual load seemed to oppress my stomach, and by the time we had reached New York city, I was exceedingly distressed. I hastened to a boarding house, kept by a colored woman, who did everything in her power to relieve me; but I grew worse until I thought in reality, I must die. The lady supposed I was dying of cholera, sent to Brooklyn after Mr. Nell; but having previously administered an emetic, I began to feel better; and when I had finally emptied my stomach of its contents, *tea and all*, by vomiting, I fell into a profound sleep, from which I awoke greatly

L*

relieved. The kindness of that lady I shall not soon forget. She had a house full of boarders, who would have fled instantly, had they known that, as she supposed, I was suffering from cholera; and instead of sending me to the hospital, as she might have done, she kept all quiet until it was over, doing all she could for my relief and comfort; yet, it was a scene of distress which I hope may never be repeated.

On the following morning, I saw in the city papers, "A Card," inserted by the owner of the poor slave on board the steamboat, informing the public that he was returning South with a fugitive slave, who, when arrested, evinced great willingness to return; who had confessed also, that he had done very wrong in leaving his master, for which he was sorry,—but he supposed that the abolitionists had been tampering with him. That was all! Not a word about his attempt to take his life! Oh no, he merely wished to allay the excitement, that the horrid deed had produced on the minds of those present.

I was indignant at the publication of such a deliberate falsehood, and immediately wrote and published that I too was on board the same boat with the fugitive; that I had witnessed an exhibition of his willingness to return to Slavery, by seeing him cut his throat, and lay on the deck wallowing in his blood; that the scene had so excited the sympathies of the soldiers present, that his owner had been obliged to hurry him out of their sight, &c.

When this statement appeared in the newspapers, it so exasperated the friends of the slaveholder, that I was advised to flee from the city, lest I might be visited with personal violence; but I assured my advisers that it was only the wicked who "flee when no man pursueth, but the righteous are bold as a lion." I therefore commenced the business that brought me to that city. Messrs. Bloss, Nell, and myself, made an effort, and raised between three and four hundred dollars for the purpose of sending Mr. Nell after Rev. N. Paul.

Most of the funds collected, we gave to Mr. Nell, who sailed from New York, and arrived safely in England, just as N. Paul was boarding a vessel to return to New York.

Had Mr. Nell acted honorably, or in accordance with his instructions, he would have returned with the agent; but he remained in England, and for aught I know is there yet. He was sent expressly after Mr. Paul, and when he left that kingdom, Nell's mission was ended. He proved himself less worthy of confidence than the agent, for he *did* return when sent for, and he did account for the money he had collected, though he retained it all; but Mr. Nell accounted for nothing of the kind; and if he has ever returned, I have not seen him. Mr. N. Paul arrived in New York in the fall of 1834, and remained there through the winter, to the great disappointment and vexation of the colonists. I wrote him concerning our condition and wants, hoping it would induce him to visit us immediately; but he had married while in England, an English lady, who had accompanied him to New York, where they were now living; nor did he appear to be in any haste about giving an account of himself to the board of managers who had employed him.

# CHAPTER XXIX.

A NARROW ESCAPE FROM MY ENEMIES.

DURING my absence in New York city, Lewis and his confederates were prophesying that I would never trouble them more, and shaking their heads quite ominously at the happy riddance. One day, our hired man entered the house and inquired of my wife, when I was expected home. She told him she did not know, having received no intelligence from me. He assured her that a letter had been received by some one in the colony; that he had seen it, and had heard Mr. Lewis speak of conveying it to her,—but as it did not come, she gave it up, supposing some mistake had been made. I had, however, written, naming the time when she might expect me; but no letter of mine reached her, during my long absence, for which she could not account. A short time before that specified for my return, a woman, whose husband was an associate of Mr. Lewis, came to my house, and urged my wife "to leave word at the village of London, to have Mr. Steward detained there, should he arrive toward evening, and by no means allow him to start for the colony after dark." My family had so often been alarmed by such warnings, and had so frequently been annoyed by the violent threatenings of Lewis, that they ceased to regard them, and paid little attention to this one.

I arrived at London on the day I had appointed for my return, but was detained there until a late hour; feeling anxious, however, to get home that night, supposing that I was expected,—I therefore hired a horse to ride the remaining fifteen miles to the settlement.

The road from London to Wilberforce led through a swamp, known as "McConnell's Dismal Swamp," and it was indeed, one of the most dreary places in all that section of country. I am certain that a hundred men might conceal themselves within a rod of the highway, without being discovered.

The horse I had engaged, was a high spirited animal, and to that fact, I doubtless owe my life. The moon shone brightly, and nothing broke the stillness of the night, as I rode onward, but the clatter of my horse's hoofs, and an occasional "bow-wow" of some faithful watch-dog.

When I reached the swamp and entered its darkened recesses, the gloom and stillness was indeed fearful;

my horse started at every rustling leaf or crackling brush, until I attempted to pass a dense thicket, when I was started by the sharp crack of a rifle, and a bullet whizzed past me, close to my ear! The frightened horse reared and plunged, and then springing as if for life, he shot off like an arrow, amid the explosion of fire arms discharged at me as I rode away. I lost my balance at first, and came near falling, but recovering it I grasped the rein tightly, while my fiery steed flew over the ground with lightning speed; nor did I succeed in controlling him until he had run two miles, which brought me to my own door.

I found my family well, and very grateful that I had arrived safely after so fearful an encounter.

When morning came I sent a person out to inquire whether any of the settlers were out the night previous, and the report was, "Israel Lewis and two other men were out all night; that they had been seen near the Dismal Swamp;" moreover, Lewis was seen to come in that morning with his boots covered with swamp mud,—these the Rev. Mr. Paul's boys cleaned for him, all of which was evidence that he it was, who had way-laid me with criminal intent.

I afterwards learned, that those three men left the settlement at dusk, for the swamp; that they stationed themselves one rod apart, all on one side of the road, each man with a loaded rifle,—the poorest marksman was to fire first, and if he did not bring me down, probably the second would; but Lewis being the best shot of the three, was to reserve his fire until the last, which they supposed I could not escape. It was quite dark in the thicket, and my spirited horse plunged in every direction so furiously, that they could take no aim at me, until he had started to run, when we were soon beyond their reach.

We had already had so much difficulty in our little colony that we were getting heartily sick of it. I was well aware that Lewis was thirsting for revenge; that he wished to do me a great wrong; and yet I was thankful on his account, as well as on my own, that he had been prevented from imbruing his hands in the blood of a fellow being.

Had he succeeded in taking my life, as he undoubtedly intended to do, he would have been arrested immediately, and most likely punished as a murderer. He had boldly threatened my life, and the colonists were expecting something of the kind to take place. Had I not arrived at the colony, it was known at London that I had started for the settlement that night, and an immediate search would have been instituted; nor could the wicked deed have brought the least peace to the mind of Lewis or his companions.

"No peace of mind does that man know,
Who bears a guilty breast;
His conscience drives him to and fro,
And never lets him rest."

## CHAPTER XXX.

DEATH OF B. PAUL, AND RETURN OF HIS BROTHER.

THE bold and wicked attempt to take my life, recorded in the preceding chapter, aroused a feeling of indignation in the community against Lewis, and completely destroyed the little influence he had left; moreover, he had now been so extensively published as an impostor, that he could collect no more money on the false pretense of raising it for the benefit of the colony. As soon as his money was gone and his influence destroyed,—many who had been his firmest friends, turned against him, and among this class was the Rev. Benjamin Paul. He had ever professed the greatest friendship for, and interest in the success of Mr. Lewis. Heretofore, whenever he went to the States he was commissioned by that gentleman's family, to purchase a long list of expensive articles, which the poor colonists were seldom able to buy; and he generally returned to them richly laden with goods, purchased with money given to the poor, sick, and destitute in the colony.

Mr. B. Paul had ever been a very proud man, but not a very healthy one. He was inclined to pulmonary diseases; but had kept up pretty well, until Lewis was effectually put down, and his own character involved in many of his notorious proceedings, together with the disappointment occasioned by his brother remaining so long in England, when his health failed, and he sank rapidly under accumulating disasters, to the grave.

The Welshmen had partially engaged him to preach for them the ensuing year, but something they had heard of him changed their minds, and they were about appointing a meeting to investigate his conduct, when they were informed of his illness, and concluded to let it pass. His son, with whom he lived, became deranged, and his oldest daughter on whom he was greatly dependent, had been dismissed from school, where she had been for some time engaged in teaching. All these unpleasant circumstances in his sickly state weighed heavily upon his proud heart; and he not only declined in health, but sank into a state of melancholy and remorse for his past course of living. As he lay pining and murmuring on his death bed, I could but reflect how different the scene from that of an apostle of the Lord Jesus Christ, who could exclaim, when about to be offered, "I have fought a good fight,

I have finished my course, I have kept the faith; henceforth there is laid up for me a crown of righteousness."

I called to see him as he lay writhing in agony, his sunken eyes gleaming wildly, rolling and tossing from side to side, while great drops of perspiration stood upon his forehead, continually lamenting his misspent time, and the life he had led! He took my hand in his cold, bony fingers, thanking me that I did not so despise him, that I could not come to see him in his sorrow and affliction. Generally, however, when he raved and talked of his wicked life, his family excluded all persons from his room except his attendants.

Pride, which had ever been his besetting sin, displayed itself in his conduct to the last, for he had a lengthy will made, dispensing some sixteen hundred dollars to different individuals, when he must have known that his whole possessions would not amount to half that sum. As I looked upon him I could but reflect on the mysterious ways of Providence. Before me lay a man, who had for years arrayed himself against me, using all his influence as a man and a minister to injure me, by setting Lewis forward in his wickedness; his family living in extravagance and a style far beyond their means, while mine had labored hard and were sometimes destitute, often harrassed and perplexed on every side by himself and party. And for what? Because I would not join hands with iniquity, and deeds of darkness. Notwithstandi ıg the contrast, when I heard his bitter lamentations and self-reproaches, I could lift my heart to God, in gratitude for His protecting goodness, which had preserved me an *honest man*. I had often erred no doubt, but it had never been designedly; and never did I value a good conscience more than when standing by the death-bed of Benjamin Paul, who now had passed the Jordan of death; and it is enough to know that his future, whether of joy or woe, will be meted out to him, by a merciful and just God,—nevertheless, his last moments on earth were such as ought to arouse every professed christian, to redoubled diligence in watchfulness and prayer, lest they fall into temptation,—lest they determine to become rich, and thereby fall into diverse and hurtful lusts, and pierce themselves through with many sorrows.

Soon after the event above narrated, a law was passed in the Province, allowing each township to elect three commissioners, whose duty it should be, to transact the public business pertaining to the township. Each township should also elect one township clerk, whose business it should be, to hold and keep all moneys, books, and papers belonging to said town; with power to administer oaths, and in fact, he, with the commissioners, were to constitute a board, possessing all the power of a court, in relation to township business.

In our colony, located in the township of Bidulph, the colored people were a large majority of the inhabitants, which gave us the power to elect commisioners from our own settlement, and therefore, three black men where duly chosen, who entered on the duties of their office, while your humble servant, A. Steward, was elected township clerk, with all the responsibility of the office resting upon him and the same power given him as though he had been born in Her Brittanic Majesty's dominion, with a face as white as the driven snow. I felt the responsibility of my office, but not more deeply than I did this assurance of entire confidence, and respect shown me by my townsmen, after all the cruel persecutions I had met; after all the accusations of theft, forgery, &c., that vicious person could bring against me.

The Rev. Nathaniel Paul, with his lady, arrived at Wilberforce in the spring of 1835, to the great joy of the colonists, to find that his brother had gone the way of all the earth, and his remains quietly resting on his own premises, where his afflicted family still resided.

In the colony there was a great deal of excitement regarding the course our agent would pursue, and all waited with anxious expectancy to see him enrich the treasury with his long-promised collections.

We had agreed, on sending him forth as an agent for the colony, to give him fifty dollars per month for his services, besides bearing his expenses

The reverend gentleman, charged, on his return to the colony, the sum specified, for four years, three months and twenty days. We spent several days in auditing his account, with increased fearful forebodings. We found his receipts to be, in the United Kingdoms of Great Britain, one thousand six hundred and eighty-three pounds, nineteen shillings; or, eight thousand and fifteen dollars, eighty cents. His expenditures amounted to one thousand four hundred and three pounds, nineteen shillings; or, seven thousand and nineteen dollars, eighty cents. Then his wages for over four years, at fifty dollars per month, left a balance against the board of several hundred dollars, which we had no funds to cancel, inasmuch as the reverend gentleman had paid us nothing of all he had collected in Europe, nor even paid a farthing toward liquidating the debts incurred for his outfit and expenses.

There was also in Mr. Paul's charge against the board of managers, an item of two hundred dollars, which he had paid to Wm. Loyd Garrison, while that gentleman was also in England; but by whose authority he had paid or given it, it was hard to determine. We gave him no orders to make donations of any kind. To take the liberty to do so, and then to charge it to our poor and suffering colony, seemed hard to bear; still we allowed the charge. Had we, in our straitened and almost destitute circumstances, made a donation of that, to us, large sum of money to Mr.

Garrison or any body else, certainly *we* should, at least, have had the credit of it; and as Mr. Garrison had made no acknowledgment of the receipt, I wrote him on the subject, and his answer will be found, heading our correspondence, in this volume.

Not a dollar did the treasurer ever receive of the Rev. N. Paul, unless we call the donations he had made without our permission, a payment. He did, it is true, award to the board, the sum of two hundred dollars, paid by him to Mr. Garrison, and fifty dollars more given by himself to Mr. Nell, on his departure from England. Not a farthing could we get of him; and in short, as far as the monied interest of the colony was concerned, his mission proved an entire failure. How much good the reverend gentleman may have done in spreading anti-slavery truth, during his stay in Europe, is not for me to say. The English, at that time held slaves; and report speaks well of his labors and endeavors to open the eyes of that nation to the sin of slavery and the injustice of the colonization scheme. It is said that he continually addressed crowded and deeply interested audiences, and that many after hearing him, firmly resolved to exert themselves, until every chain was broken and every bondman freed beneath the waving banner of the British Lion. Perhaps his arduous labors assisted in freeing the West India islands of the hateful curse of

Slavery; if so, we shall not so much regret the losses and severe trials, it was ours to bear at that time.

The indignant and disappointed colonists, however, took no such view of his mission; and knowing as they did, that he had paid not a cent of cash into the treasury, nor liquidated one debt incurred on his account, they became excited well nigh to fury,—so much so, that at one time we found it nearly impossible to restrain them from having recourse to Lynch law. They thought that the reverend gentleman must have large sums of money at his command somewhere—judging from his appearance and mode of living, and that a little wholesome punishment administered to his reverence, by grave Judge Lynch, enthroned upon a "cotton bale," might possibly bring him to terms, and induce him to disgorge some of his ill-gotten wealth, which he so freely lavished upon himself, and was withholding from those to whose wants it had been kindly contributed.

Just, as was their dissatisfaction, I was satisfied by the examination of his accounts, that he had spent nearly all of the money collected for us; his expenses had been considerable; beside, he had fallen in love, during his stay in England, with a white woman, and I suppose it must have required both time and money to woo and win so fine and fair an English lady, said also to possess quite a little sum of money, that is, everal thousand dollars, all of which our poor, little suffering colony must pay for,—the reverend gentleman's statement to the contrary notwithstanding.

We succeeded at last, after a tedious effort, in satisfying the minds of the settlers to the extent, that a violent outbreak was no longer to be feared or dreaded. When all was quiet in the colony, I ventured to make my first call on the wife of N. Paul, who was then stopping with the widow of the late Rev. B. Paul, residing some three miles from us.

The houses of the colonists were generally built of logs, hewn on both sides, the spaces chinked with mortar, and the roof constructed of boards. The lower part was generally left in one large room, and when another apartment was desired, it was made by drawing a curtain across it. When we arrived at the residence of Mrs. Paul, we were immediately ushered into the presence of Mrs. Nathaniel Paul, whom we found in an inner apartment, made by drawn curtains, carpeted in an expensive style, where she was seated like a queen in state,—with a veil floating from her head to the floor; a gold chain encircling her neck, and attached to a gold watch in her girdle; her fingers and person sparkling with costly jewelry. Her manners were stiff and formal, nor was she handsome, but a tolerably fair looking woman, of about thirty years of age: and this was the wife of our agent for the poor Wilberforce colony!

M

N. Paul had now settled his business with the colonists, and being about to leave for the States, we appealed to his honor as a man and a Christian, to call at Rochester and pay the seven hundred dollar bank debt, for which he was justly and legally holden, and relieve honorably, those kind gentlemen who had raised the money for him. He well knew the condition of our friend E. Peck, and that the names of some of our colored friends were also attached to the note; all of whom were relying implicitly on his or our honor to pay the obligation. That we had no funds in the treasury he was well aware; also, that all were deeply concerned about that debt. All this he knew; and in answer to our earnest and repeated injunction, he promised most faithfully and solemnly that he would call at Rochester, and take up the note. On those conditions he was allowed to leave the colony, and when parting with me, no more to meet in this life, his last assurance was, that he would cancel that obligation. What then could we think of his word, when we learned soon after that he passed Rochester, without calling, direct to Albany; nor did he ever return, or make any explanation of his conduct; nor give any reason why his promise was not redeemed and the money paid.

He preached in Albany until his health failed, then he was obliged to live the best way he could, and at last to depend on charity.

His disease was dropsy, from which he suffered deeply, being unable to lie down for some time previous to his death. I have been told that his domestic life was far from a peaceable or happy one, and that in poverty, sorrow and affliction, he lingered on a long time, till death at last closed the scene.

## CHAPTER XXXI.

MY FAMILY RETURN TO ROCHESTER.

I WAS now seriously meditating a return to Rochester. My purpose in going to Canada, has already been made known to the reader, as well as some of the disappointments I met, and some of the trials and difficulties I had to encounter.

Now, after laboring, and suffering persecution for about five years, my way was comparatively clear; still I wished to leave the Province and return to the States, in which prospect my family greatly rejoiced. Doubtless most persons in the position I then occupied, would have chosen to remain; but for several reasons, I did not.

Notwithstanding I had been during my youth, a poor, friendless, and illiterate slave, I had, through the mercy of God and the kindness of friends, not only obtained my freedom, but I had by the industry and perseverance of a few years, acquired a tolerable English education, established a profitable business, built for myself a good and extensive business reputation, and had laid the foundation for increasing wealth and entire independence.

Indeed, so far as a competency is concerned, I possessed that when I left Rochester. My house and land was paid for; my store also, and the goods it contained were free from debt; beside, I had several hundred dollars in the bank for future use,—nor do I boast, when I say that the comfort and happiness of myself and family, required no further exertion on my part to better our worldly condition. We were living in one of the best countries on the earth, surrounded by friends,—good and intelligent society, and some of the noblest specimens of christian philanthropy in the world. My wife and children, had not only been accustomed to the comforts, if not the luxuries of life, but also to associate with persons of refinement and cultivation; and although they had willingly accompanied me to Canada, where they had experienced little less than care, labor and sorrow, it cannot be thought very strange that they should desire to return. We were colored people to be sure, and were too often made to feel the weight of that cruel prejudice, which small minds with a perverted education, know so well how to heap upon the best endeavors of our oppressed race. Yet truth and justice to my friends, compel me to say, that after a short acquaintance, I have usually been treated with all that kindness and confidence, which should exist between man and man.

At my house of entertainment in Canada, it was not uncommon for gentlemen of my former acquaintances, to stop for a friendly chat; merchants, journeying through our settlement, after goods, would frequently call, with their money, watches, and other valuables, carefully concealed about their persons; but when they learned our name, and had become acquainted a little, they would not only freely expose their wealth, but often place all their money and valuables in my hands, for safe keeping; nor was their confidence ever misplaced to my knowledge.

Another thing: when I went to Wilberforce, I supposed that the colonists would purchase the whole township of Bidulph, and pay for it, which might have been done, had they been fortunate enough to put forward better men. Then when we had a sufficient number of inhabitants, we could have sent a member to Parliament, one of our own race, to represent the interests of our colony. In all this we were disappointed. The Canada Company, in their unjust judgment of a whole people, by one dishonest man, had stopped the sale of lands to colored persons, which of course, put an end to the emigration of respectable and intelligent colored men to that place; nor was there any prospect of a favorable change. Moreover, the persecutions which gave rise to the colony, had in a great measure ceased; anti-slavery truth was taking effect on the minds of the people, and God was raising up many a friend for the poor slave, to plead with eloquent speech and tears, the cause of the dumb and down-trodden.

These, with other considerations, influenced me in my decision to leave Canada. As soon, however, as my intentions were made known, I was importuned on all sides, by persons both in and out of the settlement, to remain awhile longer, at least. This will be seen by a reference to the appendix.

After due deliberation, I concluded to send my family to the States, and remain myself, until my year should terminate, for which I had been elected township clerk. In accordance with this determination, I made preparation to take my family to Port Stanley, forty miles distant. But what a contrast was there between our leaving Rochester, five years before, and our removing from the colony! Then, we had five two-horse wagon loads of goods and furniture, and seven in family; now, our possessions were only a few articles, in *a one-horse wagon*, with an addition of two members to our household! The settlers collected about us, to take an affectionate leave of my wife and children; but tears and sobs, prevented an utterance of more than a "God bless you," and a few like expressions. The scene was indeed an affecting one: all the weary days of our labor; all the trials and difficulties we had passed; all the sweet communion we had enjoyed in our religious and social meetings; all the acts of neighborly kindness, seemed now to be indelibly impressed on every memory, and we felt that a mutual regard and friendship had bound us closer to each other, in the endearing bonds of Christian brotherhood—bonds not to be broken by the adverse scenes incident to frail human life.

Arrived at Port Stanley, we were kindly entertained by a Mr. White, a fugitive slave from Virginia, who owned a snug little farm on the bank of Kettle Creek, and who appeared to be in a good and prosperous condition. Being detained there, waiting for a boat, on which I was anxious to see my family comfortably situated before I left them, I was aroused at an early hour on the second morning of our stay, by a loud rapping at the door; and hearing myself inquired for, I dressed myself immediately, and followed Mr. White into the sitting room, where I saw two strange men, armed with bludgeons! I soon learned, however, that one of them was the under-sheriff, who had come to arrest me for a debt of about forty dollars, and the other armed man had come to assist him. I assured them I was ready to accompany them back to London, which I was obliged to do, a prisoner, leaving my family among comparative strangers. The debt had become due to a man who had worked for us in the building of a saw-mill. I arranged the matter without going to jail, but before I could return to Port Stanley, my family, kindly assisted by Mr. White, had departed for Buffalo. The weather was cold and the lake very rough, but they safely arrived in Rochester, after a journey of three days. During their passage up the lake my oldest daughter took a severe cold, from which she never recovered.

I returned to the colony to attend to the duties of my office, and to close my business with the colony, preparatory to joining my family, who were now settled in Rochester, but in very different circumstances from those in which they had left it. I had deposited quite a sum of money in the Rochester Bank; but our continual expenditures at Wilberforce, in my journeyings for the benefit of the colony, and in the transacting of business pertaining to its interests, had left not one dollar for the support of my family, or to give me another start in business. Nevertheless, I felt willing to submit the case to Him who had known the purity of my intentions, and who had hitherto "led me through scenes dark and drear," believing he would not forsake me now, in this time of need.

Consoling myself with these reflections, I renewed my endeavors to do my best, leaving the event with my God.

M*

# CHAPTER XXXII.

### THE LAND AGENT AND THE SQUATTER.

I HAVE named, I believe, that all the colored people, who purchased lands of Lewis, could get no deed nor any remuneration for their improvements. This they thought hard and unfair. Some had built a house and barn, cleared land, &c.; but when they wished to pay for their farms, they could get no deed, and were obliged to lose all their labor.

This raised such a general complaint against the land agents, that they finally agreed to pay the squatters for their improvements, if they would leave their farms. An opportunity was soon offered to test their sincerity in this agreement. A shrewd fellow, who had been many years a sailor, named William Smith, had made valuable improvements on land, for which he could get no deed, and then he wished to leave it. His wife, also, died about this time, leaving him with eight children, which determined him to leave the colony, and after providing homes for his children, to return to his former occupation on the high seas; but he also determined not to leave without receiving the pay which the agents had agreed to give for his improvements.

"Oh yes," said they, in answer to his repeated solicitations, "you shall be paid, certainly, certainly; you shall be paid every farthing." But when the appointed day came for the pompous land agents to ride through the settlement, you might see Smith station himself at first one and then another conspicuous place on the road, hoping they would have the magnanimity to stop and pay him, especially, as he had informed them of his destitute and almost desperate condition, with eight young children to maintain, and no means to do so, after giving up to them the farm. Before them as usual rode their body servant, of whom Smith would inquire at what hour the agents might be expected. And most blandly would he be informed of some particular hour, when perhaps, within the next ten minutes, the lordly agent would fly past him, on their foaming steeds, with the speed of a "lightning train." This course they repeated again and again. One day, when all of the land agents rode through the settlement in this manner, Smith followed them on foot over fifty miles. He at last intercepted them, and they promised with the coolest indifference, that on a certain day, not far distant, they would certainly pay him all he claimed, if he would meet them at a certain hotel in London. To this he agreed; and the poor fellow returned to the colony almost exhausted.

His funds were nearly all spent, and he wished to take his children to New York; yet his only hope was in the integrity and honor of the land agents.

On the day appointed, he was at London long before the hour to meet, had arrived. He entered the village with a determined air, and saw the agents just riding up to a hotel,—but not the one they had told him to call at. He, however, waited for no invitation, but entered the hotel and inquired of the servant for his master. He said his master was not there!

"I know he is, said Smith, " and I want to see him."

The servant withdrew, but soon returned to say that his master was engaged and could not see him that day. Smith followed the servant into the hall, calling out to him in the most boisterous manner demanding to be told the reason *why* he could not see his master. The noise which Smith purposely made, soon brought into the hall one of the agents, a Mr. Longworth, a short, fat man,—weighing in the neighborhood of three hundred pounds! When he saw Smith, he strutted about, assuring him that this disgraceful uproar was quite uncalled for, and finally putting on a severe look, told him that he could not have anything for his improvements; of course not,—

he really could not expect; certainly not, &c. Smith plainly assured the agent that his "blarney" would avail him nothing; he had come by their own appointment to get his pay, and that he ceartainly should *have*—if not in the way they themselves agreed upon, he would choose his own method of getting it! Thus saving, he stepped back, threw down his woolly head, and goat fashion, let drive into the fat Englishman's "bread basket!" He sprawled about and soon recovered his standing, but continued to scream and halloo with rage and mortification, more than with pain, until he had brought to the spot landlord, boarders, and servants, to witness the affray; but Smith, nothing daunted, administered two or three more effectual butts with his hard head into the lordly agent, when the subdued and now silent English gentleman, drew from his pocket book, and carefully counted out, every dollar Smith had at first demanded. Smith accepted it pleasantly, thanked him and withdrew, amid the shouts and jeers of the spectators, which the agen. was more willing to avoid than he. That was the way the land agent paid the squatter.

It seemed, however, a little too bad, to make a fine English gentleman, feel as "flat" as Longworth appeared to feel; yet it was undoubtedly the only method by which Smith could recover a farthing. The agents, it was supposed, did not design to pay for any improvements; indeed, some very hard and unjust incidents occurred in connection with that matter, and probably Smith was about the only one, who ever received the full value of his claim.

There was committed about this time, a most shocking murder, in the London district. A farmer who had a respectable family, consisting of a wife and several children, became so addicted to the use of spirituous liquors, that he neglected both his family and farm so much, that his friends felt called upon to request the distiller, who was his near neighbor, to furnish him with no more intoxicating drink. This, so exasperated the poor, ruined and besotted wretch, that he raved like a madman—such as he undoubtedly was—crazed and infuriated, by the contents of the poisoned cup of liquid damnation, held to his lips by a neighboring distiller; a fellow-being, who for the consideration of a few shillings, could see his neighbor made a brute and his family left in destitution and sorrow. Perhaps, however, he did not anticipate a termination so fearful; yet that is but a poor excuse for one who lives by the sale of rum. When a rum seller gives that to a man, which he knows will "steal away his brains," and make him a maniac, how can he anticipate his future conduct? And who is responsible? Ah, who?

When Severin found he could get no more intoxicating beverage, he in his demoniacal rage, conceived the idea of despatching his whole family, and set about his purpose by first snatching the young babe and casting it into the fire! When the poor wife and mother came shrieking to the rescue of her darling infant, he with one furious blow, laid her a bleeding corpse at his feet! Two other young children he next murdered, and left them mingling their blood with that of their mother's, while he ran furiously after the two older ones, who were endeavoring to escape to a neighbor's for assistance; and overtaking, killed them both! When the miserable wretch had completed his hellish design, he started for his nearest neighbor, named Smith, and told him that there was a black and a white man at his house, murdering his family, requesting him to go to their assistance. Mrs. Smith, believing that Severin designed to murder her husband, insisted on his calling his young men to assist him, which he did; and on arriving at the scene of slaughter, a most horrid spectacle was before them: five dead bodies weltering in blood, aside from that of the innocent babe, whose little form lay roasted and charred, on the fatal and bloody hearthstone of the drunkard! Victims all, of an intoxicated husband and father! When the guilty man saw the mangled remains of his household, he only increased his depravity by trying to make others responsible for the wicked deed,—exclaiming in feigned anguish, "my dear wife! my poor children! I was afraid they would murder you! Oh, my lost family!" &c

Community was soon alarmed; Severin, arrested, tried, convicted, and sentenced to suffer the extreme penalty of the law.

It is sufficient for us to say, that the evidence was clear and conclusive, that he was the only murderer of his family; nor was it doubted that Mrs. Smith's suspicion was correct; yet, with all the array of positive testimony brought against him, he denied the commission of the crime to the last moment of his life! When brought out for execution, he was placed under the gallows, and the rope with its fatal noose adjusted around his neck, when one of the attorneys arose, and with great solemnity, addressed him, in the most impressive manner: "We have done," said he, "all in our power to save your life; but you are justly condemned, and in a few minutes more, will enter the presence of the All-seeing eye of Jehovah; now let me beseech you, in the name of God, to tell the truth, before you die." Severin declared himself innocent of the crime, for which he was about to suffer; but was consoled, he said, with the belief that he should, in a few short moments, meet in blissful re-union his dear, murdered wife and children in heaven, to part no more! Prayers were read; and during the reading of the Lord's prayer, at the words "Thy will be done," the hardened wretch was launched into eternity.

No room was left to doubt the fact, that Severin with his own hand destroyed the life of his unhappy and abused wife, and also that of his helpless family. Yet in one sense, may we say with the murderer, it was not he who committed the awful and inhuman deed, but boldly and truthfully charge it to man's bitterest foe—Rum! What but the maddening effects of spirituous liquors, could so demoralize, so demonize a man, as to convert the once loving husband and proud father, into a reckless fiend, a heartless savage? Oh, Rum! earth contains not another so fell a foe!

Should any who may read these humble pages, find an effectual warning in the unhappy end of Severin, one which shall induce them to pause in their course, or at once and forever abandon the use of alcoholic drinks, I shall gratefully feel that I have not written this incident in vain.

Before I left Wilberforce, the Rev. S. E. Cornish, made a visit, and preached the Word of Life to the colony, greatly to the satisfaction and comfort of the settlers. After distributing liberally of his abundance, to his poor brethren, he departed for the States, attended by the prayers and blessings of the Wilberforce colonists.

## CHAPTER XXXIII.

CHARACTER AND DEATH OF I. LEWIS.

I HAVE spoken in the preceding chapter, of a visit from the Rev. S. E. Cornish, to the colony. He had previously written me, concerning the object of his proposed visit, which was to obtain the depositions of the board of managers, relative to all the money received through their agents for the colony. He was sent to Canada then, and once afterwards, for and at the expense of A. Tappan, on business pertaining to the law-suit instituted by I. Lewis against that gentleman, for defamation of character. The depositions taken in the colony, with the expense of twice sending an agent to Canada, must have made a round sum for that kind gentleman to pay, merely for telling a truth already known!

Mr. Cornish had also been informed of my intention to leave the colony, and that my family were already gone. He, knowing something concerning the state of things, urged me to remain at least, until his arrival, as will be seen by a reference to his letter in the appendix.

As I look back on those scenes of labor and trial, I find cause for deep humiliation and gratitude to God, for His goodness and gracious protection, over my frail life, through unseen dangers of various kinds, and for his continued favors and unmerited blessings. Many of my fellow men have fallen in death's cold embrace since that time, while my health and life has been mercifully preserved.

Three of the leading characters of the Wilberforce colony are now dead. Rev. Benjamin Paul, lies in the silent grave-yard in Wilberforce, C. W. His brother, Rev. Nathaniel Paul, also sleeps the dreamless sleep of death, and his dust rests in the beautiful cemetry in Albany, N. Y.

Israel Lewis has also finished his earthly career after robbing the poor of their just dues, and persecuting those who endeavored to defend them; after living in extravagance—"faring sumptuously every day,"—he became reduced in circumstances; despised and dishonored, his proud spirit was at last broken. His health gave way; when at length, unattended and alone, he found his way to a hospital in Montreal, where he soon after died, leaving not enough of all his gains to afford him a decent burial!

Oh, what a reward "for all his labor under the

sun!" His fame, his wealth, and his law-suits, all have perished with his memory. Poor man!

Israel Lewis was born a slave, raised on a Southern plantation, and subjected to all the cruelties and deprivations of a bondman. His natural abilities were above mediocrity, but having never had the advantages of an education, or the privileges of a society calculated to cultivate and refine his natural aspiring intellect, and to direct his indomitable will in the acquirement of the more imperishable graces of the human heart, he had come to manhood with a determined, selfish disposition, to accomplish whatever gratified his vanity or administered to the wants of his animal nature.

And may we not, with propriety here inquire, whether our common Father, who has declared himself to be "no respecter of persons," has endowed men with enlarged capacities for the attainment of that knowledge and wisdom, so requisite to the elevation of character,—for the express purpose of seeing them made beasts of burden, and their superior faculties prostituted by the sensuality imposed by Slavery, and to be sold as chattels, with impunity? I tell you, nay. The day when Almighty God will avenge the work of his own hands, hasteth greatly! Were it not so, we might rejoice in the ignorance of the poor slaves, and pray that none of them may ever be endowed with a superior intellect to that of the brutes they are made to resemble. Then would the proud spirit no longer chafe, and manhood writhe in the unbroken chain; but, like the ox to the yoke or the horse to the harness, they might submit, without a conscious violation of their dearest and God given rights. But we were speaking of Israel Lewis.

A natural energy and strength of character, he had inherited; a malicious, selfish, and consequently a deceptive disposition, his life as a slave had undoubtedly bestowed upon him. Intellect must have scope, and when nothing is left within its grasp but vice, can we wonder that the slave possessing the most talent, should generally prove the greatest villain.

Uneducated as was Lewis, his quick perception, his ungoverned passions, and his native independence, not only made him a dangerous slave, but an unfaithful and overbearing companion. He, however, took a wife—a slave like himself,—whose devotedness and good sense, cannot be made manifest, more than in her willingness to leave all that was dear to her on earth, and flee from their birth-place, she knew not whither; but confiding in the professed love and protection of her husband, she cheerfully followed him to the dense forest, in search of that freedom, denied them in their native country,—submitting herself gladly to all the hardships and fearful anxieties of a fugitive slave. What to her were horsemen, armed with dirk and rifle! What though the trained and inhuman blood-hound bayed upon their track! Was not he who had sworn a life-long allegiance to her by her side! Should he be killed or retaken, what could she desire, but to be his companion still! Slavery even, bitter as was the cup, might contain for her *one sweet drop*, while connubial love lighted up their rude cabin, and sweetened their daily toil; but the additional anticipation of LIBERTY, to their domestic happiness—oh blessed hope! How it quickened their weary footsteps, and, with fixed eyes upon the star of the North, they pressed forward through every difficulty, until they finally reached Cincinnati, O. There they lived quietly, and with others, suffered the terrors of the mob, where also he was chosen agent, to seek a more safe and quiet home for his afflicted and outcast countrymen. The office was accepted, and Lewis became the founder of the Wilberforce colony.

The personal appearance of Israel Lewis was prepossessing; his manner and address easy and commanding. To those unacquainted with his private life, his ungoverned passions, and his unprincipled, revengeful disposition, he could appear the gentleman, the philanthropist, and the Christian.

His education was limited; yet he had managed to gather a sufficient knowledge of the sciences to enable him to read and write, together with quite a fund of general information; and then his shrewdness and tact accomplished all the rest. To strangers he could appear a ripe scholar, if left unquestioned. He was a good speaker, and once spake with eloquence and marked effect before the Legislature, assembled in the Senate Chamber, at Albany, N. Y.

Had the childhood of Mr. Lewis been passed under more favorable auspices; had his intellectual faculties been so cultivated as to predominate over his animal propensities, and his towering aspirations directed toward the accomplishment of acts, lofty in their benevolence, noble in their sacrifice, high in their honorable purpose, and great in their purity; I can but believe that his powerful intellect would have achieved the fame of a Lundy, or would have bequeathed to his brethren a memory like that of a Clarkson. Instead, we have found him devoting his energies to the gratification of his avarice, pride, and ambition—characteristics directly opposed to the deportment of the humble Christian, and such as our Heavenly Father has never promised to prosper. How truly has "the wise man" said, "He that is greedy of gain troubleth his own house; but he that hateth gifts shall live." How strikingly has this passage been verified in the course of Lewis! For a few paltry sums of gain, could he consent, not alone to rob the poor, for whom it was kindly given as unto the Lord, but to turn scornfully away from that poor, illiterate, and humble slave wife, whom he had, in their mutual adversity, vowed to cherish in *prosperity* as well as in all other circumstances through life. That wife, who had borne with him the sorrows of Slavery—the humble choice of a bondman! She, who fled with him, anticipating additional happiness in a life of freedom! Poor woman! Disappointment is of an earthly growth, yet God is merciful; notwithstanding we have the same authority as above, for saying that "Every one that is proud in heart is an abomination to the Lord: though hand join in hand, he shall not be unpunished."

In the hands of a righteous Judge we leave him, who, for the wealth that perisheth,—who, for worldly honor and selfish gratification, could barter his honesty and integrity, as "Esau, who sold his birth-right for a mess of pottage."

To me the lesson is an impressive one, and I am thinking it would be well for us all to examine the foundation on which we stand. If based upon the solid and broad foundation of christianity, doing to others in all things as we would they should do to us, sacrificing on all occasions our own case, and worldly honor, for the benefit of our fellow-men, and the good of our country, then indeed, we need fear no evil; if the winds of adversity howl about our dwelling, we shall find it will stand, being founded on a ROCK. But if we build upon "the sands" of fame or self-aggrandizement, and, like the towering oak, lift our insignificant heads in proud defiance of the coming storm, we may expect that our superstruction will fall! "And great will be the fall of it!"

N

## CHAPTER XXXIV.

### MY RETURN TO ROCHESTER.

HAVING closed my business in Wilberforce, I prepared to leave on the expiration of my term of office as township clerk, which was now near at hand. Notwithstanding, I ever felt a sensation of relief and pleasure, when I thought of returning to my old home and friends in the States, yet as often as I look abroad over the settlement and remember all my glowing hopes,—all my delightful anticipations of a prosperous future for those poor, struggling colonists; when I recollected with what zeal and honest purpose, with what sincerity and sacrifice I had prosecuted my labor among them,—a dark shadow of disappointment would flit across my mind, however welcome it might be. That I had firm and tried friends in the colony, I had never the least reason to doubt, not to suppose their number less after a five years residence with them; but our expectations had not been realized.

Our hope of settling a township, to be represented in Parliament by one of our own people, was now forever blasted. I remembered too, that many of the colonists had been unjustly incited against my course; but in the retrospect my heart did not condemn me. Errors many, no doubt I had committed; but I was grateful, when reviewing the whole ground, for a conscience void of offence toward God and man; and I finally took my leave of all, craving the choicest blessings of Heaven to rest upon that infant colony and its interests.

On the nineteenth day of January, 1837, I left Wilberforce, passing through Brantford, Hamilton, Queenston, Lewiston, and from thence to Rochester. During my journey, I could not avoid feeling sad and despondent, as my mind incessantly returned to the review of my mission, upon which I could look with no other decision than that of an entire failure. I had spent my time, wasted my substance for nought, and was now returning to my dependant family,—that, with myself, had been stripped of nearly every means of comfort and support.

What would my Rochester friends think of my conduct? Notwithstanding all my despondency and evil foreboding at that time, I am now well satisfied that my labor was not all in vain, but that some good did result from it.

As I drew near the city, a gloom like thick darkness overshadowed me: I thought of the unfavorable transactions which had occurred between the directors of the colony and my friends in Rochester, and fell to wondering how they would receive me.

On the twenty-third of January, 1837, I finally re-entered the city penniless; but as I soon found, not so friendless as my fears would have it. Among the first to welcome me back to my old home, was that friend of "blessed memory," Everard Peck, who had been apprised of some of the losses I had met and the trials I had passed through. This gentleman was also one of the first to propose to be one of five men, who should loan me one hundred dollars each, for five years. Through the disinterested kindness of this worthy gentleman, I was in a few days after my arrival, well established in a store of provisions and groceries. The five kind gentlemen, to whom I was so deeply indebted for the loan, were: Everard Peck, George A. Avery, Samuel D. Porter, Levi W. Sibley, and Griffith, Brother & Co.

This noble act of generosity and kindness, on the part of my friends, to furnish me with the means to commence business, especially when their prospect was anything but flattering, regarding my ever being able to refund their well-timed and gracious liberality,—affected me more deeply than all the censure and persecution I had elsewhere received. Their frown and displeasure, I was better prepared to meet than this considerate act of Christian sympathy, which I am not ashamed to say melted me to tears, and I resolved to show my appreciation of their kindness by an industry and diligence in business hitherto unsurpassed.

E. Bardwell, then a merchant on Exchange Street, next laid me under a lasting obligation by offering to sell me goods on credit; others proffered assistance by promising their continual patronage, which was to me the same as cash,—and soon the store I had opened on Main Street, was doing an extensive business. My profits were small to be sure, and I had a heavy rent to pay for my store and dwelling, yet I was making a comfortable living for my family, and laying by something to reimburse the kind friends who had helped me in the time of need, when I found that the health of my family required more of my time and assistance than ever before. My oldest daughter, who, I have before mentioned, having taken a violent cold on Lake Erie, was now confined to her bed. All that could be done to save the life of a darling child—our first born—was done; and if we sometimes went beyond our means, it was a satisfaction to us to see her enjoy some of the comforts of life of which my mission to Canada had deprived her. One physician after another was employed to stay the approach of the destroyer: some said they could cure her, if paid in advance; to all of which I cheerfully acceded, but only to see our beloved sink lower, and patiently pine away.

No one but a parent who has watched the rapid decline of a darling child, and marked with a bursting heart the approaching footsteps of the spoiler, can imagine how powerless we felt at that time. The wealth of the Indias, had we possessed it, would have been freely given, although it would have been unavailing, to shield that loved and gentle form from pain, and we were obliged to look hopelessly on, while our little patient, suffering daughter sank lower and lower every day. In vain were our parental arms outstretched for her protection; from death we could not save her. She had long since ceased to glide about the house, and soothe with her silvery tones all the childish fears of the little ones. Helpless she now lay, burning with fever, and wasting from our sight, "till soft as the dew on the twilight descending," the cold damps of death gathered on her youthful brow. One pleasant morning after passing a restless night, I observed her to gaze earnestly upward, and a moment after I called her name but received no answer.

> "Her languishing head was at rest;
> Its thinkings and achings were o'er;
> Her quiet, immoveable breast,
> Was heaved by affliction no more."

On the fifteenth day of April, 1837, she sweetly fell

asleep, aged eleven years. Sorrowfully we followed her remains to Mount Hope, where we laid her down to rest until the resurrection morning. Death had now made its first inroad in our family circle, and since then we have laid two other loved ones by her side. We sorrowed, but not without hope.

My business continued to prosper, and I concluded to buy a small variety store, containing some three or four hundred dollars worth of goods on the corner of Main and North Streets, formerly owned by Mr. Snow, but, having two stores on my hands, I did not make much by the trade.

The first summer after I returned to Rochester, the friends of temperance made a fine celebration, and gave me the privilege of providing the dinner.

I considered it not only a privilege, but an honor, and felt very grateful to the committee who conferred the favor upon me.

The celebration came off on the Fourth of July, and was indeed a splendid affair. The multitude were addressed on the public square, by some of the best speakers in the country. I laid in a large quantity of provisions of every available kind, built a bower, hired waiters, and prepared seats for five hundred to dine; but when the oration was over, and the multitude came to the table, I found that as many more seats were wanted. We, however, accommodated as many as we could, at one dollar each, and all passed off well, to the great satisfaction of all concerned.

When all was over, and the friends learned that I had on hand a large amount of cooked provision, they continued their kindness by purchasing it, thus preventing any loss on my part.

My store on the corner of Main and North Streets, was at the head of the market, and I was enabled to supply both of my stores with country produce on the best possible terms. I kept two clerks at each store, and all seemed prosperous for a time, when from some cause, which I could never understand, my business began to fail. My family had ever lived prudently, and I knew that was not the cause. I thought to better my circumstances by taking a store in the Rochester House, but that proved to be a bad stand for my business, and after one year, I removed to Buffalo Street, opposite the Court House. I ought to say, that as soon as I found that my income was getting less than my expenses, I went to the gentlemen who had loaned me the five hundred dollars, and showed them the true state of my affairs, and they kindly agreed to take fifty per cent., which I paid them.

After locating on Buffalo Street, I took in a partner, named John Lee, a young man, active and industrious, who paid into the firm three hundred dollars, with which we bought goods. With what I had on hand, this raised the joint stock to about a thousand dollars, which we were making frequent additions, and on which we had an insurance of six hundred dollars. Our business was now more prosperous than at any previous time, and we began to look up with hope and confidence in our final success. One night I returned to my home as usual, leaving Lee in the store. About twelve o'clock, Mr. Morris awoke me with a few loud raps, and the announcement that my store was on fire and a part of my goods in the street! I hastened to the place, where I found, as he had said, what was saved from the fire piled up in the street and the fire extinguished. The building was greatly damaged and the goods they rescued were nearly ruined. Now we were thrown out of business, and the firm was dissolved. With the assistance of W. S. Bishop, a lawyer, we made out the amount of damage, which was readily paid by the agent for the insurance company.

When the Fourth of July came round again, the temperance men resolved on having another demonstration, and as before, I was requested to supply the dinner, which I did, after the same manner as the year previous.

Having been thrown out of business by the fire, I began to examine my pecuniary matters, and found that I was some three or four hundred dollars in debt, which I had no means of paying. True, I had met with a great misfortune, but I felt that to be an honest man I must meet all obligations, whether legally bound to do so or not; yet it was beyond my power at that time, and I finally concluded to leave the city, and try to better my condition by some other business, or at least to clear myself from debt.

# CHAPTER XXXV.

BISHOP BROWN—DEATH OF MY DAUGHTER.

I REMOVED with my family to the village of Canandaigua, where I commenced teaching a school for colored children, assisted by my daughter. The school was sustained partly by the liberality of the citizens of the village, and partly by donations from abroad. It was continued two years, and the children made rapid progress while they were under our tuition.

Soon after I left Rochester, I visited New York city, and while there, I joined "The African Methodist Episcopal Conference." Bishop Brown, of Philadelphia, presided over the deliberations of that body, and appeared to be a man of deep piety, as well as apt in business, and was a native of one of the Carolinas. I found a pleasing acquaintance also, with Bishop Walters of Baltimore, Md. He was small in stature; but a powerful speaker, and discharged every duty with "an eye single to the glory of God." He has now gone to give an account of his stewardship, and I pray that "his mantle may fall" upon one as capable of leading our people as he. The conference consisted of some sixty or seventy ministers of the gospel, with these two Bishops at their head. The conference continued its session ten days. When it was closed, Bishop Brown, with several others, started on a visit to the West. They called at Rochester, and then passed over to Canada, where a conference was to be holden. We arrived, after a pleasant journey, at Hamilton, where the English government have a regiment of black soldiers stationed. It was common, in passing through the streets of Hamilton, to meet every few rods, a colored man in uniform, with a sword at his side, marching about in all the military pomp allowed only to white men in this *free republic*.

All being in readiness, Bishop Brown opened the conference under the authority of Her Brittanic Majesty, with great solemnity, which seemed to be felt by the whole assembly. This meeting appeared to me far more interesting than the one we had attended in New York city. The colored people were much more numerous in Hamilton, and in far better circumstances than in New York. It is a hard case to be poor in any large city, but to be both poor and black, as was the condition of the majority of our friends in New York, was indeed a terrible calamity

Every class, no matter how worthless they might be, would be allowed to rent a house in preference to a colored man. The consequence was, our people were crowded back into the most unhealthy alleys, in old dilapidated tenements unfit for human beings to dwell in, and such as could not be disposed of to any other class of people. I am happy to say, however, that a favorable change has taken place in New York, since the time of which I am speaking. Capitalists have noted the good reputation of the colored people as tenants, and have of late erected good dwellings for their accommodation. In Hamilton there was none of that wretchedness and squalid poverty, nor any of that drunken rowdyism so common in Eastern cities, perceivable among the colored people.

Our conference was largely attended by all classes, both black and white,—many of the latter invited the Bishop with his associates to their dwellings to dine, indeed we seldom took a meal at our lodgings, so constantly were we solicited by friends to accompany them home.

We also found many fugitive slaves in that city, many of whom were intelligent mechanics. Some of them took us about the place, showing us the different buildings they were engaged in erecting; quite a number were employed in building a church which appeared to be done in a workman-like manner.

In the meantime our meeting was progressing in a

very interesting manner, and when the closing services were commenced, the house was filled to overflowing; still many could not be accommodated. The preaching was solemn and impressive, and it really seemed to me that the glory of God filled the house in which we worshipped; saints rejoiced and shouted "glory to God, in the highest," while sinners trembled and cried out, "what must we do to be saved from the wrath to come." There were several hopeful conversions during the session of conference; and after its close we spent one day in making social calls, and viewing the city and its surroundings.

Burlington Bay makes an excellent harbor for shipping, while Burlington Heights loom up on the north in all their wild and terrific grandeur. Near the bay resides Mr. McNab, so notorious in the history of the Canadian revolution. We went in a large company to look at his beautiful grounds and residence, over which we were politely conducted by his amiable lady. It was indeed a lordly mansion, with its surroundings laid out in the English style of princely magnificence.

On our return to the city at evening, we were invited to attend a grand soiree, got up in honor of the Bishop's first visit to that place. Several families of colored people combined to provide the splendid entertainment, while one lady presided at the board. She was very beautiful and very dark; but a complete model of grace and elegance, conversing with perfect ease and intelligence with all, both black and white ministers, who surrounded the festive board, as well as our Irish friends, not a few of whom were present. One honest son of the Emerald Isle entered, and not understanding the matter, inquired of his brother "Pat," in rather a loud whisper, "What's all them nagurs setting to that table for?" He, however, soon satisfied himself, and all passed off quietly and in excellent order. At a late hour the company, after a benediction, withdrew and dispersed.

We left Hamilton the following morning, feeling grateful and pleased with our meeting and visit.

It was a beautiful morning; the lake was still, no sound was heard but the rushing waves, as our boat moved on through its placid waters, toward our destination, then called Fort George, now Niagara, where we took stage for the Falls.

At that place of resort, we stopped to view the stupendous work of Almighty God, and listen to the ceaseless thundering of the cataract. How tame appear the works of art, and how insignificant the bearing of proud, puny man, compared with the awful grandeur of that natural curiosity. Yet there, the rich from all parts of the world, do congregate! There you will find the idle, swaggering slaveholder, blustering about in lordly style; boasting of his wealth; betting and gambling; ready to fight, if his slightest wish is not granted, and lavishing his cash on all who have the least claim upon him. Ah, well can he afford to be liberal,—well can he afford to spend thousands yearly at our Northern watering places; he has plenty of human chattels at home, toiling year after year for his benefit. The little hoe-cake he gives them, takes but a mill of the wealth with which they fill his purse; and should his extravagance lighten it somewhat, he has only to order his brutal overseer to sell—soul and body— some poor creature; perchance a husband, or a wife, or a child, and forward to him the proceeds of the sale. While the wretched slave marches South with a gang, under the lash, he lavishes his funds in extravagant living,—funds gathered from the tears and blood of a helpless human being. Have you, dear reader, ever watched the slaveholder at such places as I have, gliding through the shady groves, or riding in his splendid carriage, dressed in the richest attire, and with no wish ungratified that gold can purchase; and have you ever been guilty of envying him, or of wishing yourself in his condition? If so, think of the curse which rests on him who grinds the face of the poor. Think of his doom in the day of final retribution, when he shall receive at the bar of a righteous Judge, "according to the deeds done in the body," and not according to his wealth and power. Think you, that the prayers, cries, and pleadings of the down-trodden slave that for years have been ascending to the throne of a just God, will never be avenged? Yea, verily, the day of reckoning hastens on apace, and though, "He bear long with them; He will surely avenge them of their adversaries; and that speedily!"

As we pursued our journey to Buffalo, we passed Grand Island, from whence Mordecai Emanuel Noah, some years ago issued a proclamation, calling on the Jews to come and build on that island the "City of Refuge," but which I believe was not responded to, as I saw it remained in its native wildness. He had also a monument erected there at the time, which might be seen from the highway and canal, consisting of a white marble slab, six feet in height, with a suitable inscription upon it, to direct the poor Jew to the City of Refuge.

It was quite conspicuous, but not so magnificent as Gen. Brock's at Queenston Heights.

Arrived at Buffalo, we held several meetings which were very interesting. The colored people were then numerous in that city, and owned one of the largest churches in Western New York. We found a large and prosperous society under the superintendence of Elder Weir, who was a good and talented man, setting a godly example for his flock to imitate. At Buffalo I parted with my pleasant and instructive traveling companion, Bishop Brown, never to meet again on the shores of time. Soon after that pleasant journey he died, and passed from his labor to reward.

Buffalo was then, as now a great place for business. Vessels from all parts of the country crowded the docks, and I then thought that it must in time become one of the largest cities in the Union. After a pleasant visit with our people there, I returned to my home in Canandaigua, where I now began to feel quite settled.

I had been requested to act as agent for the "Anti-Slavery Standard," with which I complied, and leaving my daughter to teach the school, I spent the most of my time in traveling through the country to advance the interests of that paper. .

When I returned from Buffalo, she was complaining of poor health, nor was it long before we saw that she was rapidly declining.

This beloved daughter, I had spared no pains nor money to educate and qualify for teaching. I had encountered all the trials and difficulties that every colored man meets, in his exertions to educate his family. I had experienced enough to make me fear that I should not always be able to get my children into good schools, and therefore determined at whatever cost, to educate this child thoroughly, that she might be able, not only to provide for her own wants, but to teach her younger brothers and sisters, should they be deprived of the advantages of a good school.

Well had she rewarded my labor; well had she realized all my fondest hopes and expectations,—but alas! for human foresight and worldly wisdom! The accomplishments and qualifications of a teacher were attained; and proudly we looked for the achievement of our long-contemplated design. How hard to believe that the fell destroyer was upon her track! Her education had qualified her for teaching the sciences; but now I saw, that her faith in the religion of the blessed Christ, was assisting her to teach her own heart a lesson of patience, and quiet submission to the will of Him who holds the issues of life,—and Oh, how difficult for us to learn the solomn lesson, that her wasting form, her gradual sinking away, was hourly setting before us.

Slowly her strength failed; she, however, saw our sorrowful anxiety, and would try to relieve it with a cheerful appearance. One day perhaps she would be able to walk about, which would revive our wavering hope; the next she was prostrate and suffering; then hope died and we were sad! All the spring time she languished; the summer came, the roses bloomed, and the grain began to ripen, but she was wasting away. The orchard yielded its golden harvest; the birds sang merrily on the trees, but a dark shadow had fallen on our hearthstone, and a gloom, like the pall of death, rested on our household. Her place at table was already vacant; no longer she called the little ones about her to hear them repeat their tasks,—all of which admonished us, that soon the bed where we could now see her, would be vacated; and we should no longer witness her patient smile, and know that she was still with us. The pastor of the Baptist church often called to pray with, and for, the quiet sufferer, which she appreciated very highly, for she was a Christian in every sense of the word.

On the thirtieth day of August, at about eleven o'clock, A. M., without a struggle or a groan, her spirit returned to God who gave it. "Sweetly as babes sleep," she sank into the embrace of death. Happily, triumphantly, had she seen the grim messenger approach; but she knew whom she had believed, and that He was able to keep that which she had committed to Him, unto the resurrection of the just.

She had previously made a confession of her faith in Christ, and had been buried with Him in baptism. A few days after her demise, a long, sad train wound its way to the village church yard, where we deposited the remains of our beloved,—Patience Jane Steward, in the eighteenth year of her age; and then returned to our desolate house, to realize that she had left a world of pain and sorrow, where the fairest rose conceals a thorn, the sweetest cup a bitter drop, for a home where the flowers would never fade, and where pain, sorrow and death will never come. We all felt the solemn and impressive warning, "Be ye also ready, for in such an hour as ye think not, the Son of Man cometh."

As often as I recalled her triumphant, peaceful death, her firm reliance on God, and sweet submission to His will, I could not forbear contrasting her departure with that of Mrs. Helm, whose death I have elsewhere described; and could fervently pray, that I might live the life of the righteous, that my last end might be like hers.

> "Behold the Western evening light,
>     It melts in deep'ning gloom ; .
> So calmly Christians sink away,
>     Descending to the tomb.
>
> The winds breathe low, the withering leaf
>     Scarce whispers from the tree,—
> So gently flows the parting breath,
>     When good folks cease to be.
>
> How beautiful on all the hills,
>     The crimson light is shed ;
> 'Tis like the peace the Christian gives,
>     To mourners round his bed.
>
> How mildly on the wandering cloud,
>     The sunset beam is cast,—
> 'Tis like the mem'ry left behind,
>     When loved ones breathe their last.

## DEATH OF MY DAUGHTER.

And now above the dews of night,
 The yellow star appears;
So faith springs in the breast of those,
 Whose eyes are bathed in tears.

But soon the morning's happier light,
 Its glory shall restore;
And eyelids that are sealed in death,
 Shall wake to close no more."

# CHAPTER XXXVI.

CELEBRATION OF THE FIRST OF AUGUST.

THE anti-slavery friends in Canandaigua, had resolved to celebrate the anniversary of the West India emancipation, in suitable manner in that village, for which funds had been unsparingly collected, to defray the expenses of the coming demonstration. The first of August, 1847, fell on Sunday, and our people concluded to devote that day to religious meetings, and the second to their proposed celebration.

Frederick Douglass and Mr. Van Loon, from Poughkeepsie, addressed the people on the Sabbath; and also, on the same evening, a large concourse at the Court House. The day following, there were not less than ten thousand people assembled on the beautiful grounds, belonging to the village Academy—attentive listeners all to the eloquent speeches delivered, and interested spectators of the imposing exercises.

When the vast multitude had convened, the exercises were commenced by the Rev. S. R. Ward, who addressed the throne of grace, after which, Mr. Frederick Douglass delivered an oration, in a style of eloquence which only Mr. Douglass himself can equal, followed by a song from the Geneva choir, and music by Barring's band. Rev. H. H. Garnet, editor of "The National Watchman," next spake, and with marked effect, followed by Messrs. Ward and Douglass; after which, the assemblage formed a procession, and marching to the Canandaigua Hotel, partook of a sumptuous dinner, provided by the proprietor of that house. At six P. M., they again assembled on the square, and were most eloquently addressed by both Ward and Garnet; at the close, they repaired to the ladies' fair, where they found everything in a condition which spake well for the enterprise and industry of our colored sisters. Their articles for sale, were of a choice and considerate selection, and such as sold rapidly and at fair prices. When all was pleasantly over, the ladies contributed twenty dollars toward paying the speakers present.

A most beautiful ode was composed by a warm and generous friend of the cause, which was sung in the grove, in a spirit which produced a thrilling interest. Gladly would I give the reader the whole composition, but its length makes it objectionable for this place, but should they happen to hear a soul-stirring and sublime ode, commencing with,

> "Hail! to this day returning;
> Let all to Heaven aspire," &c.,

they may know it is the one to which I refer.

It was indeed, a glorious day for the colored population generally; and many were the indications of a diminution of that prejudice so prevalent everywhere. Some, who had supposed the colored man so inferior to themselves as to be incapable of making an interesting speech, were convinced of their error, after hearing Messrs. Douglass, Ward and Garnet. Mr. Van Loon was a white clergyman, but a brother indeed; his soul illumined by the pure light of the gospel of peace; his heart full of sympathy for the oppressed; his tongue pleading eloquently for equal rights; and his hands busily engaged in breaking every yoke, resting on the necks of poor humanity. So vigorously, so zealously did he unfold the horrors of the slave system; so truthfully and faithfully did he expose the treachery of northern politicians, and so pathetically did he appeal to the humanity of every professed Christian to speak out boldly for the dumb; to shield, by the holy principles of their religion, the poor, bound, illiterate slave, from Southern cruelty and bondage,—that some of our aristocratic citizens, some of our white savans, repaid his truthful eloquence, by visiting upon him the bitterest maledictions. From the negro, said they, we will accept these statements as true,—from him, they are pertinent and forcible; but when such unpalatable truths are uttered by a white clergyman, we cannot abide, nor will we listen to them!

Let consistency blush, and justice hang down its head! Is not truth the same, whether proclaimed by black or white,—bond or free? Is a falsehood to be pardoned because uttered by a negro? If indeed, as was admitted, the sentiments expressed by our eloquent colored speakers, were *true*, could they be false, when enforced by our intellectual friend, Van Loon? Certainly not; nor would the case have been so decided by these Solons, in any other case: or where the prejudice against color had not warped and blinded their otherwise good judgments. Our speaker, however, performed his duty faithfully, and with great satisfaction to the colored people and their true friends present.

The remains of this fearless champion of liberty; this humble disciple of the despised Nazarene, now sleeps in death, beside the placid waters of the Hudson, while his cherished memory lives in the affections of thousands, who "are ready to perish," and is honored by the pure in heart, wherever his name has been known throughout the land. In the day of final reckoning, think you, he will regret having plead the cause of the bondman? Ah, no; nor can we doubt that to him will be rendered the welcome plaudits : "Well done, good and faithful servant; enter thou into the joy of thy Lord. Thou hast been faithful over a few things; I will make thee a ruler over many things." What then are the few light afflictions endured in this life, when compared with "an eternal weight of glory," awarded to the faithful in that which is to come?

Pleasant, happy, and beneficial, as had been the re-union of old and tried friends, to celebrate a glorious event, yet, like all earthly enjoyments, it was brought to a termination, reluctant as were the friends to separate. Since that day, many have been the demonstrations of grateful joy and gladness on the glorious anniversary of the emancipation of slaves on the West India Islands; and yet, in this boasted "land of the free, and home of the brave;" this famous and declared *free* Republic,—the American slave still clanks his heavy chain, and wears the galling yoke of the bondman!

# CHAPTER XXXVII.

#### CONCLUSION.

FOR several years past, anti-slavery truth has been spreading, and in proportion as light has shone upon the "peculiar institution," exposing to the world its crimes and blood,—enstamping upon its frontlet, "THE SUM OF ALL VILLAINIES,"—has the wrath of the impious slaveholder been kindled, and his arm outstretched to strengthen the chain, and press closer the yoke upon the helpless slave, proving conclusively that he loves darkness because his deeds are evil. Nor is this all; he and his apologists will insolently tell you, that *you* are the guilty ones who have tightened the bonds of the slave, increased his hardships, and blighted his prospect of freedom, by your mistaken kindness, in showing the slaveholder the enormity of his sin! Can this be so? Have we any direct influence over his human chattels? None. Then who is it that rivets the chain and increases the already heavy burden of the crushed slave, but he who has the power to do with him as he wills? He it is, who has been thrust, unwillingly perhaps, into sufficient light to show him his moral corruption, and the character of the sin he is daily committing; he it is, whose avarice and idleness induces to hold fast that which is to him a source of wealth,—and by no means to allow the same light to fall in upon the darkened intellect of his slave property, lest his riches "take to themselves wings;" or, as may be more properly said, *take to themselves legs and run away*.

What stronger proof can we ask in favor of our position, than the intolerant spirit of the South? If the system and practice of Slavery is a righteous one, instituted by an All-wise God, certainly no human power—especially one so impotent and futile as the abolition power is said to be—can ever overthrow it. Why then are the mails so closely examined, and fines imposed on prohibited anti-slavery documents? Is it beyond their power to confute the arguments adduced, or are they fearful that a ray of Northern light may fall on the mind of some listening slave, and direct him to the depot of an under-ground railroad? Judge ye!

What but this same fearful and intolerant spirit,—this over-bearing, boasting spirit, was it, that cowardly attacked a Christian Senator, while seated unsuspectingly at his desk, and felled him to the floor, bleeding and senseless? Was not the villainous blow which fell upon the honored head of CHARLES SUMNER, dealt by the infamous Brooks of South Carolina, aimed at the free speech of the entire North? Was it, think you, a personal enmity that the cowardly scoundrel had toward our worthy Northern Senator, which induced the attack? No, no. Brooks spake for the South, and boldly has it responded—Amen!

It has said through its representatives, that you Northerners are becoming too bold in speaking of our sin, and we will use brute force to repel it—an argument with which we are familiar. You have told us that we ought not to hold slaves, nor extend slave territory, which will in a measure destroy our slave market, and prove injurious to our slave-breeding population. You have told us we have no right to usurp Kansas,—no right to murder "Free State men," and no right to sustain there, a set of "ruffians" to make Kansas a slave State. You have told us, that we have no right to live on the unrequited toil of our slaves; nor to sell them to the highest bidder; nor spend the proceeds of the sale in idle extravagance. Now know, all ye Northerners, by this cowardly blow on the devoted head of your honored and respected Senator, that we shall no longer permit you to tell us such unpalatable truths, nor allow you the privilege of free speech! We have too long held the balance of power in the government to yield it now; and we give you to know, that whatever we ask of this government, we expect to obtain; nor will we hear any of your objections. When we desire you to turn blood-hound, and hunt for us our fugitive slaves, we expect you to do it, and to see them returned to their masters, without a murmur on your part. Should you object or dare refuse, we shall certainly *cane somebody*, or else do what we have threatened for the last quarter of a century,—"DISSOLVE THE UINON!" Bah!

My house has ever been open to the fugitive slaves; but more particularly when I resided in Rochester, did I have occasion to see and feel the distresses of that class of persons; and it appears to me, that the heart must be of adamant, that can turn coldly away from the pleadings of the poor, frightened, flying fugitive from Southern bondage.

For many years past, I have been a close and interested observer of my race, both free and enslaved. I have observed with great pleasure, the gradual improvement in intelligence and condition of the free colored people of the North. In proportion as prejudice has diminished, they have gradually advanced; nor can I believe that there is any other great impediment in the way to a higher state of improvement. That prejudice against color is not destroyed, we very well know. Its effects may be seen in our down-cast, discouraged, and groveling countrymen, if no where else. Notwithstanding the late diminution, it exists in many of our hotels: some of them would as soon admit the dog from his kennel, at table, as the colored man; nevertheless, he is sought as a waiter; allowed to prepare their choicest dishes, and permitted to serve the white man, who would sneer and scorn to eat beside him. Prejudice is found also, in many of our schools,—even in those to which colored children are admitted; there is so much distinction made by prejudice, that the poor, timid colored children might about as well stay at home, as go to a school where they feel that they are looked upon as inferior, however much they may try to excel.

Nor is that hateful prejudice—so injurious to the soul, and all the best interests of the negro—excluded from the professed church of Christ. Oh, no; we often find it in the house of worship, in all its cruel rigor. Where people assemble to worship a pure and holy God, who can look upon no sin with allowance—the creator of all, both white and black,—and where people professing to walk in the footsteps of the meek and quiet Jesus, who has taught us to esteem others better than ourselves; we often see the lip of some professed saint, curled in scorn at a dusky face, or a scowl of disapprobation if a colored person sits elsewhere than by the door or on the stairs. How long, O Lord, must these things be!

Of my enslaved brethren, nothing so gratifies me, as to hear of their escape from bondage; and since the passage of that iniquitous "Fugitive Slave Bill," I have watched with renewed interest the movements of the fugitives, not only from Slavery direct, but those who have been compelled to flee from the nominally free States, and ask the protection of a monarchial government, to save them from their owners in a land of boasted liberty!

The knowledge I have of the colored men in Canada, their strength and condition, would cause me to tremble for these United States, should a war ever ensue between the English and American governments, which I pray may never occur. These fugitives may be thought to be a class of poor, thriftless, illiterate creatures, like the Southern slaves, but it is not so. They are no longer slaves; many of whom have been many years free men, and a large number were never slaves. They are a hardy, robust class of men; very many of them, men of superior intellect; and men who feel deeply the wrongs they have endured. Driven as they have been from their native land; unprotected by the government under which they were born, and would gladly have died,—they would in all probability, in case of a rupture, take up arms in defense of the government which has protected them and the country of their adoption. England could this day, very readily collect a regi-

O*

ment of stalwart colored men, who, having felt the oppression of our laws, would fight with a will not inferior to that which actuated our revolutionary forefathers.

And what inducement, I ask, have colored men to defend with their lives the United States in any case; and what is there to incite them to deeds of bravery?

Wherever men are called upon to take up arms in defense of a country, there is always a consciousness of approaching wrong and oppression, which arouses their patriotism and incites to deeds of daring. They look abroad over fields of their own cultivation; they behold too, churches, schools, and various institutions, provided by their labor, for generations yet to come; they see their homes, their cherished hearthstone, about to be desecrated, and their wives and little ones, with their aged sires, exposed to the oppression of a ruthless foe. Then, with what cheerful and thrilling enthusiasm, steps forward the husband, the father, the brother, and bares his bosom to the sword,—his head to the storm of the battle-field, in defence of his country's freedom, and the God-given rights of himself and family! But what sees the oppressed negro? He sees a proud and haughty nation, whose Congressmen yearly meet to plot his ruin and perpetuate his bondage! He beholds, it is true, a few Christ-like champions, who rise up with bleeding hearts to defend his cause; but while his eye kindles with grateful emotion, he sees the bludgeon of the South—already reeking in the blood of freemen—raised and ready to fall with murderous intent upon the head of any one, who, like the illustrious Sumner, dare open his mouth in defence of Freedom, or speak of the wrongs of the poor negro, and the sins of the Southern autocrat!

What inducement then, has the slave to shoulder his musket, when the American drum beats the call, "To Arms! To Arms!" Does he not remember that the wife of his bosom; the children,—"bone of his bone, and flesh of his flesh,"—and the rude hearthstone they for a time are allowed to surround, belong not to himself, but to the tyrannical master, who claims dominion over all he possesses. As his property then, let the slave owner go forth in defence of his own, and lay down his life if he please; but the poor slave has no home, no family to protect; no country to defend; nor does he care to assist in sustaining a government that instead of offering him protection, drives him from the soil which has been cultivated by his own labor,—to beg at the hand of England's Queen, "life, liberty, and the pursuit of happiness."

Humiliating as it is for an American citizen to name these things, they are nevertheless true; and I would to God that America would arise in her native majesty, and divest herself of the foul stain, which Slavery has cast upon her otherwise pure drapery!

Then would she be no longer a hissing and by-word among the nations; but indeed what she professes to be, "the land of the free, and the home of the brave;" an asylum for the oppressed of every clime.

But should the monarchial government of England call for the services of the colored man, freely would his heart's blood be poured out in her defence,—not because he has a particular preference for that form of government; not because he has ceased to love his native country,—but because she has acknowledged his manhood, and given him a home to defend. Beneath the floating banner of the British Lion, he finds inducements to lay down his life, if need be, in defence of his own broad acres, his family and fireside,—all of which were denied him under the Stars and Stripes of his fatherland. But a short time ago, the colored men of Cincinnati, O., were promptly denied the privilege they had solicited, to join with other citizens, in celebrating the anniversary of WASHINGTON's Birth Day! Oh, no; there must be no colored man in the company, met to honor him who still lives in the heart of every American citizen,—"the father of his country,"—and yet, who scorned not to sleep beside his faithful negro! Nor did the nephew of the illustrious General, despise the command of the black regiment, which Gen. Jackson so proudly commended for their bravery, and bestowed upon it his personal thanks, for their services on the field of battle.

Do the Northern or Free States of the Union think to clear their skirts of the abomination of Slavery, by saying that they own no slaves? Very true. But is the poor, flying fugitive from the house of bondage, safe one moment within your borders? Will he be welcomed to your homes, your tables, your firesides? Will your clergymen bid you clothe and feed him, or give him a cup of cold water, in the name of a disciple of that holy Christ, who has said,—"inasmuch as ye have done it unto one of the least of these little ones, ye have done it unto me?"—Or will your own miserable Fugitive Slave Law, close the mouth of your clergy; crush down the rising benevolence of your heart; and convert you into a human blood-hound, to hunt down the panting fugitive, and return him to the hell of Slavery? Oh, my God!—the fact is too horrible to acknowledge, and yet it is a stubborn one. Not on one foot of land under the broad folds of Columbia's banner, can the slave say, "I am free!" Hungry, naked, and forlorn, he must flee onward; nor stop short of the outstretched arms of an English Queen. Yet, thanks be to our Heavenly Father, that all have not bowed the knee to the Southern autocrat or slave power. A few noble souls, thank God, remain, who, in defiance of iniquitous laws, throw open wide their doors to the trembling, fleeing bondman, whose purses are freely emptied to supply his wants, and help him on in his flight to the British dominion. But can these out-gushings of a benevolent heart—the purest impulses of a noble nature—be permitted to flow out spontaneously, in open daylight? Alas, no! You must be quiet; make no noise, lest an United States' Marshal wrest from you the object of your Christian sympathy, and impose on you a heavy fine, for your daring to do to another as you would he should do to you.

Is not the necessity of an *"under ground railroad,"* a disgrace to the laws of any country? Certainly it is; yet I thank God, that it does afford a means of escape to many, and I pray that the blessings of Heaven may ever rest upon those who willingly superintend its interests. Oh, my country! When will thy laws, just and equal, supersede this humiliating necessity!

Is my reader about to throw the blame of our nation's wrong on England, and accuse her of first tolerating Slavery? We admit it; but did she not repent of the evil she had done, and speedily break every yoke, and let the oppressed go free? Certainly; no slave now breathes in England's atmosphere. But, say you, her white poor are slaves to the aristocracy, from which sentiment I beg leave to differ. Oppressed they may be, and doubtless are, as the poor are apt to be in any and every country; but they are not sold in the market, to the highest bidder, like beasts of burden, as are the American slaves. No Englishman, however poor, destitute, or degraded he may be, but owns himself, his wife and children; nor does he fear that they be sold and torn from his embrace, while he is laboring for their support. . Poverty, my friend, does not comprise the bitterness of Slavery, no more than "one swallow makes a summer,"—nor does it consist solely in ignorance and degradation. Its bitterness arises from a consciousness of wrong; a sense of the violation of every right God has given to man, and the uncertainty of his future, over which he has no control.

If the American people flatter themselves with the idea of getting rid of the hated negro race, by colonizing them on the sickly soil of Liberia, or any other country, they will surely find themselves mistaken. They are Americans; allied to this country by birth and by misfortune; and here will they remain,—not always as now, oppressed and degraded,—for all who have any interest in the matter, well know that the free colored people, are rapidly advancing in intelligence, and improving their condition in every respect. Men of learning and genius, are now found among those with fleecy locks, and good mechanics with dusky complexion.

This marked improvement in the condition and rapid advancement in intelligence among our people, seems to have alarmed the colonizationists, and made them fearful that those very down-trodden slaves, who have for years labored for nought; whose blood and tears have fertilized the Southern soil, may, perchance, become their equals in intelligence, and take vengeance on their oppressors for the wrongs done them; and lest they should do so, they would gladly remove them to some far-off country.

Yet here, in North America, will the colored race remain, and ere long in my opinion, become a great people, equal with the proud Anglo-Saxon in all things. The African has once been a powerful nation, before Christian Englishmen invaded her coasts with rum, and incited her chiefs to war, by purchasing with gaudy, but worthless trinkets, her conquered captives; and we have every reason to believe, that though her glory as a nation has departed, that her sons will yet be acknowledged free men by the white population of this country.

There have been black generals in the world before Napoleon was born, and there may be again; and to-day, notwithstanding all the prejudice against color, that everywhere exists in this guilty nation, there are men of talent among us, inferior to none on the earth; nor are their numbers few, though rapidly increasing.

Well may the South arouse herself, form societies, replenish its treasury with a tax imposed on the free colored people, to defray the expense of sending manumitted slaves to Liberia!

Listen a moment to the cant of the colonizationists. Hear him talk of the duty he owes to Africa, and how happy, how intelligent, how prosperous everything is in Liberia. But when that delightful country asks to be taken into fellowship with the United States, and to have her independence recognized—ah, then he lifts his hands in horror and begs to be excused from so close a relation.

This is all cant, in my humble opinion; and when I see men so anxious to send the negro out of their sight, I feel quite certain that they are conscious of having deeply wronged him, and think to remove him, to atone for their guilty consciences. Would they refuse to acknowledge the independence of Liberia, if their interest in the colored people was genuine, especially when several other nations had done so? Oh, no. But that is not "*the rub.*" How could one of our lordly nabobs of the South, sit in Congress with perhaps one of his own manumitted slaves as a representative from Liberia or Hayti! He would die of mortification. Very well then; but let him talk no more of sending colored men to that country to make them free men.

The colored people generally, I am happy to say, have a right conception of the colonization plan, and will never be induced to go to Africa, unless they go as missionaries to the heathen tribes, who certainly should have the gospel preached to them. Some, from a sense of duty, may go as teachers,—which is all well enough,—but certain it is, that no amount of prejudice or abuse, will ever induce the colored race to leave this country. Long have they been oppressed; but they are rising—coming up to an elevated standard, and are fast gathering strength and courage, for the great and coming conflict with their haughty oppressors.

That there must be ere long, a sharp contest between the friends of Freedom and the Southern oligarchy, I can no longer doubt.

When our worthy ministers of the gospel, are sent back to us from the South, clothed with a coat of tar and feathers; when our best and most sacrificing philanthropists are thrown into Southern dungeons; when our laboring men are shot down by haughty and idle Southern aristocrats, in the hotels of their employers, and under the very eye of Congress; when the press is muzzled, and every editor, who has the manliness to speak in defence of Freedom, and the wickedness of the slaveholder, is caned or otherwise insulted by some insignificant Southern bully; and when at last, our Mr. SUMNER is attacked from behind, by a Southern, cowardly scoundrel, and felled senseless on the floor of the Senate chamber, for his defence of Liberty,—then, indeed, may Northern men look about them! Well may they be aroused by the insolence and tyranny of the South!

And for what *is* all this? Do not our Southern men know, that if light and truth are permitted to reach the minds of the people, that Kansas will be lost to them as slave territory, wherein the Southern slave-breeder can dispose of his own flesh to the highest bidder! Hear them talk as they do, in their pious moments, with upturned faces, in solemn mockery, of returning the negro to his *native* Africa! How many pure Africans, think you, can be found in the whole slave population of the South, to say nothing of their nativity? Native Africa, indeed! Who does not know, that in three-fourths of the colored race, there runs the blood of the white master,—the breeder of his own chattels! Think you, that a righteous God will fail to judge a nation for such flagrant sins? Nay, verily. If the All-wise God, who has created of one blood all nations of the earth, has designed their blood to commingle until that of the African is absorbed in that of the European,—then is it right, and amalgamation of all the different races should be universally practiced and approved. If it be right for the Southern slaveholder, to cruelly enforce the mixture of the races, to gratify his lust, and swell the enormity of his gains, certainly it cannot be wrong to amalgamate from choice and affection. Let us ask then, why did our Omnipotent Creator make the marked distinction? Certainly not for the purpose that one race might enslave and triumph over another; but evidently, that each in his own proper sphere might glorify God, to whom their respective bodies and spirits belong. Why, indeed, was the black man created, if not to fulfil his destiny *as a negro*, to the glory of God?

Suffer me then to exhort you, my countrymen, to cease looking to the white man for example and imitation. Stand boldly up in your own national characteristics, and show by your perseverance and industry, your honor and purity, that you are men, colored men, but of no inferior quality. The greatest lack I see among you, is unity of action, pardonable, to be sure, in the eyes of those who have seen your oppression and limited advantages; but now that many of you have resolved to gain your rights or die in the struggle, let me entreat you to band yourselves together in one indissoluble bond of brotherhood, to stand shoulder to shoulder in the coming conflict, and let every blow of yours tell for Freedom and the elevation of your race throughout the land. Speak boldly out, for the dumb and enslaved of your unfortunate countrymen, regardless of the frowns and sneers of the haughty tyrants, who may dare lift their puny arm, to frustrate the design of the Almighty, in preserving you an unmixed and powerful race on the earth.

While I would not that you depend on any human agency, save your own unyielding exertion, in the elevation of our race; still, I would not have you unmindful of, nor ungrateful for, the noble exertions of those kind white friends, who have plead the cause of the bondman, and have done all in their power to aid you, for which, may the God of the oppressed abundantly bless them.

Let your attention be given to the careful training and education of the rising generation, that they may be useful, and justly command the respect of their fellow-men. Labor for a competency, but give not your whole attention to amassing the wealth that perishes; but seek to lay up for yourselves "treasures where moth doth not corrupt, nor thieves break through and steal."

'Suppose not, my brethren, that your task is a light one, or one that can be performed without years of patient toil and unyielding perseverance. Our oppressors are not very ready to credit our exertion,—too often forgetting the effects of our long degradation, and vainly expecting to see us arise at once, to the highest standard of elevation, able to cope successfully with those who have known no such discouragements or disadvantages, as has been our lot to bear.

These and many other obstacles must be bravely met, and assiduously removed,—remembering that Slavery has robbed some of us, and prejudice many others, of that perseverance so necessary to the accomplishment of any enterprize; but in the elevation of ourselves and race, let us never falter and grow weary, until we have reached the elevated station God designed us to occupy, and have fitted the rising generation to fill and improve it after our earthly course is finished and we leave to them the stage of action.

Allow me, however, to entreat, that no success which may attend your determined efforts; no position which you may attain,—may ever so occupy your mind, as to cause you to forget for one moment, the afflictions of your countrymen, or to cease to remember the groaning millions in bonds, until every slave shall triumphantly chant the song of deliverance from Slavery's dark prison house.

Bear with me, my dear brethren, while I claim a friend's license, to say, that I would not that you place implicit confidence in any of the political organizations of the present time; but remember that the majority of those parties are diligently laboring for their own interest. Look you then to yours; are you less capable of securing your rights than they? Never was there a time when indolence and supineness among us, would be so unpardonable as now, nor when so much depended on our active and judicious exertions.

Let us not forget, that in the past, we could and did truthfully complain, that we had no helper,— bound and crushed beneath an overwhelming weight of prejudice and ignorance, we lay helpless at the feet of our political spoilers. A favorable change has since been effected in the public sentiment; and now that we see thousands who are willing to aid us, and as many more who will not hinder our labor,—shall we fold our hands in idleness?—or shall we renew our energies, in the cause of freedom and of our own advancement? Although we may not implicitly rely upon the political exertion of others, let us not fear to co-operate with the friends of liberty everywhere, as far as a good conscience will permit, and our limited privileges will allow, by our determined zeal for the right, make our influence felt in the nation. See what wrong and oppression our white brethren have met in Kansas, from the slave power; and let their noble deeds of patriotism; their liberal sacrifices for freedom, be not only our example, but an incentive to do our duty. Have they more at stake in that mighty struggle than we, that they should leave their homes of refinement and comfort, take their lives in their hands and bravely contend for their rights, surrounded by scenes of blood and carnage? Certainly not. No people on the earth can have greater incentives to arouse them to action, than the colored people of this country now have; I trust therefore, that our future independence and prosperity, will suffer nothing from the inactivity of our race.

Some may entertain the belief that the African

slave trade is entirely abandoned. I think not. Often are seen strange, suspicious looking vessels, lying along the African coast, for no other purpose than that of kidnapping the poor, ignorant natives. Stealthily the slave-trader lands his wicked crew, in the vicinity of some negro village or cluster of huts, and when a favorable opportunity occurs, he and his men rush upon the frightened African, burn their huts, and amid the shrieks of the captives, and the groans of the helpless and aged, who have been trampled down in their rude haste to secure the young and able-bodied natives, bear them to the vessel, where they are stowed away in the hold of the ship, which bears them to Christian (?) America, where they are sold as slaves.

Some years ago, a woman engaged in washing clothes, near the sea coast, had a lad with her to take care of her two younger children—one a young babe—while she was at work. They wandered away a short distance, and while amusing themselves under some bushes, four men, to them strange looking creatures, with white faces, surrounded them; and when the lad attempted to run away, they threw the infant he held in his arms, on the ground, and seizing the other two children, bore them screaming with fear, to the ship. Frantic and inconsolable, they were borne to the American slave market, where they were sold to a Virginia planter, for whom they labored sorrowfully and in tears, until old age deprived them of farther exertion, when they were turned out, like an old horse, to die; and did die destitute and uncared for, in their aged infirmity, after a long life of unrequited toil. That lad, stolen from Africa's coast, was my grandfather.

It is not, however, necessary for us to look beyond our own country, to find all the horrors of the slave traffic! A tour through the Southern States will prove sufficient to satisfy any one of that fact; nor will they travel over one of them, before—if they have a heart of flesh—they will feel oppressed by the cruel outrage, daily inflicted on their fellow-beings. The tourist need not turn aside to seek evidences: he will very readily observe the red flag of the auctioneer floating over the slave pen, on which he may read in large letters, waving in the pure air of heaven, "SLAVES, HORSES, AND OTHER CATTLE, *in lots to suit purchasers!*" He may halt a moment, and look at the multitude, collecting under the folds of that infamous banner, where will be found a few gentlemanly appearing slave holding planters, superbly mounted, and perhaps with their servants in waiting; but the larger number he will find to be drunken, coarse, brutal looking men, swaggering about in the capacity of slave-traders.

Let him enter the low, dingy, filthy building, occupied by human merchandize, and he will there behold

P

husbands and wives, parents and children, about to be sold, and perhaps separated forever! See the trader, as he examines with inhuman indifference the bones and sinews, the teeth and joints of the *articles* on hand, even of females, and hear him make inquiries concerning her capabilities, that would make a savage blush! And see the miserable woman lift her red and swollen eyes to the face of the heartless trader, and the next moment cast a dispairing glance over the motley crowd, in search of a compassionate look—a pitying eye. Should she see one countenance wearing a kind, humane expression, it will most likely bring her frantically to his feet, where, kneeling, with uplifted hands, she pleads: "Oh, Massa, do buy me! Do buy me and little Sam! He be all of the chil'ens I got left! O, Lord! O, Lord! Do, Massa, buy me, and this one baby! Oh, do Massa!" But the weight of the cow-hide drives her to the auction block, where in mock solemnity she is represented as "an article of excellent breed, a good cook, a good seamstress, and withal a good Christian, a ra'al genewine lamb of the flock!"—and then she is struck off to the highest bidder, who declares that he "won't have the young'un any' how, 'cause he's gwine to drive her down to Lousianny."

He may see, too, the wild, dispairing look of some frightened young slave girl, passing under the lustful gaze of some lordly libertine, who declares himself "in search of a fancy article for his own use!"

'One after another is taken from the block, until all are disposed of, amid the agonized wail of heartbroken wives and mothers, husbands and fathers, and the piercing screams of helpless children, torn from a parent's embrace, to be consigned to the care of strangers.

Nor need I inform our traveler of the inhuman method generally approved, in hunting with trained blood-hounds, kept and advertised for the purpose of recapturing any poor slave who may attempt to escape from this cruel bondage. He may perchance, come across the mangled and lifeless body of some fugitive, which has just been run down and torn in pieces by the dogs of the hunter! Should he stop a few moments, he will soon see a hole dug in the ground, and the remains of the slave pitched into it, covered sufficiently to hide the unsightly mass from view, and there will be an end of the whole matter! "Shall I not visit for these things? saith the Lord; and shall not my soul be avenged on such a nation as this?"

In giving to the public this unvarnished, but truthful narrative, of some of the occurrences of my humble and uneventful life, I have not been influenced by a vain desire for notoriety, but by a willingness to gratify a just and honorable request, repeatedly made by numerous and respected friends, to learn the truth concerning my connection with the

Wilberforce colony; the events which there transpired during my stay, and the cause of my losing a hard-earned property. Regarding the affairs of the colony, I have, therefore, endeavored to be particular,—believing that duty to myself and brethren, required me to give them the within information; but nothing have I set down in malice. Much more might have been said ralative to some of the leading characters in that settlement, had I not been fearful of its assuming the character of a personal enmity or retaliation. He who knows and will judge the actions of men, will bear me witness, that I have cherished no such feelings toward any of those who then lived, but now sleep in death.

In justification, however, of my statements regarding the character of Mr. Lewis, I will call the attention of the reader to some of the many letters received from good and eminent men, to show that I was not alone in the low estimate of his virtues. Gladly I leave that unpleasant subject, hoping that nothing in our past history will serve to becloud the bright future beginning to dawn on the prospects of our disfranchised and oppressed countrymen.

# CORRESPONDENCE.

LETTER FROM A. STEWARD TO WM. L. GARRISON.

MR. GARRISON,

Dear Sir:—In a recent examination of the business transactions between the Board of Managers of the Wilberforce Colony, and their agent Rev. N. Paul, I find a charge made by him, and allowed by the board, of the sum of two hundred dollars, which he paid to yourself. Finding no receipt or acknowledgment from you, I write to ask you to favor me with one, or an explanation of the facts in the case, either of which will greatly oblige me, as I design to make it public. Truly Yours, &c.,

A. STEWARD.

Canandaigua, N. Y., May, 1856.

MR. GARRISON'S REPLY TO A. STEWARD.

DEAR SIR:

You state that Rev. N. Paul, as agent for the Wilberforce Settlement, U. C., in rendering his accounts on his return from England, charged the Board of Managers with the sum of two hundred dollars, paid by him to me while in England; that said sum was allowed by the board; adding that you do not recollect of my acknowledging or giving credit to the Settlement for it.

In reply, I can only assure you that there must be a mistake in regard to this item. I borrowed no money, nor had I any occasion to ask a loan of my friend Paul, my expenses being defrayed by funds contributed by friends in this country; nor could I with propriety receive, nor he give me any part of the money contributed for the benefit of the Wilberforce Settlement; hence, a loan or gift from him, could have been nothing more than a personal matter between ourselves. Moreover, had he at that time or any other, given me in good faith the sum named as belonging to the Settlement, (believing that as we were laboring together, for the interest of one common cause, the board would not hesitate to allow it,) he would certainly have demanded a receipt, which it would have pleased me to give, of course, that he might satisfy the board that their liberality had been disbursed according to their wishes, or his judgment. But receiving no money from your agent, will be a sufficient reason for not acknowledging it, or giving due credit to the Settlement.'

I can account for this charge on his part, in no way, except that as he was with me a part of the time I was in London, and we traveled together a part of the time, during which, he ably and effectively assisted me in exposing that most iniquitous combination, "The American Colonization Society,"—he charged to me, (that is, to my mission) sundry items of expense which he undoubtedly believed justly incurred by his helping me to open the eyes of British philanthropists to the real design of that society; and I shall ever remember with gratitude, his heartiness and zeal in the cause and in my behalf. I owe much to the success that so signally crowned my mission, to his presence, testimony, and eloquent denunciation of the colonization scheme. I, however, received no money from him, and can but think that the above explanation was the occasion of his making the charge, and which I trust will leave on his memory, no intentional wrong.

WM. L. GARRISON.

Boston, Mass., June, 1856.

### FROM MR. BAKER TO A. STEWARD.

MR. A. STEWARD,

Dear Sir:—Israel Lewis, the former agent of your Settlement, last spring represented to me the suffering condition of your poor, and requested that I should forward some goods, for which I should be paid; I did so, and sent goods to the amount of one hundred thirty-six dollars and ninety-eight cents. The goods were sold at cost.

I am also endorsed on a note for two hundred thirteen dollars and ten cents, which falls due 24th of this month, and which I shall have to pay. This note was given by Lewis for the purpose of raising money to fit out Mr. Paul, on his mission to England. I was promised that the money should be here to meet it.

I have heard nothing from Lewis or this business since, and as I understand you are the agent, I must look to you to make provision to meet the note, and pay for the goods. Good faith requires that all contracts by your agency be fulfilled.

Yours, Respectfully,

CORNAL BAKER.

New York City, Dec., 1833.

---

### FROM MR. L. A. SPALDING TO A. STEWARD.

DEAR FRIEND:

In August last, Israel Lewis, accompanied by Rev. Nathaniel Paul called upon me and exhibited a power of attorney, signed by you as president of the trustees of the colony, authorizing Lewis to take loans, &c., for the benefit of the colony.

Feeling a deep interest in the progress of the colony, I agreed to become security with E. Peck, at the Bank of Rochester, for the payment of seven hundred dollars, which soon was raised by Lewis on the note, for the benefit of the colony. I was in hopes to have seen you. E. Peck and myself, both are willing to aid you in your noble enterprise,—and may others feel the same disposition. But as we have families and friends, who look to us for support and protection, it is proper that we should have your personal pledge to save us from embarrassment.

We know your character *well*, and we have also great confidence in Israel Lewis, and the others engaged with you,—but none of them are so thoroughly known to us as yourself.

Our asking for your personal pledge, does not arise from any fears that the note will not be paid; but as it was signed to aid you, we think it proper that you should respond by guaranteeing that we shall not be injured.

I accordingly copy the note in question, and write a guarantee which I wish you to sign and hand to my brother.

I feel much anxiety in regard to your progress; in your forming schools; religious and temperance societies; and in your taking every measure to elevate the unfortunate colored man who may go to your colony for protection and improvement.

       Very Respectfully Yours,
Austin Steward.    LYMAN A. SPALDING.
Lockport, N. Y., 1831.

---

From the Conventional Board, Philadelphia, Pa., to A. Steward.

Mr. Austin Steward, Wilberforce, U. C.,

    Esteemed Friend:—I am charged by the conventional board, to inform you that at the last session of the general convention, you was duly elected their *General Corresponding Agent*, for the Wilberforce Settlement and parts adjacent. Respectfully and in an official capacity, would I ask you to accept the appointment.

And in pursuance of the said appointment, the board would be happy to have at least a monthly correspondence from you, on all such matters as may, in your opinion, be thought conducive to the prosperity of the settlement, the elevation and future happiness of the free people of color.

In particular, we would wish you to give as accurate an account as possible, of the number of settlers; the number of acres as purchased; at what price; what number are improved and under culture; what number of houses or tenements are in the Settlement, &c., &c.

What are your present prospects in regard to crops; your political advantages or disadvantages.

We would also respectfully ask you to inform us, what number of settlers might emigrate there each year, without injuring the Settlement. Also, what kind of machines you most need; also, what are the terms for which laborers are contracted for and how paid.

The board have been thus particular, because they rely with full confidence on your *patriotism* and capability, which have been unanimously assigned to you.

You will perceive our object is, to contribute, as far as lays in our power, *pecuniary* aid, and assist in securing you such *agricultural* and *mechanical* emigrants as, in your opinion, the Settlement may need; and in all our recommendations to you, we shall endeavor to have an eye to character, knowing full well that by that alone you must *stand* or *fall*.

We have been informed here by a letter (purporting to be written by a Mr. Stover), that the Canada Company actually refuses to sell land to colored persons; and that they are anxious to buy out the colored settlers at Wilberforce.

Be pleased to inform me if that be a fact, with its particulars; and if there be any disadvantages in purchasing land by colored emigrants.

The board would be happy to know if you have had any news from your agent in England. If any, what are his prospects?

You will please be particular and candid in stating your wants (as well as disadvantages) to us, as we will do our utmost to satisfy

P*

them, as well as promote the happiness of the settlers, and the prosperity of the Settlement.

Be pleased to answer as soon as possible, for we as brothers in common, feel deeply interested.

With sentiments of sincere friendship,

I remain, yours,

JUNIUS C. MORRELL.

A true copy from the record.

---

### Resolutions passed by the Board of Managers of the Wilberforce Colony.

At a meeting of the Board of Managers, held September 30th, 1831, to call the Agents to an account:

Resolved, That the Report of N. Paul be accepted, and unanimously agreed to.

At a meeting of the Board of Directors, all the members present, March 18th, 1832:

Resolved, That we disapprove of the conduct of Israel Lewis, in his being absent so long, and also his not communicating with the Board of Directors, and not informing them from time to time, how he is prosecuting his agency.

Resolved, That the chairman of this board be instructed to write to said Lewis, to return home, and lay before this board his doings.

At a meeting of the Board, held April 1st, 1832, all the members and Israel Lewis present with them, he made the following Report, and resigned his office as agent, which was accepted:

Lewis said that seven hundred dollars was all that he had collected. That he paid one hundred and fifty dollars for board in New York, thirty-five dollars for clothes, and two hundred dollars to N. Paul, as an out-fit for England.

## CIRCULAR.

THE BOARD OF MANAGERS FOR THE COLONY,

*To the Christians and Philanthropists in the United States:*

We, the undersigned inhabitants and Board of Mauagers for the Colony of Wilberforce, beg leave to state that the frost cut off the crops in this part of the country last year, and some of the colonists are in great need of assistance. And we flatter ourselves that when the peculiar circumstances of this infant Settlement are duly considered, this appeal, to a generous and discriminating public, will not be made in vain.

The board are sensible from the cause above stated, that the inhabitants of Wilberforce will be *compelled* to ask *aid* from the friends of humanity in the States, or they must *suffer*.

Under these circumstances they commissioned the Rev. James Sharp, as their agent, and sent him to the States; but owing to the opposition of Israel Lewis,—who had been formerly employed as agent, but was removed from the agency—his labors were almost wholly lost to the board.

We would simply say, that Lewis was acting for a *certain* company here; but we have made inquiries, and find but *one man* in Wilberforce that belongs to said company, and he is an old man, in his dotage. That man is *Simon Wyatt*. We might say *more*, but we think there has been enough written to satisfy the public.

In consequence of the unfaithfulness of Israel Lewis, and the numerous agents that may be looking around the country after him, the board have come to the conclusion to dispense with a traveling agent for the present.

And we would humbly request Lyman A. Spalding, Esq., of Lockport; E. Peck, Esq., of Rochester; Rev. Dr. Budd, of Auburn; Charles Davis, Esq., of Ludlowville, Tompkins County, N. Y.; Aruthur Tappan, Esq., city of New York; to act as receivers for the Colony. The above named gentlemen, will see that the funds which they may receive, be faithfully applied according to the wishes of the donors.

All money placed in each of the banks at Rochester and a duplicate sent on to the Colony, may be cashed here without any discount.

To Christians we appeal: by the brotherhood of Christ, and by their own hopes of being united in him, to extend to us the means of obtaining bread; give us, in the name of Jesus, of your abundance; give us, as God has blessed you, for the poor among us want bread and clothing.

It is to be hoped that every clergyman in the States, will lay this circular before their respective congregations, and give every person an opportunity to throw in their mite into the treasury of the Lord !

AUSTIN STEWARD, <i>Pres't</i><br>
JOSEPH TAYLOR, <i>Sec'y.</i><br>
PHILIP HARRIS,<br>
JOHN WHITEHEAD,<br>
PETER BUTLER,<br>
SAMUEL PETERSON,<br>
WILLIAM BROWN.

---

FROM REV. J. BUDD TO A. STEWARD AND OTHERS.

MESSRS. PAUL AND STEWARD:

I have ever taken a great degree of interest in the welfare of your colony, and have in various ways, brought it before the public.

It has pained me deeply to learn that there are divisions among you. The whole deportment and manner of Lewis, who has been here, has evidently impressed the public in his favor. Although I do not wish to take ground as his advocate, to the extinction of others, I am not inclined to think him dishonest from the testimony now before me.

But, apart from him, my present impression is that the most effectual way for you to promote the cause of the Colony, is not, at this stage of the business, to appear before the public in a hostile attitude to Lewis.

I know some excellent and prominent gentlemen in this quarter, who think he is unkindly treated; at any rate, while the investigation, lately commenced at Albany, is going on, it appears to me not wise in you to put forth any further publication reflecting upon Lewis. He may have acted imprudently; but he has excited himself very much, and should the idea prevail that you and he are in a state of collision, it would be very bad for you.

I consider your Colony as a very important matter, and will do all in my power to promote your welfare, but it is very material not to prejudice the public against you.

Before I move in the matter, I wish to know the real state of the matter between Lewis and the Colony. As soon as I can know that he has defrauded you and deceived the public, I will not hesitate to give my views on the subject, and put forth any efforts in my power for your advancement.

There should no sectarian or party feeling be allowed to creep into your institution.

I thank you for naming me as a receiver for your Colony, and should anything come to me, I shall hand it over to James S. Seymour, Esq., Cashier of the Bank of Auburn, who should have been named instead of me. I hope you will put his name in my place, or at any rate, name him with me, for he has been from the first, much interested in your behalf.

If you will allow me, I will briefly say, that my opinion is, your best way to relieve your immediate wants, would be to issue a brief circular, stating the failure of your crops, your newness of settlement, &c., &c.; and call upon the public for help, without naming Lewis or alluding to your difficulty with him; let your papers be properly authorized, and say that the agent you employ is not engaged in getting funds to pay for land, found schools, &c., but to get *immediate* provisions for the Colony.

If you will send an agent here and prepare your circular in this way—let it be short—and I will print it and give copies of it to him for circulation, free of charge.

With many prayers for the prosperity of your Colony,

I am your Friend,

JOHN BUDD.

Auburn, N. Y., May, 1833.

---

REPLY TO J. BUDD BY A. STEWARD.

TO THE REV. J. BUDD,

Sir :—We feel under renewed obligation to you, for your friendly advice; but we have already sent out several copies of our circular to different places, and probably some of them have been printed before this time.

We have no object in view, but truth, justice,—the greatest good of the Settlement, and of our brethren in general. Israel Lewis has, however, collected large sums of money, for our relief, of which we have not had the benefit. Nearly two years ago, he was appointed agent for the Colony, to collect funds to build a meeting-house, to endow schools, &c. In less than one year he received more than two thousand dollars, which he squandered; and we have neither *meeting-house* nor *schools*, nor never *will have*, so long as the money goes into the hands of Lewis. All that we would have forgiven him gladly, if he would consent to be *still* and not *usurp* the agency *against* the wishes of the people.

Sir, is it not expected that he would appear well; as you say, that "the whole deportment and manner of Lewis, who has been in this place, evidently have impressed the people in his favor,"—while collecting money with the eye of the public upon him. But follow him home into another kingdom, and there see the man in his true character; stripped of his borrowed plumage,—and we will guarantee that you would agree with us, in believing that he *is* an *arch hypocrite.*

We should be sorry to prejudice the public against our Settlement, more especially when we are actuated by the purest motives,—that of preventing the Christian public from being imposed upon, by drawing large sums from them for us, as they suppose, when in *truth* such sums *never* reach us at all.

Sir, we know that you are actuated by the purest motives, but you are deceived in the character of the man, (Lewis). When I was living in the States and only saw him there, collecting money for the poor, I thought him honest as you now do; but two or three years' residence in Wilberforce Colony, has abundantly satisfied me that his object is to get money, that he may live in a princely style, and not for the benefit of the poor as he pretends.

Such are the true facts in the case. We should be glad to have the name of James S. Seymour, Esq., added to the list, and any other prominent citizen you may think would help the cause.

In regard to the investigation at Albany, we do not see how the public are to arrive at the facts in the case from any statement Lewis may make; for all his statements that I have seen in print, are positively void of truth, in the most essential part, so that they are of little or no importance at all unless substantiated by other testimony.

The circular contains no testimony that has not been heretofore laid before the public. Mr. Benjamin Paul recently wrote a letter to the editors of "The Baptist Register," in which he stated that Lewis had fed and clothed the colonists like a father, which is not true; and so sensible was Paul of the fact, that when the letter reached here, together with the surprize it created wherever Lewis was known, that Paul cheerfully contradicted it, confessed that he was mistaken, and thus made it known to the public.

We certainly have no sectional feelings in the matter, though Lewis has labored hard to impress the public with a contrary belief; and he has even brought false charges of the basest kind against our most respectable citizens, all to draw the attention of the public from the true facts in the case.

It is a general time of health here in the Colony. The season is very favorable; our crops look well, and with the blessings of God we shall raise enough to supply our wants this year.

Yours, with due respect,<br>
In behalf of the Colonists,<br>
A. STEWARD.

Wilberforce, June, 1833.

---

FROM A. STEWARD TO G. BANKS AND OTHERS.

MESSRS. BANKS, WILBER, BROCKENBERG & HARRIS:

I have received a communication through your corresponding secretary, Mr. James C. Brown, and I hasten to answer it. The last communication I have received from Mr. N. Paul, was in December, 1833, at which time he was vigorously prosecuting his mission, as will more fully appear by the annexed copy of said letter, which I cheerfully send you. His return is expected daily.

[COPY OF N. PAUL'S LETTER.]

MY DEAR BROTHER STEWARD:

When I last addressed you, I informed you that I expected to leave this country before a return letter from you could be expected. I therefore stated, if I remember correctly, that you need not write.

I now find that I shall be detained much longer than I then calculated; and this detention is owing to the Slavery question. The friends of the cause, advised me to forego my object, until that question was settled; and then they would turn their attention to my cause, and render me what assistance they could.

All their united strength was needed now, while that question was pending. But thanks be to God, that is now settled. On the first day of August next, will be the proudest day that ever Britain knew; for from that time henceforth, there will not remain a single slave throughout His Majesty's dominions.

The friends of the cause are now turning their attention to Slavery in the United States, and are about to form a society for the abolition of Slavery throughout the world. They all think highly of our Settlement, and will give it their cordial support.

The leading abolitionists have given me letters of recommendation throughout the Kingdom, and have appointed one of their most effective men to travel with me,—his name is John Scoble, a very ready, intelligent, earnest, and an eloquent speaker. I think I can do more now in one month, than I could in three before the question was settled in regard to their own slaves.

You will at once see that although the people concluded my object to be an important one, yet, they generally thought that they ought to lend all their aid in removing the stain from their own land first. This stain is now effectually effaced, and my meetings are exceedingly crowded. I addressed an audience at Norwich of from three to four thousand persons, week before last, when about five hundred dollars was collected. So you see I am getting on. I start, the Lord willing, next week for Scotland, and shall spend the winter there and in the North of England. In the spring I shall return and take passage for Canada. I doubt not, that you are anxiously looking for my return; yet, you cannot want to see me more than I want to return; but I tell you now as I have told you before, that I shall not return until I have done all that can be done by my labor.

Yours,

N. PAUL.

Sirs:

The above copy will give you all the recent information we have received concerning the mission of our foreign agent.

Please accept my kindest regards, with my acknowledgments of your distinguished consideration, while I remain,

Yours truly,<br>AUSTIN STEWARD.

Wilberforce, U. C.

---

### From A. Steward to Mr. Nell.

Dear Sir:
We are glad to acknowledge your favor of October last, and to hear of your safe arrival in England, your health and fair prospects.

Since my removal to Wilberforce, I have opened a school, which Mrs. Steward has engaged to teach for one year; while I shall probably devote my time to traveling through the States, for the benefit of the Colony, which is indeed poor, and in want of some assistance; and yet, not a dollar have we in the treasury to help them with.

Mr. Paul has not returned, though we are daily expecting him. Our friends in New York, still have confidence in his pledge to do right; and we are anxiously expecting its fulfilment.

Your wife, Mrs. Nell, and the children are well, and we are still doing all in our power for their comfort; but my means, in consequence of having been so much abroad the past season, are limited; by which you will see, my dear Sir, the necessity of remitting funds to me, that I may make your family more comfortable in all things, without distressing my own.

The settlers are well, and are looking with hopeful expectancy for you to do something handsome for them, in which I do hope they may not be disappointed. Lewis is still in New York. We have appointed another agent, named Scott, but who is doing nothing for the Colony now.

May the blessings of God rest upon you, and your endeavors; your good deportment put to silence your enemies; may they who foresee that you will cheat the poor colored children, be sadly mistaken, and your good deeds finally enrol your name on the proud list of philanthropists, headed by a Wilberforce and a Clarkson.

Yours, in great haste,<br>
AUSTIN STEWARD.

Wilberforce, Dec., 1835.

---

FROM L. A. SPALDING TO A. STEWARD AND OTHERS.

DEAR FRIENDS:

I have received a letter from Israel Lewis, New York, requesting me to forward fifty dollars to the treasurer of the Wilberforce Colony, which I will do at the first convenience. I sent fifty dollars some time since, which I presume was received

I have also received a letter from B. Lundy, who speaks very flatteringly of the Settlement; but gives me some information relating to Lewis, which will injure you, unless you act wisely.

Now I suggest for your consideration, whether it would not be best to keep perfectly quiet relative to him, until after he returns and settles with the directors. If he cannot then satisfy you, he will no doubt surrender up his documents and agency like a man, and leave you to appoint another.

By all means you must agree among yourselves, not suffering any difference of opinion to become public. Your enemies will seize upon this, and injure your prospects; besides, you gain nothing by it. Your friends too, could then say that you acted imprudently. I hope to have a good account of the settlement of your difficulties if any should exist.

Respectfully your Friend,<br>
LYMAN A. SPALDING.

AUSTIN STEWARD & BENJ. PAUL.

Lockport, N. Y., 2d Mo., 4th, 1832.

## CORRESPONDENCE.

FROM REV. S. E. CORNISH TO A. STEWARD.

DEAR STEWARD:
I have this day received your letter, and God willing, I will be with you in the course of ten or twelve days. Please to keep your people together, until I come. I will see that they be not oppressed by that notorious Israel Lewis. I believe him to be one of the worst men living, whose deeds will yet come to light. Do stay in the Colony and keep all things as they are until I come.
Yours, with high esteem,
SAMUEL E. CORNISH.

P. S.—I am glad that Mrs. Steward is in Rochester; your Colony is by no means suited to her talents and refined mind. She never could be happy there. My love to all the Colonists; I will do every thing for them in my power. S. E. C.

---

FROM B. LUNDY TO A. STEWARD AND OTHERS.

ESTEEMED FRIENDS:
Again I take this method of communicating some private information to my personal friends, relative to my proceedings in Mexico. My last visit to that country, (like the one preceding), having been prolonged far beyond the time which I had anticipated, I feel it incumbent on me to explain the causes thereof especially to such as take an interest in the enterprize in which I have engaged, and those who have kindly assisted me with means to defray the expenses of my journey, &c.

Soon after the date of my last printed letter, which was issued from this place, I went to New Orleans, with the intention of taking a passage by sea, to some port in Mexico; but after waiting in that city about two weeks, and finding no opportunity to obtain one, I proceeded up the Red River, and journeyed through Texas again by land. My health continued very good for some length of time; but when I reached the middle part of the Texas country, it was my misfortune to come again in contact with the direful "cholera," and again I was the subject of its virulent attacks. My detention was great, and affliction severe; though I finally expelled the disorder as I had done before. My sufferings were somewhat aggravated in several instances, by the fearful prejudices of the people among whom I traveled. I was very anxious to get through my journey, and often assayed to travel before I was in fact well enough. The consequence was, that I frequently took relapses, and sometimes had to lie out under trees, even in time of rain, within sight of houses, the people being unwilling to give me shelter therein, fearing that my disorder was contagious.

At length I reached the Mexican town of San Antonio de Bexar, and there I tarried, until I had got pretty well rid of the cholera. I then pursued my journey to Monclova, the seat of government for the State of Coahuila and Texas, in company with several Mexican gentlemen and foreigners. Previous to this time, I had traveled several hundred miles entirely alone, and generally encamped in the woods or plains at night. On my arrival at Monclova, I was doomed to encounter "misfortune" of a very different character. Here I found that the Englishman, (mentioned in my other letter), with whom I had contracted to petition for two grants of land, *had totally failed in his application*. The petition had been laid before the Governor, and he was about issuing the grants, when he received a *decree* from the Legislature—which was then in session—forbidding him to grant any more land, under any pretext. This measure was taken to prevent the great land speculators from carrying on their swindling operations in Texas. An act was soon after passed by that body, repealing all their Colonization laws; and thus every hope that I had so fondly entertained, and each fair prospect, seemingly so near its realization, *was instantly blasted and utterly destroyed!* If ever the fortitude of man was tried, mine was then. If ever stoic philosophy might be successfully called to the aid of human courage, I felt the necessity of invoking it upon that occasion. Nearly two years of toil, privation and peril, have been wasted. My sufferings had been great, though my spirit soared on the bouyancy of hope. Now the fair superstructure of an important enterprise, whose ideal magnitude had employed my mind, to the exclusion of many hardships endured, suddenly vanished from my sight, and left before me a hideous and gloomy void with no other encouragement than total disappointment, conscious poverty and remediless despair! What *should* I then have done? My health was restored, but my detention and consequent expenses had been so great that my funds were nearly exhausted. I came to the country for an important purpose; and I reasoned with myself thus; although my way is closed in this State, cannot something be done *elsewhere?* I will not boast of the stoutest heart among men, but mine *must not quail.* Something further *must* be done if possible, and I will try.

In the course of my travels, I had seen a part of the adjoining State of Tamaulipas, and had been informed that the colonization laws thereof were liberal. I was even aware that some parts of it are more suitable for the culture of the sugar cane, than any tract I could have obtained in Coahuila and Texas. And upon a little reflection, I determined to make further investigations in Tamaulipas, and had been informed of the State. As soon as my horse was a little rested, I set out, *alone,* on a journey of between four and five hundred miles, part of the way through an awfully mountainous region, and much of it an uninhabited wilderness. I encamped out almost every night, during the whole journey; very seldom near any human habitation. I had no fire-arms nor anything to defend myself against the ferocious beasts of the forest, which I had evidence to convince me were frequently numerous, and not far distant. In two weeks I reached the city of Matamoras, in the State of Tamaulipas, quite destitute of funds, after parting with almost every disposable article belonging to my wardrobe, &c. The people of this place being all perfect strangers to me, I did not for a while unfold to them the real object of my visit; but instead thereof, I opened a shop, and commenced working at my old trade—the saddling business. I soon got as much work as I could do—supported myself, replenished my pocket, made some acquaintance with a number of people, and obtained more information respecting the Colonization laws of the State. A few weeks elapsed, while I was employed in this way. I then mounted my horse again, and proceeded to the capital of the State; and after negotiating for some time with the Governor and Council of the State, I succeeded in obtaining a grant of land, upon advantageous terms. I then performed another journey of almost two hundred and fifty miles, "alone," to Matamoras again; and soon thereafter embarked for the United States.

My friends will thus perceive that I have not been idle; though much time has been occupied in my last expedition. I shall not attempt to excite their sympathy by exhibiting the twentieth part of what I have suffered. I do not even like to look back upon some of the scenes through which I have passed. But thanks to a kind and all-sustaining Providence, complete success has at last crowned my exertions. I strove hard to command it; and I leave it to others to say whether I have *deserved* it or not.

The terms upon which I have obtained my grant of land will be noticed in a public address, which I shall forward with this letter.

Since my arrival in this place, I have been confined by sickness; but am now convalescent, and shall visit my friends to the eastward, as soon as circumstances will permit. I cannot close this communication, without an expression of my sincere thanks to those kind friends who rendered me assistance in defraying the expenses of my last Mexican tour. Their favors will be most gratefully remembered, and I shall feel myself under additional obligations to labor for the melioration of the condition of the poor and suffering *slave*.

In the next number of the "Genius of Universal Emancipation," I shall insert the names of those who contributed to aid me in the prosecution of my enterprise; and correct information relative to all proceedings therein, will be given in the pages of that work, as the business connected with it progresses.

I am, most respectfully, your Friend,

N. & B. Paul,                                                          B. LUNDY.
Austin Steward,
Rev. J. Sharp.
Nashville, 5th Mo., 1835.

THE END.

www.ingramcontent.com/pod-product-compliance
Lightning Source LLC
Chambersburg PA
CBHW020238240426

43672CB00006B/568